NGOs AND HUMAN RIGHTS ACTIVISM

NGOs and Human Rights Activism

Puran Chandra

FORWARD BOOKS
NEW DELHI • GUWAHATI • VISAKHAPATNAM

FORWARD BOOKS
4649-B/21, Ansari Road
Darya Ganj, New Delhi - 110 002
Ph.: 23263193 / 9811582579 / 09435116718
Fax: 011-23263193
Email: ektabooks@yahoo.com
www.akanshapublishinghouse.com

NGOs and Human Rights Activism

First Published 2011
ISBN 978-81-909742-0-2

PRINTED IN INDIA

Published by Forward Books, New Delhi and Printed at S.N. Printers, Delhi.

Contents

Preface

> "Men often oppose a thing nearly because they have had no agency in planning it, or because it may have been planned by those whom they dislike."
>
> —*Alexander Hamilton*

These days NGO is the term understood more or less by everybody everywhere. Simultaneously, Human rights awareness is gradually reaching far and wide. NGOs have been instrumental in making human rights activism more vocal in different geographical locations where violation of human rights take place. And they seek the redressal of the grievance of victims.

In fact, NGOs have immensely influenced and contributed to human rights issues all over the world. We have amply addressed all vital factors in this connection in this book.

The role of NGOs in the realm of human rights activism is elaborately discribed in the present volume under the following chapters:--Introduction; Human Rights Activism; Judicial Activism and Human Rights; National Democratic Movements and Human Rights; NGOs and HR Protection; NGOs and Women's Rights; NGOs' Influence; NGOs and Mechanism of Commission on Human Rights; Human Rights Organisations in Developing Countries; Role of NGOs in Human Rights Activism; NGOs and Civil Society; Some Notable NGOs; Red Cross and Red Crescent and Bibliography etc.

Hopefully, this will prove a vade mecum to one and all concerned.

In preparation of this work we have extracted vital information from different standard works, reports and news items, available in printed and digital form. We express our thankfulness to the authors, copyright holders and the sources. Simultaneously, we acknowledge our gratefulness to all those who extended all assistance and guidance while working on this project. My publishers deserve all appreciation for their keenness and executing this work superbly in the present shape.

Comments and criticism are welcome from all users to make this more comprehensive and informative.

—Author

1

INTRODUCTION

> "Value are desirable states, objects, goals, or behaviours, transcending specific situations and applied as normative standards to judge and to choose among alternative modes of behaviour."
>
> —*Schwartz (1992)*

These days NGO is the term understood more or less by everybody everywhere. Simultaneously. Human rights awareness is gradually reaching far and wide. In fact, NGOs have been instrumental in making human rights activism more vocal.

India has also seen a phenomenal mushroom growth of NGOs operating in different areas with different missions. By 2010 thousands and thousand NGOs are operating here.

In common parlance, a Non-governmental organization (NGO) is any local, national or international citizens' group (i.e., not part of a government) which does not work for profit. This simple definition also means that organizations under the label of NGOs have an extremely broad range of functions. NGOs work in fields as diverse as law, refugee work, human rights and disarmament; their work can range from influencing policy or organizing communities around special issues to providing technical or medical assistance to conducting research. Over the last some decades the role of NGOs in local and international affairs has grown tremendously. By way of example, 54,000 new organizations were set up in France between 1987 and 1994; in less than a decade, 27,000 in Chile. The amount of development assistance flowing through NGOs has more than doubled since 1980.

Most of this growth reflects a desire on the part of citizens to influence their own lives and environments. Because of their flexibility, NGOs provide a unique channel through which ordinary citizens can participate in decisions which they feel affect their lives - that could be anything from housing to arms control.

Remarkably, in the 1945 San Francisco meetings in which the United Nations Charter was drawn up and signed, 42 NGOs were invited to participate by the US government. They presented draft texts for the Charter, parts of which were eventually incorporated, including this passage from Article 71: "The Economic and Social Council may make suitable arrangements for consultation with Non-governmental organizations... That laid the foundations for cooperation between the UN and NGOs. The Council granted consultative status to a limited number of NGOs, which meant that these NGOs could participate in some debates and, in some cases, place items on the agenda. Other NGOs, however, could cooperate in the field with the specialised agencies. It was probably in the field more than anywhere else that the presence of NGOs began to be felt strongly. Specialised agencies and bodies such as the UN Development Programme and the UN High Commissioner for Refugees realised early on that NGOs offered them crucial resources and expertise.

For example, without the cooperation of humanitarian organizations -ranging from CARE to Medecins Sans Frontieres

(Doctors Without Borders) - it would have been virtually impossible to meet the needs of refugees fleeing war. Many of these specialised agencies have their own relationships with NGOs; they can coordinate NGO efforts, provide funds for NGO projects or even receive funds from NGOs for their own programmes.

Remarkably, the cooperation of NGOs has also furthered the goals of the UN in other areas such as disarmament, human rights, education, the environment and science. Beginning with the 1992 UN Conference on Environment and Development in Rio de Janeiro, the broader participation of NGOs in addressing global issues became a fact. Over 1500 organizations were accredited to participate in the conference. In this and subsequent international conferences, such as the World Conference on Human Rights (Vienna), the International Conference on Population and Development (Cairo), the World Summit for Social Development (Copenhagen) and the Fourth World Conference on Women (Beijing), NGOs have shaped many of the points on the agendas, some of which have already become law. In short, NGOs participate in the UN system in four ways. They raise issues, such as women's rights and the environment, which then get placed on the world's agendas. They shape decisions taken by the UN, though it can be said that they are much less influential in politics than in the social and humanitarian fields. They enter into partnership with the UN to help carry out its objectives and programs in the field. Finally, they serve as important watchdogs of the UN, observing, criticising and reporting on its role.

NGOs and the Human Rights Protection Within the UN System

The acknowledgment of the dignity of the human being, and the promotion of the respect of an individual's rights, is the story of along struggle through the centuries and civilisations, a struggle in which architects of peace and justice have early on sought to pool their resources, be it at the local, national or more recently international level. At all the stages of this long march activities have been undertaken by NGOs. NGOs include tens of thousands of non-profit associations, foundations, groups, and volunteers, They are very diverse, in structure, composition and objectives. Some deal with education, others are activists, and yet others deal with technical projects, material assistance or information. NGOs are also professional and commercial organisations, trade union Cooperatives, youth movements, feminist organisations, religious associations, research centres, etc. Of diverse political, cultural or religious affiliation, each NGO specialises in a particular sector of society. The term "NGO" is thus simplified, it is the tree which hides the forest of which the variety constitutes its resources. By using this term, one therefore should riot fall prey to generalities with reference to these thousands of organisations. One would commit a serious error by trying to unify something that cannot be unified. However, there are several characteristics for all the NGOs. Before the NGO Conference in Paris in 1968, Rene Cassin explained that in the field of human rights, NGOs performed three main functions:

> "First of all, they (NGOs) represent on the one hand, ordinary men and women, all members of the world community and on the other, official national and international bodies. They were the first to make widely known though official channels, the principles of the Universal Declaration of human rights to uninformed individuals. NGOs are truly invaluable for the dissemination of information.

Secondly, and based on this primary function, NGOs play an important role in the education of the citizen, a role which the authors of the Universal Declaration considered of prime importance, even more important than all other measures which could be undertaken at the national or international level; NGOs are the tools is by which human rights can be made known and respected.

Finally, of the three functions of NGOs is that of catalysts thereby encouraging officials bodies to act. It is impossible to say how many problems concerning human rights would not have been brought to the attention of these organs were it not for the initiative or the indirect action undertaken by NGOs.

Actors of development, agents of information, inbitiators of proposals, in the field of the protection of human rights, NGOs are present at all stages of the proceeding. They are at the origin of most of the norms and are indispensable for the shaping of public opinion thereby ensuring that these norms are actually implemented. Within international institutions, law and practice are not always on the same wavelength, The rift between the fundamental needs of peoples and the UN debates is widening and the NGOs are the only ones who can build bridges between these two realities on per.

NGOs and the United Nations

It is pertinent to note here that the history of the United Nations is closely linked to the activities of NGOs. From its inception, the United Nations Organisation sought to define its relationship with NGOs.

The International Human Rights Charter

The World War II ended with a terrible toll of massacres, and destruction never known before as such by humankind. All over, architects of peace, utopic, great and generous, multiplied their initiatives. At the universal level, these men and women rapidly encouraged their governments to reconstruct universal organisation which received, with their impetus, the name of United Nations. In order to avert another tragedy, architects of peace operated in three major ways: encouraged reconciliation, refused violence (peaceful conflict resolution, action in favour of disarmament), promoted justice and the respect for human rights.

These considerations have been reiterated in the objectives of the United Nations, whose Charter starts with the following words: "we, the Peoples of the United Nations..". Article I of the Charter signed in San Francisco on 26 June 1945, describes as the major aim: "to develop friendly relations among nations based on respect for the principles of equal rights and self-determination of peoples" (al.2) "in promoting and encouraging respect for human rights and for fundamental freedoms for all without distinction as to race, sex, language, or religion" (al. 3).

During its first session (London, January 1946), the General Assembly already considered a draft declaration on human rights which was then transmitted to its Economic and Social Council (ECOSOC) in order to contribute to the activities of the Commission on Human Rights, which was going to be set up. At the end of 1947, the Commission decided to adopt a Human Rights Charter composed of a declaration, a covenant and implementation mechanisms. A year later, in Paris, the General Assembly adopted the Universal Declaration of Human Rights which had been prepared by the Commission. The drafting and the adoption of the 'Covenant took almost ten years. In December 1966, the General Assembly finally adopted two Covenants, one on economic, social and cultural rights, the other on civil and political rights. These three documents constitute the international human rights Charter In their elaboration, the proposals and the untiring work of the NGOs have been significant.

A Status for NGOs

This active role of NGOs in the foundation of the world organisation is exemplified by the fact that the UN Charter already provides that "the Economic and Social Council may make suitable arrangements for consultation with nongovernmental organisations which are concerned with matters within its competence" (Article 71). On 21 June 1946, ECOSOC created a Committee entrusted with non-governmental organisations to examine matters concerning NGOs seeking to obtain consultative status. Initially, the Committee was composed of five member states. Since 1981, the Committee is composed of 19 members, who are elected for a four year term. The criteria for the obtention of consultative status have also evolved and it is resolution 1296 (XLIV) of 25 May 1968 which establishes the arrangements for consultation with nongovernmental organisations. According to this resolution, NGOs wishing to obtain consultative status must meet 11 principles: the organisation shall be concerned with matters falling within the competence of ECOSOC, the organisation shall be of representative character and of recognised international standing and the aims and purposes of the organisation shall be in conformity with the spirit, purposes and principles of the Charter of the United Nations. Resolution 1296 reiterates the distinction made in the UN Charter between the participation (of non member states) and the consultation (of NGOs). In order to organise this consultation with accredited NGOs:

(a) Organisations which are concerned with most of the activities of the Council (general consultative status, category 1);

(b) Organisations which have a special competence in, and are concerned specifically with, only a few of the fields of activity covered by the Council (special consultative status, category II);

(c) Organisations which the Council considers can make occasional and useful contributions to the work of the Council or its subsidiary bodies (Roster).

The ECOSOC Committee on non-governmental organisations is presently composed of the following 19 states: Burundi, Ethiopia, Lesotho, Lybia, Sudan, Cyprus, Iraq, Oman, Philippines, Bulgaria, USSR, Chile, Cuba, Costa Rica, Nicaragua, France, Greece, Ireland and Sweden. Members meet every two years to examine and report on the requests of NGOs for consultative status, requests which must be submitted, at the latest, six months prior to the session of the Committee. The following session of the Committee being held in January 1991, the deadline was in May 1990. Moreover, the Committee also examines periodic reports submitted by NGOs with consultative status with regard to the use of their status in the contribution to the work of the United Nations. Over the years, the biannual sessions of the Committee have taken on greater importance in view of the large number of NGOs having obtained consultative status and the sensitive subjects which are being dealt by NGOs in their interventions at the United Nations.

The Rights of NGOs

NGOs in consultative status with ECOSOC have acquired a certain number of rights which enable them to be heard and to contribute to the work of the United Nations, be it with regard to standard setting or the supervisory mechanisms. It is beyond the scope of this paper to enter into any further detail in particular the special rights accorded to organisations in category I or the distinctions between NGOs in category II and those on the roster. In general, NGOs with consultative status can assist in all the meetings of ECOSOC and its bodies, in particular the Commission on Human Rights and its Sub-Commission, the UN Crime Congress and the Commission on the status of women. They can also submit written or oral statements, which is very important for the debates within the subsidiary organs of ECOSOC, in particular the Commission on Human Rights. Furthermore, NGOs can submit their proposals, information and complaints within the framework of the special procedures of the Commission on Human Rights and its Sub-Commission.

The Commission and the Sub-Commission

The Commission on Human Rights is an organ of the Economic and Social Council (ECOSOC). Its annual session at the Palais des Nations in Geneva is an immense forum, during the course of which virtually every question of human rights is discussed. The Commission consists of 43 Member States. Dozens of other States and about a hundred non-governmental organizations (NGOs) also participate in its work. The issues inscribed on the agenda of the Commission are nearly the same each year: the delegates have dozens of annual reports to examine, in particular that of the Sub-Commission, that of the Working Groups of the Commission (on minorities, enforced disappearances, human rights defenders, the mentally ill), and that of the special Rapporteurs and Representatives, of experts (Advisory Services Program) and of the U.N. Secretariat. The UN Sub-Commission is composed of 26 independent experts nominated by the Commission for a period of four years. It meets annually in August at the Palais des Nations in Geneva. The Sub-Commission is the principal sub-organ of the Commission on Human Rights and carries out work on behalf of this body. It acts as a think-tank by examining problems and obstacles to the realisation of human rights, and by drafting standards and principles. Most of the UN human rights declarations and conventions began their lives in the Sub- Commission.

The Sub-Commission also works as a catalyst; it examines the situation of human rights in the world and draws the attention of the United Nations to serious human rights violations and to situations which have been neglected or forgotten. The Sub-Commission has three Working Groups which meet before its session: the Working Groups on Indigenous Populations, on contemporary Forms of Slavery and on Communications. The former two attract hundreds of witnesses who come to Geneva to contribute to their discussions, The Working Group on Communications however meets in closed session. As stated above, under each item on the agenda, nongovernmental organisations (NGOs) in consultative status with ECOSOC have the right to submit written and oral statements to the Commission concerning the subject under discussion. The written statements should be addressed before the end of the year to the Secretariat of the United Nations (the statements have to be translated).

Obviously, this is not possible if the NGO wishes to comment on one of the reports submitted to the Commission, which are circulated only during the course of the session. With regard to oral interventions, each NGO has the right to make a speech of no more than 10 minutes under each agenda item. Each year, the number of NGO participants increases. This is why the UN Secretariat kindly invites NGOs to intervene only when they have a substantial contribution to make.

Other Forms of Consultations

Notwithstanding the NGOs in consultative status with ECOSOC, hundreds of other NGOs are associated with the activities of the United Nations. Several special procedures of the Commission and its Sub-Commission thus allow for direct access of NGOs without consultative status to certain activities. This is the case with the working group on indigenous populations, at which representatives of any organisation of indigenous peoples or working to protect indigenous rights can participate. Since 1985, the United Nations even have a special fund to cover the travel expenses of several indigenous representatives who wish to attend the annual session of the Working Group. It is a voluntary fund which has received contributions from the Governments of Australia, Canada, Finland, the Netherlands, Norway, Sweden, Switzerland, and of several NGOs.

The fund is administered by the Secretariat and Board of Trustees, composed of: Mr. A. Willemsen Diaz (Guatemala), Chairman; Mr. L. Danfjeld (Norway); Mr A. Sene (Senegal); Mr H. Tauroa (New Zealand); Mr. D. Turk (Yugoslavia). In 1988 and 1989, the fund provided travel grants to 27 and 39 indigenous representatives respectively. For 1990, it could only provide 21 travel grants. This can be explained, in part, by the fact that the extension of the meetings to two weeks increased the expenses considerably. The annual session of the group which is held in Geneva during the summer before the session of the Sub-Commission has thus become the largest forum of indigenous peoples.

Likewise, the working group of the Commission on enforced or involuntary disappearances which provides for a regular forum for the victims themselves or their relatives. On a more general level, the Department of Public Information (DPI) of the United Nations grants a status to several hundred organisations, often of a national character, which receive regularly information on the activities of the United Nations, and which can participate at public sessions and the seminars organised by the UN Secretariat.

Conference of NGOs (CONGO) in Consultative Status

The obtention of consultative status enables every NGO to contribute to the protection of human rights within the framework of its own programme and priorities. However, experience shows that on this level too, there is strength in unity. By being regrouped, NGOs view their force of proposal increase considerably. The UN bodies also benefit from a closer cooperation between NGOs, since it is easier to consult one spokesperson instead of each NGO separately. The Conference of NGOs in consultative status (CONGO) responds to this dual need by bringing together the majority of NGOs with consultative status. CONGO is entrusted to ensure that NGOs with consultative status are able to carry on their consultative functions to their full potential. CONGO is now officially recognised as the major partner of ECOSOC.

Remarkably, in its work, in Its special committees and sub-committees, CONGO increases its exchange of ideas between such varied NGOs. The Special NGO committees for disarmament, on development and on human rights have organised official meetings, conferences and seminars, in order to formulate proposals concerning the activities at the United Nations. In the field of human rights, a special committee brings together NGOs active In Geneva. This special committee has sub-committees on racism and on the status of women. The NGOs represented at the headquarters of the United Nations in New York also have their special Committee, whose role is no doubt less well known, but as important, since it is in New York that ECOSOC human rights meetings and the commissions of the General Assembly are held. It is also in New York that decisions are taken with regard to the general budget, that is to say derisions concerning the funds available for the human rights programme of the United Nations. The NGOs associated with the Department of Public Information are also regrouped in the Executive Committee NGO/ DPI, which transmits the proposals of national NGOs and participates in the organisation of meetings.

On a daily basis, the United Nations is often disappointing. A large bureaucracy, the polarization of power blocs, the defence of national interests, raison d'etat and interminable debates on procedures. But, sometimes, it is useful to make the balance: in 55 years, the United Nations has prepared and adopted more international community has over the past centuries.

International Instruments

After the adoption of the Universal Declaration of Human Rights and the International Covenants, dozens of general principles, declarations and conventions were adopted with regard to different rights. In the preparatory work, which sometimes took years in different working groups, the role of NGOs was not only important but instrumental. Therefore, a few example only are given to illustrate the role of NGOs. In the course of these last few years, the UN General Assembly has adopted two international conventions of great importance/one against torture, the other on the rights of the child. In both cases, a sustained and well coordinated effort on the part of a handful of specialised NGOs led to the inclusion of a number of elements into the draft convention. This endowed these two Conventions with more effectiveness since the NGOs were able to express the needs and problems of the victims of human rights violations.

The Convention on the Rights of the Child was the result of a ten year drafting process and negotiations. UN observers agree that the contribution of NGOs to the drafting of many of the Convention's articles was essential. However, at the beginning of this process, the NGOs dealing with the rights of the child had little or no experience in drafting such international instruments. In a memorandum submitted to the NGO Symposium on 4 May 1990, Nigel Cantwell of Defence for Children international (DCI) explained how NGOs finally set up an ad hoc working group in order to coordinate the work on the Convention and to present a more coherent NGO policy. This ad hoc group submitted a concise report containing proposals to the negotiators. The ad hoc group became the fully fledged representative for the governments. According to Cantwell, 15 substantive items proposed by NGOs were incorporated into the draft. NGOs are having a similar experience with the preparation of a draft declaration on enforced or unvoluntary disappearances.

During the 42th session of the Sub-Commission (August 1990), the 26 experts decided to transmit their draft declaration to the Commission on Human Rights. NGOs have been active supporters in this drafting process. At the forefront were the Latin American organizations for victims and others close to disappeared persons, notably the Latin American -Federation (FEDEFAM) which has been submitting testimony to the working group of the Commission for years. In 1986 FEDEFAM had submitted a draft declaration of its own to international authorities. In addition to proposals made by victims came those formulated by international non-governmental organizations, These NGOs were active at every stage of the discussion process, putting forward proposals and commenting on debates.

For NGO efforts to be effective, they had to meet two

conditions. First of all, it had to be shown that enforced disappearances were not an exclusively Latin American practice the cases put before the Commission's working group concerned a growing number of African and Asian countries. The well-documented cases submitted by FEDEFAM itself, which has consultative status with ECOSOC, also concerned disappearances in other regions. During the Sub-Commission's 42nd session FEDEFAM addressed cases in Morocco and Turkey. The second condition turned on the consensus of NGOs, In this respect the work of the ICJ was essential since it ensured that the final draft would reflect the diverse concerns of a wide number of organizations. To make certain the Commission will transmit the draft to ECOSOC. NGOs will now have to pool their efforts on the political front.

Of course, before proposing draft declarations and then conventions, it is necessary to promote within the UN system the recognition of general legal principles which will be defined later in international instruments. And the role of NGOs in this regard is also very significant. Let us examine some of the recent initiatives:

- Right to compensation: a Canadian organization, the War Amputees of Canada, initiated the process leading to a UN study on the right to compensation since 1988, the organization has been working in the Sub-Commission to obtain reparation from the Japanese Government for injury suffered by its members - former prisoners of war-during the second world war.

  After the timid response to its claim for war-crimes compensation, War Amputees of Canada decided to raise the broader issue of the right to compensation of victims of all gross human rights violations by holding an international conference on the topic.

The Sub-Commission subsequently took up the question, entrusting a study on it to Mr van Boven. Meanwhile, War Amputees of Canada has obtained consultative status with ECOSOC and is pressing its claims against the Government of Japan. At the organization's instigation, the first international meeting of former prisoners of war took place in Amsterdam in May of 1990. Groups in Australia, New Zealand, the United Kingdom the Netherlands the the United States have now formed an alliance with War Amputees of Canada to seek reparations from Japan.

* *Popular participation:* over the last ten years, a large number of NGOs have been actively involved in promoting the recognition of the right to development as a fundamental human right, These efforts were coordinated in particular within the NGO Committee on Development, and this has led to the adoption by the UN General Assembly of a declaration on the right to development. In this debate on the right to development many NGOs introduced the notion of popular participation in the Recovery and Development Process was held in Harare. This conference stressed the concepts of democratic development and the creativity and self-reliance of people as an integral element of development. The African Charter adopted during that conference the role of people and their organisations as crucial in designing policies and programmes to solve the economic and human problems of Africa.

In the present book, we have made an attempt to address all crucial and important issues pertaining to NGOs and Human Rights Activism. Citing instances from India and other countries the information contained herein have become of utmost use to the readers.

In the next chapter, we will introduce you to human rights activism.

2

HUMAN RIGHTS ACTIVISM

The Beginning

Since the adoption of the Universal Declaration of Human Rights in 1948, an elaborate system of mechanisms has been created to ensure the advancement of universal human rights, as well as to deal with violations of human rights as they occur. At the centre of this system are two types of mechanisms: formal monitoring of States compliance with international treaties, and extra-conventional mechanisms or special procedures, working groups, special rapporteurs and special representatives of the Secretary-General - which deal with burning issues as they arise. Once the Universal Declaration of Human Rights was adopted, the Commission on Human Rights set out to turn the principles that it defined into international treaties. When States ratify international treaties, they agree to engage in a review process of their human rights legislation and practice by groups of independent experts.

It is remarkable that the first human rights instrument to establish an international monitoring system was the Convention on the Elimination of Racial Discrimination, adopted by the General Assembly in 1965. This convention not only defined and condemned racial discrimination, but also committed States to amend policy which creates or perpetuates racial discrimination. It was also revolutionary in its provision for national measures towards the advancement of specific racial or ethnic groups. Today, the convention has 148 States parties. The Committee on the Elimination of Racial Discrimination was established in 1969 when the Convention went into force. It consists of 18 independent experts, nominated and elected by States parties to the convention. States submit to the Committee periodic reports on their legislation and practices relevant to the convention's provisions. The Committee can also investigate and attempt to reconcile complaints made by one State against another, as well as communications from individuals.

It is significant to note that in 1966, after two decades of debate, the International Covenant on Economic, Social and Cultural Rights and the International Covenant on Civil and Political Rights were adopted. The Covenant on Economic, Social and Cultural Rights addresses the right to work, to form trade unions, to have social security, to protection of the family, to a standard of living, health and education. The Covenant on Civil and Political Rights defends the right to life - that no one can be subjected to torture, enslavement, forced labour, arbitrary detention - and such freedoms as movement, expression and association. These two treaties, which entered into force in 1976, now have 137 and 140 States parties, respectively. Much of the long debate focussed on the question of one treaty versus two. The prevailing belief was that civil and political rights were already legislatively defined in most countries and could therefore be reviewed by a monitoring body. Economic, social and cultural rights at the time were considered goals and less enforceable, even though the Universal Declaration itself had identified the two sets of rights as equally important.

Thus, only the Covenant on Civil and Political Rights

stipulated creation of a monitoring body - the Human Rights Committee—which was mandated to study reports from States parties, to make comments and recommendations, to consider complaints from one State against another and to, consider complaints from individuals. It was not until 1985 that a Committee on Economic, Social and Cultural Rights was created as a treaty body by the United Nations Economic and Social Council, Unlike the other committees, whose members are elected by States parties to the conventions, the members of the Committee on Economic, Social and Cultural Rights are elected by all members of the Economic and Social Council. Three subsequent conventions also established treaty bodies: the Convention on the Elimination of All Forms of Discrimination against Women (161 ratifications), which entered into force in 1981 and established the Committee on the Elimination of Discrimination against Women; the Convention against Torture and Other Cruel, Inhuman or Degrading Treatment or Punishment (104 ratifications), which entered into force in 1987 and established the Committee against Torture; and the Convention on the Rights of the Child (191 ratifications), which entered into force in 1990 and established the Committee on the Rights of the Child.

Further, a Second Optional Protocol to the International Covenant on Civil and Political Rights aimed at the abolition of the death penalty was adopted in 1989 and is monitored by the Human Rights Committee. In ratifying any of these treaties, States willingly subject their legislations and policy to international monitoring which is based on a dialogue and cooperation between the relevant United Nations committee and participating States. All of the committees are made up of independent, non-governmental experts. Following ratification, each country submits an initial comprehensive report on legislation which relates to the principles of the convention. To review reports, as well as any additional information provided by non-governmental organizations (NGOs), specialized agencies, special rapporteurs or working groups, the Committee meets with the representatives of the State, generally high-level delegations. Formal comments are subsequently forwarded to Governments. In reviewing the reports the different committees use additional sources of information to varying degrees.

The input of non-governmental organizations (NGOs) is central to the operation of the Committee on Economic, Social and Cultural Rights, says Dr. Philip Alston, the Committee's Chairman. "NGOs are essential in providing details and case studies which would not be available from Government sources. In the case of economic rights, we need to know what is happening in practice because legislation is marginal. Therefore, we are dependent on information from the field. We were the first committee to make NGOs a full partner in the sense that we devote a part of our session at the beginning to information from NGOs which we use in debate with Government representatives." In addition to these functions, committees play a significant part in the mobilization of public awareness with the organization of such activities as international years, decades and world conferences.

The relationships which Committee members have developed with States representatives have proven to be an important factor in the advancement of human rights on the national level. Committees guide States over the long term in the revision of law and policy which impact human rights, especially as international debate focuses on more and more broadly defined rights.

According to Dr. Alston, who has chaired the Committee

on Economic, Social and Cultural Rights since 1991, "The main development of recent years is the mainstreaming of economic and social rights. We have been able to persuade other actors to see economic rights as human rights, in particular bringing the right to housing to the top of the agenda of the Habitat Conference (Istanbul)." Based on Government reports and United Nations estimates of 100 million homeless worldwide and 1 billion people inadequately housed, the Committee adopted General Recommendation No. 4 on the right to adequate housing. In response, several Governments have abandoned forced eviction plans and are focusing on guaranteed housing. According to Dr. Alston, "The Dominican Republic, for example, which had been criticized for six years for inadequate housing, invited us to do an on-the spot survey and meet with non-governmental agencies."

The Government of the Philippines reported to the Committee new programmes to relocate and house evicted and homeless and to increase the amount of public spending on new housing. Since 1990 the Committee had been expressing concern about reports of massive homelessness and forced eviction in Panama. In 1996, a Committee mission was invited by the Government to analyze the country's serious housing shortage. "The mission was a tremendous success," says Dr. Alston, "resulting in a much stronger dialogue about housing, amendment of legislation and new housing policy, including commitment to restraint from further forced evictions and bulldozing of existing housing".

Besides addition to housing, efforts are aimed toward universal recognition of the rights to food, health and education as human rights. The Committee persuaded Zimbabwe to abandon the charging of fees for primary education, a policy incompatible with the Covenant. The newest of the treaties, the Convention on the Rights of the Child, is the most universally ratified human rights convention (only two United Nations Member States - the United States and Somalia - are not parties) and it has enjoyed great momentum in a very short time. According to UNICEF, reports from more than 40 countries have been reviewed. Of these, 14 States have incorporated the Convention into their constitutions and 35 have passed new laws or amendments conforming with the Convention. These have taken the form of laws to protect children in general; revisions of laws related to child abuse, child labour and adoption; extensions of the length of compulsory education; protection of child refugees and minority children; and reform of juvenile justice systems.

The committees, however, are hindered in their work by two major factors: their reliance on States for submission of reports, which are sometimes delayed by years. A recent breakthrough, says Dr. Alston, is that two treaty bodies - the Committee on Economic, Social and Cultural Rights and the Committee on the Elimination of Racial Discrimination -have adopted a policy that non-reporting cannot be permitted to have its own rewards. "If a country reported once, it is appropriate for the committee to step in proactively as long as the problem can be dealt with in an orderly dialogue."

Remarkably, three of the six treaties that established monitoring committees also stipulated a procedure - which States parties have the option to ratify - for the consideration of individual complaints. According to the Covenant on Civil and Political Rights (which has 84 ratifications of the optional protocol), the Conventions on Racial Discrimination (14 ratifications) and on Torture (28 ratifications), individuals may submit complaints pertaining to a ratifying State directly to the United Nations. Efforts are under way to finalize an optional protocol creating such a mechanism for the Convention on the Elimination of All Forms of Discrimination Against Women. Consensus at the Vienna Conference in 1993 also prompted the drafting of an Optional Protocol to the Covenant on Economic, Social and Political Rights. If an individual communication concerning a violation of civil or political rights is considered admissible by the Human Rights Committee, it is brought to the attention of the State involved, which is then obligated to submit an explanation. Any final decision on whether or not the Covenant has been violated is made public. In respect of the principle of non-interference in States' internal affairs, it was several years before the United Nations was compelled to act on the many individual complaints it received outside the purviews described above. These, traditionally, were forwarded to non-governmental organizations. As of 1959, confidential lists cataloguing complaints, but not intended for action, were circulated to the Commission on Human Rights and to the Sub-Commission on the Prevention of Discrimination and the Protection of Minorities. In 1970, resolution 1503 of the Economic and Social Council established a confidential procedure involving the Commission on Human Rights and its Sub-Commission, to examine communications received from individuals and groups alleging systematic and gross violations of human rights.

In case reasonable evidence of a consistent pattern of gross violations is identified, the matter is forwarded to the Commission. But, as with all other mechanisms, the procedure is designed to promote, as a primary course of action, dialogue with States. In the framework of this procedure, the Government concerned has the option to present its opinion.

Non-Conventional Mechanisms

During the last four decades, individual complaints have

generally come to be taken up by the United Nations network of thematic working groups and special rapporteurs, as well as country rapporteurs, put in place to take more vigorous steps toward elimination of heinous human rights violations. Today, special rapporteurs are on the front lines, investigating and intervening as necessary in individual cases and emergencies. "Historically, the United Nations did not consider its role to call on Member States to account for human violations in the absence of the treaty body mechanisms, which offered clear standards and mechanisms," says Nigel Rodley, the Special Rapporteur on Torture. "These inhibitions began to erode when the Working Group on Enforced and Involuntary Disappearances, established in 1980, began to take up individual complaints and to seek visits to States."

Blatant violations of human rights taking place in crisis situations around the world often prompt States to call for a more aggressive response by the United Nations. The Commission on Human Rights will then appoint a special rapporteur or working group to investigate. Rapporteurs work in such areas as extra judicial, summary or arbitrary executions; torture; the independence and impartiality of the judiciary; jurors and assessors and the independence of lawyers; religious intolerance; the use of mercenaries; freedom of opinion and expression; racism, racial discrimination and xenophobia the sale of children, child prostitution and child pornography; the elimination of violence against women; and the effects of toxic and dangerous products on enjoyment of human rights.

There are also special rapporteurs assigned to specific countries: among them Afghanistan, Burundi, Congo, Cuba, Equatorial Guinea, Iran, Iraq, Myanmar, Nigeria, occupied Palestine, Bosnia and Herzegovina, Croatia, Federal Republic of Yugoslavia, Rwanda and Sudan. Special rapporteurs are free to use all resources, including individual communications and reports from non-governmental organizations, in preparation of reports. Much of their research is done in the field conducting interviews with both authorities and victims and gathering on-site evidence whenever possible. Special rapporteurs can also avail an urgent action procedure to intercede with governments on the highest level. From 1992 to 1996 the Special Rapporteur on Summary and Arbitrary executions, for example, made 818 urgent appeals on behalf of more than 6,500 persons to 91 different countries and received replies in roughly half of the instances. The reports, of the special rapporteur are made public by the Commission on Human Rights and thus contribute to publicizing violations and the responsibility of Governments.

In 1995-1996, the Special Rapporteur on Torture sent 68 letters to 61 Governments regarding 669 cases, as well as 130 urgent appeals on behalf of nearly 500 people. Forty-two countries responded on 459 of those cases. Among them, for example, were the prosecution by Chile of persons responsible for criminal excesses, reform in the country's penal code and reform of its code of criminal procedure. Following an extensive visit to Pakistan and co-operation with authorities there, the special rapporteur was able to report abolition of corporal punishment and the use of fetters in prisons.

The mandate of the Special Rapporteur on Myanmar is to address the human rights situation in the country, follow the question of transferring power to a civilian government, drafting a new constitution, lifting restrictions on personal freedoms and the restoration of human rights. Such a mandate is very sensitive, as it relates to the nature of a Member State's administration and difficult to carry out in the face of Government non-compliance. In effect, the Special Rapporteur brings violations and recommendations regarding that State to the attention of the United Nations, which by adopting a resolution can then attempt to coerce cooperation. Special rapporteurs submit annual reports to the Commission on Human Rights. These reports are also used by committees in preparation of their discussions with States.

Naturally, as mandates have been created or revised to respond to crisis, overlaps exist. Dr. Alston says, "There has been considerable blurring of the distinctions, particularly in the sense of involving treaty bodies in emergency situations, which require dramatic responses not suitable to the means at committees' disposal. Calling in the representatives of Bosnia and Rwanda is questionable because methods of operation are not of the sort that are going to change the situation. Special rapporteurs are in a better position to respond proactively in relation to violations. They can expose and raise the stakes on violating Governments."

In response to a changing world, greater demands from States and the universal recognition of more comprehensively defined rights, the mechanisms established to guarantee the rights defined by the Universal Declaration of Human Rights - in practice as well as in law - have become increasingly complex. These mechanisms were created less as 'part of a plan but rather as needs arose. All efforts were put toward the resolution of human rights crisis resulting from war, poverty and oppression. In recent years, the mandates of peace-keeping operations increasingly have included a human rights component, which has frequently been critical to a mission's success. Virtually every United Nations body and specialized agency is involved to some degree in the protection of human rights.

When the Universal Declaration of Human Rights was adopted first although not legally binding, it had a tremendous impact on subsequent debate at the international level, as well as frequently the national level. In some parliaments the Declaration is still cited in the enactment of new legislation. Now, as then, the United Nations is critical in providing an environment for debate, negotiation and study. It has been most effective when engaged with States in long-term efforts to incorporate human rights into national law, in giving voice to non-governmental organizations and in elevating universal awareness about human rights.

UN Honour to Human Rights Activists

In 1998, six Human Rights prizes were awarded for courage and determination in Promoting Human Rights. The United Nations initiating honouring five individuals for their courage and determination in promoting and protecting human rights, with a sixth award honouring all Human Rights Defenders throughout the world since that year. The individuals are: Sunila Abeyesekera of Sri Lanka; Angelina Acheng Atyam of Uganda; Jimmy Carter of the United States; Jose Gregori of Brazil; and Anna Sabatova of the Czech Republic.

The presentation of the six United Nations Human Rights Prizes at United Nations Headquarters in New York on 10 December was one in a series of gala events marking the fiftieth anniversary of the adoption of the Universal Declaration of Human Rights. Previous awardees include Nelson Mandela, Eleanor Roosevelt, U Thant, Bishop Abel Muzorewa and Dr. Martin Luther King, Jr. The Prizes were awarded by United Nations Secretary-General Kofi Annan. Around the world, voices have been raised to condemn violations of human rights, defend people's rights and lead the fight against injustice. These are the voices of people who found inspiration in the Universal Declaration of Human Rights.

Notable Awardees

- **Sunila Abeyesekera** of Sri Lanka, the Executive Director of INFORM, one of the key human rights organizations in her country. An activist for almost 30 years, her work focuses mainly on women's rights, armed conflicts and conflict resolution. She has played a key role in lobbying and advocacy work within the United Nations human rights system.
- **Angelina Acheng Atyam** of Uganda, a nurse-midwife and mother of six, is a founding member and vice-chair of the Concerned Parents Association, a group of Ugandan parents who came together to demand action when their daughters, 139 girls from the St. Mary's School, were abducted by the Lord's Resistance Army in October 1996. Ms. Atyam has been a powerful spokesperson, giving voice to the concerns of thousands of families whose children have been stolen. She has worked tirelessly to secure the release of children in rebel captivity. She has also worked to bring national and international attention to the plight of the captive children, by travelling to Europe and the United States.
- **Jimmy Carter,** former President of the United States of America, has committed himself to the cause and international defence of human rights. Mr. Carter has been involved in activities ranging from defending religious minorities in Eastern Europe to working to eradicate river blindness. He did outstanding work in bringing a peaceful solution to the civil war in Liberia, The Carter Center, in Atlanta, Georgia (USA), played a significant role in brokering peace talks between the warring parties.
- Jose Gregori of Brazil has been involved in human rights since the 1950s. He was a student at Sao Paulo University when the military regime took power in Brazil. During that period, he cooperated closely with groups in trying to reestablish democracy. He now heads the recently created National Secretariat for Human Rights. He has been active in strengthening national and regional cooperation in defence and promotion of human rights.
- **Anna Sabatova** of the Czech Republic has been involved in human rights activities for the past 30 years. She was sentenced to three years in prison for distributing leaflets that reminded Czechoslovakian citizens that to vote in parliamentary elections is not a duty, but a right. She is one of the founding members of "Charter 77", a centre of civic resistance.
- **Human Rights Defenders:** This Prize has been given in honour of all Human Rights Defenders. The commitment among ordinary people to human rights is represented by thousands of courageous individuals worldwide who struggle to promote and protect the fundamental rights of others in their communities or in other parts of the world.

The United Nations Human Rights Prizes are awarded every five years to recipients who have made outstanding contributions to the promotion and protection of the human rights and fundamental freedoms embodied in the Universal Declaration of Human Rights and in other relevant United Nations instruments. The Prize was established in 1966 by General Assembly resolution 2217/XXI, and the first awardees were honoured in 1968. Before the 1998 awards, 28 individuals and seven organizations had received the Human Rights Prize, Selection is determined by a special United Nations committee composed of the President of the General Assembly, the President of the Economic and Social Council, the Chairman of the Commission on Human Rights, the Chairman of the Commission on the Status of Women and the Chairman of the Sub- Commission on the Prevention of Discrimination and Protection of Minorities. Nominations may be made to the committee by United Nations Member States and specialized agencies and by non-governmental organizations in consultative status with the United Nations.

Human Rights-Activism in Two Guatemalan Land Disputes: A Case Study

To begin with, in 1993, human rights activists undertook a 10-day march to the Communities of Population in Resistance of the Sierra (CPRs) in northwestern Guatemala. This is one of three concentrations of internal refugees - the others are in the Ixcan and the Peten - that remain beyond .' government control after more than a decade of offensives by the Guatemalan army. The marchers were a cross-section of the human rights community, including Catholic and Protestant clergy, foreign solidarity activists, journalists and militants of the Guatemalan left. The land where you are going is holy land, watered with the blood of innumerable martyrs', a Catholic bishop told the marchers:

> You are going to meet the crucified Christs of the Population in Resistance. You are going to see them with your own eyes, you are going to hear them, you are going to touch them. You are going to help them come down from the cross,..

The marchers forgave the bishop his hyperbole. This was part of his diocese, the Department of El Quiche, where the Guatemalan army murdered hundreds of Catholic leaders during a counter-insurgency drive against the Guerrilla Army of the Poor in the early 1980s. Many CPR leaders were Catholic catechists before the army burned their villages and corralled most of the population into closely watched 'model villages'. As the bishop made contact with the CPRs in the early 1990s, death squads tried to dissuade him by murdering one of his lay workers.

They also killed Myrna Mack Chang, a Guatemalan anthropologist knifed to death outside her office; her offence was serving as a liaison with the CPRs. Led by her sister Helen, Mack's colleagues pressed the case, until it led to the army intelligence units that surround Guatemala's weak civilian presidency. Internationalists are significant players in the struggle to democratise Guatemalan society, but their work is being complicated by conflicts between peasants that cannot be reduced to the moral dichotomies that so often move foreigners to become involved in the Third World. What has made Guatemala such a popular destination for activists is the terrible human rights record of the army, a Praetorian institution that has dominated the country since the early 1960s. Because the military's lack of accountability puts it squarely in the way of a more democratic society, human rights activism in Guatemala — to pressure the state to respect international law has been difficult to distinguish from solidarity activism - to support the left against state repression. Whether internationalists refer to themselves as solidarity activists or human rights monitors, their main task has been to bring international pressure to bear on the military.

Resultantly, many newly arrived activists have assumed that any conflict involving human rights can be reduced to the army versus 'the people', with the latter represented by the dissident organisations with which they happen to work. Since the left's popular organisations need all the international support they can get, they have been all too happy to agree, by assuring foreign supporters that hostile peasants are manipulated by the army. That peasants might have their own reasons for distrusting the left, or quarrelling among themselves, is something that has been slow to enter the picture, with the result that human rights activists can find themselves in a more partisan position than they anticipated. Now that the army-guerrilla fighting is dying down, and will hopefully end in a United Nations-brokered peace agreement in 1996, many of the conflicts coining to the surface involve land. Even though such disputes have been complicated by the war, they also reflect a long history of competition for land, not just between *ladinos* and the Maya-speaking *indigenas* who make up half the country's population, but among Mayas. Because of the obvious challenges posed by the Guatemalan army, until recently internationalists tended to consider peasant competition over land a secondary problem. Typically, the refugees they accompanied were coming home to dispute property with peasants who were still organised into the army's civil patrols. This made it easy to attribute problems to army manipulation. Then in 1994-95, in the Ixcen region, returning refugees organised by the left and accompanied by foreigners found themselves in conflict with other groups organised by the left.

In other parts of Guatemala, the army vs. the people paradigm can still guide how internationalists insert themselves into disputes between peasants.-Such is the case in northern Quiche, around the three Ixil Maya towns of Nebaj, Cotzal and Chajul, which the Guerrilla Army of the Poor (EGP) used to claim as a bastion of support. The Ixils of Chajul have a long record of defending their land against usurpers. This is where, in 1975, the EGP launched its armed struggle by assassinating a well-known ladino plantation owner. Chajul is also the town where the Guatemalan army killed Petrocinio Menchii, an event memorialised by his sister, the winner of the 1992 Nobel Peace Prize, in the most dramatic passage of 1, *Rigoberta Menchii*. Since the early 1990s, and thanks in part to the arrival of foreign activists, human rights has come out of the closet in northern Quiche. Most Ixils seem pleased by this. But those of Chajul have divided feelings, because internationalists are supporting their antagonists in land disputes. One conflict is with the CPRs of the Sierra. To escape army offensives, this Mayan peasant population settled on Chajul land which is so fertile that now they do not want to leave. Chajul's other dispute is with the K'iche' Maya village of Los Cimientos, which has a national-level title to land which the Chgjules believe to be part of their own municipal grant. In each case, internationalists operating on the army vs. the people paradigm have decided to support the other party against the Chajules. These are very particular conflicts, but the kind of challenge that Chajul poses to the human rights movement is increasingly common. No longer must human rights activists in Europe and the United States confine themselves to writing letters to far-off heads of state, or pressuring their own government to take action. Now they can take action themselves. Thanks to jet travel and the growing influence of human rights activism, outsiders can be at the scene of a crisis within days. Prior to arrival, they have decided to get involved on the basis of information that has been filtered and simplified by long-distance reporting. At the scene, they must attend to a wider and more contradictory range of voices, including those of presumed victimisers who claim to be victims too. If the victimisation starts looking mutual, whose grievances are to be given priority?

Another issue cuts to the very definition of a human rights abuse, in terms of state involvement. By definition, a violation revolves around a failure by agents of the state to respect due process, whether by directly misusing their authority or by failing to use it to protect citizens' rights. This also holds where state authority is weak, as is often the Case among subordinate groups like peasants, and part of the population is pitted against another, for reasons that extend beyond the state's authority, to competition over land or other long-standing enmities. Yet human rights agencies can invoke their mandate only by attributing responsibility for violations to the state.

In the next chapter we will try to illustrate judicial activism and human rights.

3

Judicial Activism and Human Rights

Judiciary is the custodian of the Constitution. An independent judicial system is perhaps better than any other institution to maintain the perfect equilibrium between the liberty of the individual and the power of the State, In a democratic socialist republic like ours, everyone is under a duty to act in co-operation and co-ordination with everyone else. If, while dealing with cases, the judiciary finds that a law requires a change, or a particular legislation is essential for fulfilling the objective of the Constitution, or that it would serve better the rule of law if the executive adopts a particular line of action, there can be no objection; instead it becomes the duty of the Court to point out the lacuna in the law or in its execution and implementation. In fact, courts can issue directions to the executive and the legislature to perform their obligatory duties.

"To quote Lord Denning the Judges alone can deal with the instant case, to remedy the wrong in the case which is before them. If you wait for the legislation you may wait for years and years and that can't affect the instant case-only the future cases. The independence of judiciary is the "live wire" of our judicial system. The judiciary under our constitutional scheme has been performing positive anti-creative function in securing and promoting human rights to the people. The Apex Court in India in the exercise of its jurisdiction may pass such decree or make order as is necessary for doing "complete justice" in any cause or matter pending before it. The Supreme Court under article *32* of the Constitution has the power to issue any orders, directions or writs, whichever may be appropriate, for the enforcement of fundamental rights enshrined in the Constitution. Similarly the High Courts have the power under article *226* of the Constitution to issue any order, directions or writs, whichever may be appropriate, for the enforcement of fundamental rights or for any other purpose. In this regard the power of the High Courts is wider than the Supreme Court. The judiciary in India has exercised this power in the most creative manner. It has devised new strategies, forged new tools and broadly interpreted the letter of law to ensure the protection of human rights to the people."

Article 21 of the Indian Constitution provides:

> No person shall he deprived of his life or personal liberty except according to procedure established by law. Thus, it is clear that a person can he deprived of his right to life and liberty only according to "procedure established by law". From the very commencement of the Constitution, the significance of the words "procedure established by law" has been a subject matter of judicial consideration. The judicial consideration started in 1950 itself in the case of *A.K. Gopalan v. State of Madras*. In this case, the Supreme Court was divided while interpreting the expression "procedure established by law". The majority view held that "procedure established by law" meant the procedure enacted by the Parliament and State Legislature. The minority wanted to apply "due process clause" of the U.S. Constitution. It was argued by the petitioner that under the Constitution of the United States of America, the corresponding provision was found in the 5th and 14th Amendments,

where the provision, inter alia, was "that no person shall be deprived of his life or liberty or property except by due process of law". It was contended that the Indian Constitution gave the same protection to every person in India except that in the United States "due process of law" had been construed by its Supreme Court to cover both substantive and procedural law, while in India only the protection of procedural law was guaranteed and that the word "due" made no difference to the interpretation of the words in article 21. The word "established" has a wider meaning than the word "prescribed". The word "law" did not mean "enacted law" because that would be no legislative protection at all. If that definition was accepted, any Act passed by the Parliament or the State Legislature which was otherwise within its legislative power, could destroy or abridge this right. On the basis of the same reason, it was further argued that if that was the intention, there was no necessity to put this as a fundamental right in Part III at all. Regarding the meaning of the word "law", it was argued that it meant *jus,* that is, law in the abstract sense of the principles of natural justice and not lax, that is, "enacted law".

Remarkably, Chief Justice Kania gave four points which distinguished the American Constitution from article 21. Firstly, in the American Constitution, the word "liberty" was used, simpliciter, while in India it was restricted to "personal liberty. Secondly, in the American Constitution, the same protection was given to property, while in India, the fundamental right in respect of property was contained in article 31. Thirdly, the word "due" was omitted altogether and the expression "due process of law" was not used deliberately .under the Indian Constitution. Lastly, the word "established" was used and was limited to "procedure" in article 21. Rejecting the contention for the petitioner, Chief Justice Kania held that the word "law" must mean enacted law". The word "established" according to *Oxford Dictionary* means to fix, settle, institute or obtain by enactment or agreement. According to him, the word "established" itself suggested an agency which fixed the limits. The dictionary would show that this agency could be either the legislature or an agreement between the parties. He felt that, therefore, there was no justification to the meaning of *jus* to "law" in article 21. The, expression "procedure established bylaw" seemed to be borrowed from article 31 of the Japanese Constitution. But in order to determine the meaning of "law" in the phrase "procedure established by law", other articles of that Constitution which expressly preserve other personal liberties in different clauses had to be read together. These articles of the Japanese Constitution had not been incorporated in the Constitution of India in the same language. It was not shown that "law" means jus in the Japanese Constitution. The word "due" in the "due process of law" in the American Constitution was interpreted to mean "just" by the Supreme Court in America. The deliberate omission of the word "due" form article 21 lent strength to the contention that the justiciable aspect of law, that is, to consider whether it was reasonable or not by the court, did not form part of the Indian Constitution.

The other judges constituting the majority opinion also expressed the same view. Justice Das (as he then was) cited the meaning of the word "establish" given in the *Oxford English Dictionary* and Annandale's edition of the *New Gresham Dictionary*. According to this *New Gresham Dictionary*, the word "establish" meant amongst other things, to find permanently; to institute; to enact or decree; to ordain; to ratify; to make firm. He observed that in that sense the word "established" would mean enacted" and "established by law" would, therefore, mean "enacted by law" and if that meaning was accepted, "law" must mean "State-made law" and not the principles of natural justice. He discarded the fear that it would give supremacy to the legislatures in the following words:

> This absolute supremacy of the legislative authority has, however, been cut down by Article 21 which delimits the ambit and scope of the substantive right to life and personal liberty by reference to a procedure and by Article 22 which prescribe the minimum procedure which must be followed.

He also rejected the introduction of American doctrine of "due process" in article 21 because he felt that the word "due" did not find place in article 21 so as to qualify the procedure. The contrary view was expressed by Justice Mahajan and Fazal Ali. Justice Mahajan stated that article 21 laid down substantive law as giving protection to life and liberty in as much as it said that these could not be deprived except according to "procedure established by law". It meant that before a person could be deprived of his right to life and liberty, there should exist, as a condition precedent, some substantive law conferring authority for doing so and the law should further provide for a mode of procedure for such deprivation. He felt that article 21 gave complete immunity against the exercise of despotic power by the executive. The article gave immunity also against invalid laws which contravened the Constitution. It also guaranteed that there should he some form of proceeding before a person could be condemned in respect of his life and liberty. He remarkably stated that the article negatived the idea of fantastic arbitrary and oppressive forms of proceedings.

Fazal Ali, J, viewed that "law" in article 21 meant "valid law" and with reference to procedure for the deprivation of personal liberty it concluded four elements or qualifications as explained by Wills." These elements were

(1) Notice

(2) Opportunity to be heard'

(3) Impartial tribunal

(4) Orderly course of procedure

Justice Fazal Ali observed that these qualifications were independent of any claim of the judiciary through the "due process clause" and could be part of the phrase "procedure established by-law". Such elements could be found in the normal interpretations of the "law of the land" in English. Halsbury had observed:

> It seems to me that there should be added to this list the following rights which appear to have become well established the right of the subject to have any case affecting him tried in accordance with the principles of natural justice, particularly the principles that a man may not be a judge in his own cause, and that no party ought to be condemned unheard, or to have a decision given against him unless he has been given reasonable opportunity of putting forward his case ....

The Gopalan's interpretation of the expression "procedure established by law" was also followed in the cases of *Collector of Malabar v. E. Ebrahim Hajee and Ram Chander Prasad v. State of Bihar* in these cases also the Supreme Court held that "procedure established by law" meant procedure enacted by law made by the State, that is, the Parliament or the State Legislatures. The Court did not favour the interpretation of the word "law" in the abstract sense embodying the principles of natural justice. However, Lakhanpal v. Union of India, shows a change in the judicial approach. No doubt the detenue was not given any tight to represent at the time of review of his case, but the Court held that the detenue must he given such an opportunity on the ground of principles of natural justice.

The Supreme Court took more than 25 years to free itself from the shackles of Gopalan. This feat was achieved in Maneka Gandhi v. Union of India, which did it through Bank Nationalisation case. In Bank Nationalisation case the court held that fundamental rights conferred by Part III were not distinct and mutually exclusive rights, The Court reyersed the view of Gopalan that article 22 of the constitution was a complete code and that articles 19,21 and 22 had different dimensions. This led justice Bhagwati (as he then was) to say in Maneka Gandhi that article 21 could not be divorced from article 19, or, for that matter article 14, which takes care of arbitrariness-the purpose of natural justice also being to take care of arbitrariness; and so natural justice is read in article 21. Justice Bhagwati observed:

> The attempt of the Court should be to expand the reach and ambit of the fundamental rights rather than attenuate their meaning and content by a process of judicial construction.

Justice Bhagwati sought help from article 14 in making the procedure under article 21 as fair, just and reasonable. In *E.P. Royappa v. State of Tamil Nadu,* the Court had held:

> (E) quality is antithetic to arbitrariness,
>
> In fact equality and arbitrariness are sworn enemies; one belongs to the rule of law in a republic, while the other, to the whim and caprice of an absolute monarch. Where an act is arbitrary, it is implicit in it that it is unequal both according to political logic and constitutional law and is therefore, violative of Article 14.

Justice Bhagwati Held:

> The principle of reasonableness, which legally as well as philosophically is an essential element of equality or non-arbitrariness pervades Article 14 like a brooding omnipresence and the procedure contemplated by Article 21 must answer the test of reasonableness in order to be in conformity with Article 14. It must be "right and just and fair" and not arbitrary, fanciful or oppressive; otherwise, it would be no procedure at all and the requirement of Article 21 would not be satisfied.

Thus, Justice Bhagwati read articles 14 and 19 in article 21 in order to make the "procedure" under "procedure established by law" as "fair, just and reasonable".

Among the concurring opinions in this case, Justice Chandrachud (as he then was) also held that mere prescription of some kind of procedure could not ever meet the mandate of article 21. The procedure prescribed by law must be fair, just and reasonable, not fanciful, oppressive or arbitrary. But he cautioned that "due process" should not be read into article 21. He pointed out:

> The content which has been meaningfully and imaginatively poured into "due process of law" may, in my view, constitute an important point of distinction between the American Constitution and ours which studiously avoided the use of that expression .... Our Constitution too strides in its majesty but, may it be remembered without the due process clause ....

Justice Chandrachud did not allow the entrance of American due process clause because one right leading to another and that another to still other would produce "grotesque result".

In fact, the fear was that once "procedural due process"

was allowed to become a part of Article 21, it would be difficult to stop "substantive due process". Chief Justice Beg, who joined the majority opinion stated:

> The field of "due process" for cases of preventive detention is fully covered .' by article 22, but other parts of that field, not covered by Article 22, are "unoccupied" by its specific provisions. I have no doubt that, in what may be called "unoccupied" portions of the vast sphere of personal liberty, the substantive as well as procedural laws must satisfy the requirements of both Articles 14 and 19 of the Constitution.

Thus, "substantive" as well as "procedural due process" was introduced in article 21 of the Constitution. Justice Krishna Iyer, who agreed with the majority but delivered a separate opinion also observed:

> 'Procedure established by law, with its legal potentiality, will reduce life and liberty to a precarious playing if we do not ex-necessitate import into those weighty words an adjectival rule of law, civilized in its soul, fair in its heart and fixing those imperatives of procedural protection absent which the processual tail will wag the substantive head .... Processual justice is writ patently on Art. 21. It is too grave to be circumvented by a black letter ritual processed through the legislature.

Thus, according to Justice Krishna Iyer also, procedure must be "fair, just and reasonable". But he added to the opinion of Justice Bhagwati by taking "law" also reasonable. He interpreted the expression "procedure established by law" in such a manner as to reach the conclusion that "law" and "Procedure" must be "fair", just and reasonable".

He explained:

> What is fundamental is life and liberty. What is procedural is the manner of its exercise. This quality

> of fairness in the process is emphasised by the strong word 'established' which means settled firmly not wantonly or whimsically. If it is rooted in the legal consciousness of the community it becomes "established" procedure. And law' leaves little doubt that It is normally regarded as just since law is the means and justice is the end.

Once the principles of natural justice have been read into article 21 of the Constitution there is nothing to prevent the Court from construing "law" as reasonable law. It will be very strange indeed, if article 21 leaves the legislature free to dispense with "fair play in action" while authorising the violation of basic human right to life' and personal liberty.

In *M.H. Hoskot v. State of Maharashtra,* Justice Krishna Iyer quoted Justice Bhagwati's and his own opinion in Maneka and held:

> "Procedure established by law" are words of deep meaning for all lovers of liberty and judicial sentinels. Amplified, activist fashion, "procedure" mean "fair and reasonable procedure" which comports with civilised norms like natural justice rooted firm in community consciousness-not primitive processual barbarity nor legislated normative mockery.

After Maneka, article 21 has become counterpart of "procedural due process". Just as in United States "due process" clause is used to maintain prison discipline, similarly in India, procedural fairness under article 21 encouraged the Summit Court to bring prison reforms.

In *Sunil Batra (1) v. Delhi Administration,* Justice Krishna Iyer observed:

> True, our Constitution has no "due process" clause or the VIII Amendment, but in this - branch of law, after Cooper .... and Maneka Gandhi ... the consequence

> is the same. For what is punitively outrageous, scandalizing unusual or cruel and rehabilitively counter-productive, is unarguably unreasonable and arbitrary and is shot down by Arts. 14 and 19 and if inflicted with procedural unfairness, falls foul of Art. 21.

In *Jolly Varghese v. Bank of Cochin,* Justice Krishna Iyer delivering the judgment, observed:

> the high value of human dignity and the worth of the human person enshrined in Art. 21, read with Arts. 14 and 19, obligates the state not to incarcerate except under law which is fair, just and reasonable in its processual essence.

While saving the prisoners from prison torture, Justice Krishna Iyer again applied the concept of fair procedure in Sunil Batra (II) v. Delhi Administration arid held:

> It is imperative, as implicit in Art, 21, that life or liberty shall not be kept in suspended animation or congealed into animal existence without the freshening flow of fair procedure.

Remarkably, this trend of the Supreme Court was evident in the subsequent cases as well. When the Summit Court was passing through the continuous process of maneuvering "due process" under article 21, A.K. Roy proved to be a deadly stroke. In this case it was contended that the National Security Act, 1980 must be struck down on the ground that it interfered with the liberties of the people. Chief Justice Chandrachud, while delivering the majority judgment rejected the contention and held that the court could not invalidate on the specious ground that it was calculated to interfere with the liberties of the people.

Notably, it is submitted that the Chief Justice's refusal to examine the justness of the law under article 21 was born out of a narrow construction of that article which may not be consistent with the decisional law that had grown in the recent past. It Is really shocking that Justice Bhagwati (as he then was) was party to this decision, who himself had become the creator of "due process" under article 21 in Maneka. It is even more surprising that while delivering the minority opinion In Bachan Singh (which was delivered after this judgment) he gave the example of law of preventive detention to prove the existence of "due process" and in this case, he joined hands with Chief Justice Chandrachud to state that the power to judge the justness of preventive detention was not possessed by the court.

A year later, Ranjan Dwivedi, joined the row of cases which recognized the entry of due process. In this case, the Supreme Court did not hesitate to admit that it was difficult to hold in view of Maneka and E.P. Royappa etc. that the substance of the American doctrine of "due process" had not still been infused into the conservative text of article 21.

In *Olga Tellis v. Bombay Municipal Corporation,* Chief Justice Chandrachud, while delivering the judgement, following the row of cases beginning with Maneka, held that the procedure prescribed by law for the deprivation of the right conferred by article 21 must be fair, just and reasonable. It was pointed out:

> The procedure prescribed by law for depriving a person of his... right to life, must conform to the norms of justice and fair play. Procedure which is unjust or unfair in the circumstances of a case, attracts the vice of unreasonableness, thereby vitiating the law which prescribes that procedure and consequently, the action taken under it ....' The substance of the law cannot be divorced from the procedure which it prescribes for, how reasonable the law is, depends upon how fair is the procedure prescribed by it.

Chief Justice Chandrachud also observed that if a law was found to direct the doing of an act which was forbidden by the Constitution or if for the performance of an act, it compelled the adoption of the procedure which was impermissible under the Constitution, it was liable to be struck down. It is submitted that when the Summit Court is ready to strike down the "law" which prescribes unreasonable "procedure" that does not mean that only "procedure" should be reasonable but that the "law" prescribing that procedure must also be reasonable. The court may not be wanting to allow substantive due process directly along with procedural fairness but indirectly and impliedly it has expressed so. In *Kartar Singh v. State of Punjab,* the Supreme Court has once again reiterated that the "procedure" contemplated by article 21 is that the procedure must be "right, just and fair" and not arbitrary, fanciful or oppressive. In order that the procedure is right, just and fair", it should conform to the principles of natural justice, that is, "fair play in action". Thus, the Summit Court by adopting a new approach to the expression "procedure established by law" has marked a watershed in the history of development of human rights in our country and this affords protection not only against executive action but also against legislation and any law which deprives the person of his human rights would be invalid unless it prescribed a procedure for such deprivation which is "reasonable", fair and just".

Fair Procedure and Public Interest Litigation

One of the most important task before the State is to protect and promote the human rights of the people. But the question is that if the State misperforms or does not perform this important task, how to make it accountable for its actions or inactions and how to enable the "poor and oppressed" class of people to enjoy their basic human rights. Perhaps, "public interest litigation" is a partial answer to this. With the active assistance of the social activists and public interest litigators, the judiciary in India is promising innovative remedial attention for vindication of the governmental commitment to the welfare and relief of the oppressed and in protecting and promoting human rights of the people.

The concept and procedure of public interest litigation in India have been fashioned by the Supreme Court of India. They are still in the process of formulation and concretization. Public Interest Litigation is concerned not with rights of one individual but the interest of a class or group of persons who are either the victims of exploitation or oppression or are denied their constitutional or legal rights and who are not in a position to approach the courts for redressal of their grievances. It seeks to help the victims of governmental lawlessness or repression.

In India, justice was only a remote and even, theoretical proposition for the mass of illiterate, underprivileged and exploited persons in the country till the concept of public interest litigation was accepted as a part of our constitutional jurisprudence. They were unaware of the law or even of their legal rights, unacquainted with the niceties of procedure involved, and too impoverished to engage lawyers, file papers and bear heavy expenditure on dilatory litigation. Thus, the vested interests that exploited them were emboldened to continue with their cruel and even illegal practices with cynical contempt for the law. This vast underprivileged section of the society found themselves utterly helpless. Nor could anyone else take-up their case for lack of locus standi or any direct interest in the matter. Thus, the activist judges expressed the opinion that the present legal and judicial system was a "colonial legacy" unsuited to our condition. They expanded the concept of locus standi from "traditional individualsim" to "community orientation of public interest litigation" and thus relaxed the formalities of procedure.

The liberalisation of the rule of locus standi was necessitated only because of the new constitutionalism blazed in Maneka Gandhi and refined and extended in post-Maneka cases. In Maneka, the court expanded the scope of right to "life" and "personal liberty" by considering "procedure" under "procedure established by law" as "fair, just and reasonable". The concept of fair procedure led to Apex Court to leave the adversary procedure and adopt the new Innovation of public Interest litigation to give relief to prisoners, undertrials, workers, bonded labourers, women, children and many others. The Summit Court also used this tool for the protection of environment, which is an essential clement needed to live a healthy life.

Justice Krishna Iyer observed:

> It is procedural rules ... "which infuse life into substantive rights which activate them to make them effective",.... The truth is that a few profound issues of processual jurisprudence great strategic significance to our legal system face us and we must zero-in on them as they involve problems of access to justice for the people beyond the blinkered rules of "standing" of British Indian vintage.

In *Fertilizer Corporation Kamgar Union, Sindri v. Union of India,* Justice Krishna Iyer emphasised the importance of public interest litigation:

> Law... is a social auditor and this audit function can be put into action only when some one with real public interest ignites the jurisdiction .... In a society where freedoms suffer from atrophy and activism is

> essential for participative public justice, some risks have to be taken and more opportunities opened for the public-minded citizen to rely on the legal process and not be repelled, from it by narrow pendency now surrounding locus standi.

Justice Bhagwati, who was party to Krishna Iyer's opinion in Fertilizer Corporation, gave a comprehensive exposition to his concept of public interest litigation in *S.P. Gupta v. Union of India.* According to him, the traditional rule, that judicial redress was available only to an aggrieved party, was "a rule of ancient vintage". Formulating the concept of public interest litigation, he observed:

> Where a legal wrong or a legal injury is caused to a person or to a determinate class of persons by reason of violation of any constitutional or legal right or any burden is imposed in contravention of any constitutional or legal provision or without authority of law or any such legal wrong or legal injury or illegal burden is threatened and such person or determinate class of persons is by reason of poverty, helplessness or disability or socially or economically disadvantaged position, unable to approach the Court for relief, any member of the public can maintain an application for an appropriate direction, order or writ in the High Court under Art. 226 and in case of breach of any fundamental right of such persons, in this Court under Art. 32 seeking judicial redress for the legal wrong or injury caused to such person or determinate class of persons.

It must not be forgotten that procedure is but a handmaiden of justice and the cause of justice can never be thwarted by any procedural technicalities. The Court would therefore unhesitatingly and without the slightest qualms of conscience cast aside the technical rules of procedure in the exercise of its dispensing power and treat the letter of the public minded individual as a writ petition and act upon it. Today, a fast revolution is taking place in the judicial process; the theatre of the law is fast changing and the problems of the poor are coming to the forefront. The Court has to innovate new methods and devise new strategies for the purpose of providing access to justice to large masses of people who re denied their basic human rights and to whom freedom and liberty have no meaning.

It is an essential element of the rule of law that every organ of the state must act within the limits of its power and carry out the duty imposed upon it by the Constitution or the law. If breach of duty is caused by the state and injury is caused not to any specific or determinate class or group of persons but to the general public. And if no one can maintain an action for redress of such public wrong or public injury, it would be disastrous for the rule of law because it would be open to the state or public authority to act with impunity beyond the scope of its power. Where the observance of the law is left to the sweet will of the authority bound by it without any redress, if the law is contravened, the courts cannot countenance such a situation. Therefore, the court relaxed the strict rule of standing which insisted that only a person who had suffered a specific injury could maintain an action for judicial redress and adopted a broad rule which gave standing to any member of the public who was not a mere busy body or a meddlesome interloper but who had sufficient interest in the proceeding. The Apex Court broadened this rule because:

> (I)t is only the availability of judicial remedy for enforcement which invests law with meaning and purpose or else the law would remain merely a paper parchment. It is only by liberalising the rule of locus standi that it is possible to police the corridors of power and prevent violations of law.

It is submitted that Maneka's creation of "fair, just and reasonable" procedure protected the life and liberty of exploited through the expansion of the rule of locus standi by permitting the public-minded persons to seek the judicial redress for those whose life and liberty is at stake but they cannot protect it due to poverty or any other incapacity. The post-Maneka judicial activism impressed upon the Summit Court to liberate itself from clutches of the traditional technicalities of procedure which is to be followed for access to justice, Maneka made the procedure "fair, just and reasonable" in order to give protection from the executive action which is unfair and unreasonable.

In People's *Union for Democratic Rights v. Union of India,* Justice Bhagwati (as he then was) further elaborated the principle of public interest litigation.

Justice Bhagwati explained the scope and importance of public interest litigation in the legal aid movement, which is part of "fair, just and reasonable" procedure under article 21. He pointed out:

> (P)ublic Interest litigation which is a strategic arm of the legal aid movement and which is intended to bring justice within the reach of the poor masses, who constitute the low visibility area of humanity, is a totally different kind of litigation from the ordinary traditional litigation which is essentially of an adversary character... but it is intended to promote and vindicate public interest which demands that violations of constitutional or legal rights of a large number of people who are poor, ignorant or in a socially or economically disadvantaged position should not go unnoticed and unredressed. That would be destructive of the rule of law which forms one of the essential elements of public interest in any democratic form of government.

Justice Bhagwati (as he then was) again elaborated the importance of public Interest litigation in *Bandhua Mukti Morcha v. Union of India:* Public interest litigation is not in the nature of adversary litigation but it is a challenge and all opportunity to the government and its officers to make basic human rights meaningful to the deprived and vulnerable sections of the community.

The Constitution makers have also deliberately and advisedly not used any words restricting the power of the court to adopt any procedure which it considers appropriate in the circumstances of a case for the enforcement of a fundamental right.

If in the process of new judicial activism to control unfair procedure, any aspersion is cast on the executive that should not be taken in a wrong spirit. The Apex Court also admitted:

> When the Court entertains public interest litigation, it does not do so in a cavilling spirit or in a confrontational mood or with a view to tilting at executive authority or seeking to usurp it, but its attempt is only to ensure observance of social and economic rescue programmes, legislative as well as executive, framed for the benefit of the have-nots and the handicapped and to protect them against violation of their basic human fights, which is also the constitutional obligation of the executive. The Court is thus merely assisting in the realisation of the constitutional objectives.

The highest judiciary allowed the public spirited persons to come forward and become God fathers for the protection of human rights of the poor and ignorant. Due to the efforts of such public-spirited persons, Hussainara cried for the release of undertrials and echo was heard in Khatri and

Kadra Pehadiya. Free legal aid was made part of "fair, just and reasonable" procedure to protect the fundamental rights of the poor. Sunil Batra and Sheela Barse brought the inhuman and degrading condition of prisons and prisoners before the human rights conscious Court. P.N. Thumpy Thera v. Union of India made the court to endorse Francis Coralie Mullin and observed that "the right to life has recently been held by this Court to connote not merely animal existence but to have a much wider meaning to Include the finer graces of human civilization." Bandhua Mukti Morcha made right to live with human dignity a fundamental right under article 21. Neeraja Chaudhary released and directed for the rehabilitation of bounded labourers. Olga Tellis recognizing right to livelihood as a part of right to life.

In *Rakesh Chandra v. State of Bihar,* the Supreme Court in a public interest litigation, after not being satisfied with scheme furnished to it for improving conditions of mental hospitals, decided to monitor its management and a Committee was set up for this purpose.

In *Kishen v. State of Orissa,* the Supreme Court treated the letter of the petitioner as public interest litigation wherein it was alleged that there were starvation deaths of the inhabitants in the districts of Koraput and Kalahandi of State of Orissa due to utter negligence and calousness of the administration and government of Orissa. The Supreme Court pointed out that It is the duty of the government to prevent such deaths and directions were Issued to reconstitute the Natural Calamities Committee to keep a watch on the measures taken and which may be taken in future to prevent deaths due to hunger, poverty and starvation.

In *A.S. Mittal v. State of U.P.* where irreversible damage

was caused to the eyes of the patients in eye camps, a public Interest litigation was filed by the petitioner espousing the cause of unfortunate victims. The Court directed the State government to pay Rs. 12,500/- to each of the victims and Rs. 5000/- as costs to the petitioner for espousing the cause of victims and prosecuting it with deligence.

In *Parmanand Katara v. Union of India,* the Supreme Court laid emphasis, on professional ethics of medical profession in a public interest litigation. The Court held that when an injured citizen is brought for medical treatment, he should instantaneously be given medical aid to preserve life and thereafter procedural criminal law should be allowed to operate in order to avoid negligent deaths.

It is feared that the executive may find little comfort with the court's new role in settling matters of administration over which it has little expertise or no claim. The court is already looked upon as a hostile branch of the government by the executive and public interest litigation contains all potentials for a possible confrontation between the court and the executive.

It is also feared that the concept of public interest litigation will encourage vexatious litigants to file a large number of cases and as a result, the judicial process will be abused causing further delay in the administration of justice and opending a floodgate of litigation.

Justice Krishna Iyer rejecting this fear in *Bar Council of Maharashtra v. M.V. Dabholker,* observed:

> The possible apprehension that widening legal standing with a public connotation may unloose a flood of litigation which may overwhelm the judges is misplaced because public resort to court to suppress public mischief is a tribute to the justice system.

The Australian Law Reform Commission also opposed this argument:

> The idle and whimsical plaintiff, a dilettante who litigates for a lark, is a spectre which haunts the legal literature, not the court.

Justice Krishna Iyer also pointed out in *Fertilizer Corporation Kamgar Union v. Union of India:*

> We cannot be scared by the fear that all and sundry will be litigation happy and waste their time and money and the time of the Court through false and frivolous cases.

In People's Union for Democratic Rights. Justice, Bhagwati (as he then was) pointed out that there was misconception in the mind of some lawyers, journalists and men in public life that public interest was unnecessary A cluttering up the files of the court and adding to the already staggering arrears of cases pending in the court for years. Those who were decrying public interest litigation did not realise that It is only the moneyed who have so far had the golden key to lock the doors of justice" and then for the first time the portals of the court were being thrown open to the poor and the downtrodden, the ignorant and the illiterate and that their cases were coming before the courts through public interest litigation.

The Judiciary has been very cautious in entertaining the public interest litigations. From case to case it has evolved various principles. Frivolous or vexatious writ petition in the name of public interest litigation, filed mala fide and arising out of enmity between the parties cannot be allowed. The Court has to protect the society from so called protectors.

Mere obsession based on religious belief or personal

philosophy cannot be treated as legal disability entitling third party as 'next friend" to file public interest litigation.

Public Interest Litigation espousing cause of an individual permissible only if it falls within the purview of policy decision of general application. It cannot be used to remove distress of any particular individual or satisfy that individual's whims, however pious that may be. Coverting individual dispute into public interest litigation should be discouraged.

In *Janata Dal v. H.S. Chowdhry,* the Supreme Court has beautifully summarised the scope and object of public interest litigation, the horizon of which is widely extended and which at present constitute a new Chapter in justice delivery system acquiring a significant degree of importance in the modern legal jurisprudence practised by Courts in many parts of the world, based on the principle Liberty and Justice for all.

Thus, the concept of public interest litigation which has been and is being fostered by judicial activism has become an increasingly important one setting up valuable and respectable records, especially in the arena of human rights and legal treatment for the 'unrepresented and under-represented'.

Protection Against Exploitation

Human rights are part and parcel of human dignity which is adequately secured by various provisions of the Constitution of India. The importance of the concept of human dignity is well examplified by its inclusion in the national and international basic legal texts. The preamble to the Constitution of India assures among other things "dignity of the individual". Personal liberty and human dignity are most cherished values of our Constitution. These are the necessary epitomes which help in the development of an individual's personality and in the realisation of human rights. Right to life under article 21 of the Constitution means right to live with human dignity and free from all kinds of exploitation.

In addition to this, article 23 specifically prohibits traffic in human beings and *begar* and other similar forms of forced labour. Employment of children in hazardous employment is prohibited by article 24 of the Constitution. The State is expected to direct its policy towards securing that the health and strength of workers, men and women, and the tender age of children are not abused and that the citizens are not forced by economic necessity to enter evocation unsuited to their age or strength. Children are required to be given opportunities and facilities to develop in a healthy manner and in conditions of freedom and dignity. The childhood and youth are required to be protected against exploitation and against moral and material abandonment.

But in spite of the clear mandates of the Constitution, there has been exploitation of the people in various parts of the country and they have been living the life which is below human dignity.

Bonded Labour

There has been existence of bonded or forced labour in large parts of the country. The practice of bonded labour is based on exploitation by a few socially and economically powerful persons trading on the mise and suffering of large number of men and women and holding them in bondage. It is not only an affront to basic human dignity but also constitutes gross violation of human rights.

The President promulgated Bonded Labour System (Abolition) Ordinance, 1975 on 24 October, 1975. This

Ordinance was replaced by the Parliament by the Bonded Labour System (Abolition) Act, 1976.

Basically, this Act was enacted with the object of giving effect to article 23 of the Constitution and to strike against the system of bonded labour which had been a shameful scar on the Indian social scene even after independence." Though technically bonded labourers were freed in 1975 yet the system of bonded labour or forced labour exists in different parts of country even after twenty years have passed when legislature attempted to abolish it. Peter Davies, Director of the Anti-Slavery Society, at a meeting of the working group on slavery, a subsidiary body of U.N. Commission on Human Rights, Geneva, criticised the Indian Government's performance in tackling the problem, saying that the action taken by it was "at best deficient" and "at worst non-existent". He also implied that political will to deal with the problem in a time bound manner was lacking in India. There are many reasons which are responsible for the failure of the Bonded Labour System (Abolition) Act, 1976. Some of the reasons are as under. First, there has not been proper identification of the bonded labourers.

The process of identification and release of the bonded labourers is a process of discovery and transformation of non-being into human beings. It has usually been found that the administration instead of identifying the bonded labourers, denies the existence of bonded labourers. Secondly, most of the workers are totally ignorant or unaware of their right and entitlements. Thirdly, sometimes vested interests obstruct the proper implementation of the beneficial provisions of laws. Fourthly, the inadequate punishment to those who violate the labour laws, makes it impossible to ensure the observance of beneficial provisions for the have-nots. In that case the welfare provisions remain only as paper tigers without any teeth or claws. Lastly, rehabilitation of the liberated bonded labourers is yet another factor which is required to be looked into in its proper perspective. Psychological rehabilitation must go side by side with the physical and economic rehabilitation. During the recent years, the judiciary, particularly the Apex Court, has played an important role in making right to live with human dignity a reality for millions of Indians and has protected them from exploitation. The Supreme Court has not only given the widest possible meaning to the fundamental rights enshrined in articles 21 and 23 but also took into consideration the various factors which were responsible for the failure of various other social welfare laws. The true scope and ambit of the expressions "begar" and "other similar forms of forced labour, have been most eloquently explained by the Supreme Court in a monumental case of *People's Union for Democratic Rights v. Union of India.* In this case, the writ petition was filed by way of public interest litigation concerning the working conditions of workmen employed in the construction work of the various projects connected with the Asian games. In the petition, it was pointed out that the workers did not get the minimum wages as prescribed under the Minimum Wages Act, 1948.

The violation of various other laws, such as Employment of Children Act, 1938; Contract Labour (Regulation and Abolition) Act, 1970; the Inter-State Migrant Workmen (Regulation of Employment and Conditions of Services) Act, 1979 and Equal Remuneration Act, 1976 etc., was also alleged. Defending the public interest litigation, Bhagwati, J., (as he then was), pointed out that public interest litigation is intended to bring justice within the reach of the poor masses, who constitute the low visibility area of humanity and is totally different from the ordinary traditional litigation which is essentially an adversary in character. The rule of law, which is a part of Must, fair and reasonable procedure" under article 21 of the Constitution, does not mean that the protection of the law must he available only to a fortunate few or that the law should be allowed to be prostituted by the vested interests for protecting and upholding the status quo under the guise of enforcement of their civil and political rights. It was further pointed out that so far the courts have been used only for the purpose of vindicating the rights of wealthy and affluent. It is only the moneyed who have so far had the golden key to unlock the doors of justice. But, now for the first time the portals of the Court are being thrown open to the poor and the down-trodden, the ignorant and the illiterate. Dwelling on the scope of article 23 of the Constitution, Bhagwati, J. (as he then) speaking for the court observed:

> (Article 23) Is clearly designed to protect the Individual not only against the State but also against other private citizens. Article 23 is not limited in its application.... The sweep of Article 23 is wide and unlimited and it strikes at "traffic in human beings and begar and other similar forms of forced labour" wherever they are found.

It was pointed out that the word begar used in article 23 is not a word of common use in English language, It is a word of Indian origin which like many other words had found its way in the English vocabulary. It is very difficult to formulate a precise definition of the word "begar," but there can be no doubt that it is a form of forced labour under which a person is compelled to work without receiving any remuneration for it. It is thus clearly a form of forced labour. Now it is not only begar which is prohibited under article 23 but also "all other similar forms of forced labour", whenever they are found.

Explaining the meaning of "other similar forms of forced labour", the Court observed:

> We do not think it would be right to place on the language of Art. 23 an interpretation which would emasculate its beneficial provisions and defeat the very purpose of enacting them. We are clear of the view that Article 23 is intended to abolish every form of forced tabour. The words "other similar forms of forced labour" are used in Art. 23 not with a view to imparting the particular characteristic of "begar' that labour or service should be exacted without payment of any remuneration but with a view to bringing within the scope and ambit of that Article all other forms of forced labour and since 'begar 'is one form of forced labour, the Constitution makers used the words 'other similar forms of forced labour'.

Another important question which arose before the court for consideration was whether there was any breach of article 23 when a person provides labour or service to the state or to any other person and is paid less than the minimum wage for it. Lamenting on this question, Bhagwati, J., (as he then was) observed:

> That where a person provides labour or services to another for remuneration which is less than the minimum wage, the labour or service provided by him clearly falls within the scope and ambit of the words "forced labour" under article 23.

What is prohibited under article 23 is "forced labour", that is labour or service which a person is forced to provide and 'force' which would make such labour or service 'forced labour' may arise in several ways. It may be physical force which may compel a person to provide labour or service to another or it may be force exerted through legal provisions such as a provision for imprisonment or fine in case the employee fails to provide labour or service or it may even be compulsion arising from hunger and poverty, want and destitution.

From the above observations, it is clear that the Supreme Court has given the widest possible interpretation to the various phrases used in article 23 of the Constitution. This interpretation of the Supreme Court, it is submitted, would make right to live with human dignity, a living reality for millions of workers who are doing forced labour for one reason or the other.

In Sanjit Roy v. State of Rajasthan, the Supreme Court relied on the Asiad Workers case and held that the payment of wages less than minimum wage amounts to 'forced labour' and hence Violates article 23 of the Constitution. The Court pointed out that no work of utility and value can be allowed to be constructed on the blood and sweat of persons who are reduced to state of helplessness on account of drought and scarcity conditions. The State could not under the guise of helping persons extract work of utility and value without paying them the minimum wage.

In *Labourers Working on Salal Hydro-Project v. State of J&K,* the Supreme Court treated a letter addressed by Peoples' Union for Democratic Rights and based on a news/report, as writ petition. In the letter it was alleged that the labourers coming from the different parts of the country to the site of Salal Hydro-project in the State of J&K were being exploited and they were being denied the right to live with human dignity. The Supreme Court directed the observance of the various labour laws and also pointed Out that the minimum wages must be paid to the workmen directly without any deduction save and except those authorised by the statute.

Bandhua Mukti Morcha v Union of India, is yet another

landmark judgment of the Supreme Court where the bonded labourers have been protected from exploitation. In this case the petitioner was an Organisation dedicated to the cause of release of bonded labourers; in the country. Justice Bhagwati (as he then was) while describing the true condition of bonded labourers remarked that they are non-beings, exiles of civilization, living a life worst than that of animals, for, the animals are at least free to roam about as they like and they can plunder or grab food whenever they are hungry. But these outcastes of society are held in bondage, robbed of their freedom and they are consigned to an existence where they have to live either in hovels or .' under the open sky and be satisfied with whatever little wholesome food they can manage to get, inadequate though it be to till their hungry stomachs. Not having any choice, they arc driven by poverty and hunger into a life of bondage, a dark bottomless pit from which, in a cruel exploitative society, they cannot hope to he rescued.

In Bandhua Mukti Morcha, the Supreme Court noticed the causes of failure of Bonded Labour System (Abolition) Act, 1976. In the present case, the State tried to escape the liability of releasing the bonded labourers by saying that there were no bonded labourers in the State of Haryana. The petitioner made a survey of some of the stone quarries in Faridabad district and found that there were large number of labourers from different states of the Country who were working under inhuman and intolerable conditions' and many of them were bonded labourers. The petitioner described in the letter, which was treated by the Supreme Court as writ petition, that there was violation of the various constitutional provisions and the statutes which were not being implemented or observed in regard to the labourers working in those stone quarries.

The Supreme Court in Bandhua Mukti Morcha also found that there was violation of the various social welfare laws by the State and the workers were being denied of their right to have 'just and humane conditions of work'. The Court observed:

> The right to live with human dignity enshrined in article 21... includes protection of health and strength of workers, men and women, and., just and humane conditions of work and maternity relief.

Mere liberation of the labourers from bondage without making arrangements for their rehabilitation will serve no useful purpose and may even create a very real problem as to livelihood of the labourers so set free. There is a specific provision for the rehabilitation of the bonded labourers after their release from the bondage.

Neeraja Chaudhary v. State of M.R is a landmark decision of the Supreme Court on rehabilitation of the bonded labourers. The brief facts of this case were that the petitioner, a Civil Rights Correspondent of Statesman, wrote a letter to the Supreme Court pointing out that about 135 labourers; were released from bondage in 1982 from Faridabad and they were brought back .' to their respective villages in Madhya Pradesh. But they were not rehabilitated even after six-months of their release and they were living on the verge of starvation. Bhagwati, J. (as he then was) speaking for the Court observed:

> It is the plainest requirement of Articles 21 and 23 of the Constitution that bonded labourers must be identified and released and on release, they must be suitably rehabilitated. The Bonded Labour System (Abolition) Act, 1976 has been enacted pursuant to the Directive Principles of State Policy with a view to ensuring basic human dignity to the bonded

> labourers and any failure of action on the part of the State Government in implementing the provisions of this legislation would be the clearest violation of Article 21 apart from Article 23 of the Constitution.

Thus, from the above observations of the Supreme Court, it is amply clear that it is not enough merely to identify and release bonded labourers but it is equally, perhaps, more, important that after identification and release, they must he properly rehabilitated. Because without rehabilitation, they would be driven by poverty, helplessness and despair into serfdom once again, Poverty and destitution arc almost perennial features of Indian rural life for large numbers of unfortunate ill-starved humans in this country and it would be nothing short of cruelty and heartlessness to identify and release bonded labour merely to throw them at the mercy of the existing socio-economic system which denies to them even the basic necessities of life such as food, shelter and clothing. We, who have not experienced poverty and hunger, want and destitution, talk platitudinously of freedom and liberty but the words have no meaning for a person who has not even a square meal per day, hardly a roof over his head and scarcely one piece of cloth to cover the shame.

Thus, the petitioner rightly urged in Neeraja Chaudhry that failure on the part of the state government to ensure the proper rehabilitation of the freed bonded labourers amounted to violation of the fundamental right of the bonded labourers to live with human dignity under article 21 of the Constitution.

In *Mukesh Advani v. State of M.P.*, a public interest litigation was filed by one Mukesh Advani, advocate, by addressing a letter to one of the judges of the Supreme Court and annexing thereto a cutting from the *Indian Express* dated 14 September, 1982, depicting the horried plight of bonded labourers, working in stone quarries at Raisen in Madhya Pradesh, In the letter it was also alleged that the working conditions of the workers were of the 18th century vintage and not even a single legislation enacted for the welfare of labour was implemented or respected.

As a part of the social action litigation this letter was treated by the Supreme Court as writ petition under article 32 of the Constitution. The Court directed the District Judge, Bhopal to ascertain the existence of bonded labour as it was alleged in the letter. The District Judge in his report submitted that there were no bonded labourers at relevant time but there was total absence of implementation of labour laws. Therefore, the Supreme Court concentrated in giving directions to the government for taking suitable steps for implementation of labour welfare legislations in their true spirit. The Supreme Court stressed that the labourers be protected against the unauthorised exploitation by paying less than the minimum.

In *Shankar v. Durgapur Project Ltd.*, Calcutta High Court held that the State cannot deprive a worker of decent standard of life, which under article 43 of the Constitution, the State should endeavour to secure. To do an act contrary, to article 43, i.e., to deprive a person of decent standard of life, would be violative of article 21 of the Constitution. The court pointed out that compelling a person to live to sub-human conditions also amounts to the taking away of his life not by execution of a death sentence but by a slow and gradual process of robbing him of all his human qualities and graces, a process which is more cruel than sending a man to gallows. To convert human existence into animal existence no doubt amounts to taking away human right to life, because a man lives not by his mere physical existence or bread alone but by his human existence.

In *P. Sivaswami v. State of A.P.*, the Supreme Court once again stressed the need for effective rehabilitation of the released bonded labourers. The Supreme Court pointed out that the financial assistance of rupees 738 per family of the freed bonded tabour was certainly inadequate for rehabilitation. And unless there was effective rehabilitation, the purpose of the Bonded Labour System (Abolition) Act, 1976 would fail and the steps taken by the Supreme Court be rendered ineffective and there would be mounting frustration.

Similarly, in *Balram v. State of M.P.*, the Supreme Court once again stressed the need for rehabilitating the bonded labourers. In this respect the Supreme Court issued certain directions to the central government and its officials to release adequate funds to meet its liability under the scheme framed under the Bonded Labour System (Abolition) Act, 1976. The Court further directed that collector and such other officers who have been assigned the responsibility of supervising rehabilitation shall ensure that the full amount intended for the freed labourers reaches them.

It is obvious from the analysis of various above mentioned cases that the judiciary has shown deep concern for the basic human rights of the bonded labourers and issued the suitable directions for ensuring the protection and promotion of their human right to live with human dignity.

Thus, to uphold righteousness in society and protecting basic human rights of citizens, judicial activism has laid foundation and made easy access to natural justice. NGOs' role in this direction is also praiseworthy.

4

National Democratic Movements and Human Rights

It has been well accepted fact that the law is an instrument of class domination, of disorganizing the disadvantaged, of fracturing their emergent unity, and disorienting the people's struggles for a just society. This critique provides raw, bloody, here-and-now accounts of the actual suffering of subjugated Indian citizens. The radical critique of law has a practical summoning urgency. In any struggle to transform or limit the Indian state power, the state law both as ideology and as repression has also to be combatted. Implicit in the critique of the law is a vision of counter law, an alternate legality which will base itself on moralities, ideologies and practices not merely different from but superior to those of the state law. If we ask precisely what these may consist of, no clear answers emerge as of now except perhaps scientific socialism with a human face. The agonizing perplexities of this face have not as yet moved political discourse and practice in the radical critique.

This is indeed, to use Pierre Bourdieu's difficult phrase, the "theory of practice" of those who through a variety of struggles seek to limit or transform the Indian state. The critique is valuable and must not be ignored. And, surprisingly, or perhaps not, it carries a message similar in result, to the Gandhian and Sarvodaya critiques of a law, stressing its basic irrelevance to the totality of moral and spiritual development of human beings, individual and collective. If ever the history of the critique of Indian state and law implicit, for example, in Jayaprakash Narayan's Total Revolution during the seventies is deciphered, we will learn how close in idiom at least (though not in ideological terms) the radical and the Gandhian critiques of the law and state in India tend to converge. Both acknowledge as a starting point the negative face of the law and the state; both postulate as a terminus of people's struggle transcendence, of some kind, from the law, the most visible and powerful symbol and instrumentality of domination. There are, of course, various ways of perceiving and articulating this contradictory reality of state law in India.

In piloting the Indian Constitution through the Constituent Assembly, Dr. B.R. Ambedkar articulated it as follows:

> On 26th January, 1950, we are going to enter into a life of contradictions. In politics we will have equality and in social and economic life we will have inequality. In politics we shall be recognizing the principle of one man, one vote, one value. In our social and economic life, we shall, by reason of economic structure, continue to deny the principle of one man, one vote. How long, shall we continue to live this life of contradictions? How long shall we continue to deny equality in social and economic life? If we continue to deny it for long, we will do so by putting our democracy in peril. We must remove this contradiction at the earliest possible moment or else those who suffer from inequality will blow up the structure of democracy which the Assembly has so labouriously built up.

A man who fought Mohandas Gandhi and the Indian National Congress on the historic issues of justice for dalits was acclaimed, both inside and outside the Constituent Assembly, as a modern Manu! Thus began the Indian state and the law their pursuit of a democracy for the dalits—a path in which the state and law constructs and reconstructs the disadvantaged classes, primarily, for the advantage of the governing elites. Ambedkar does not use the notion of contradictions rigorously. And it is not to be thought that contradictions can be either created or resolved by strokes of the legislative pen. But the important thing to note is that Babasaheb is here portraying the dialectical tension within the structuration of the Constitution of India, and therefore of the Indian legal order, and therefore, to some extent, of the Indian state formative practices inaugurated by the Constitution itself. In proclaiming a desired social order, the Constitution enables its prime users in the state to legitimate state and class power. It provides the political logic to the progressive laws for the disadvantaged in terms of symbolic political capital for the governing elites.

At the same time, the Constitution and progressive laws provide powerful sources of sustained critiques of state power in the direction of delegitimation. The Constitution and progressive legislation flowing from it serve at the one and same historic moment to legitimate and delegitimate class and state power. They furnish on the one hand a powerful habitat for aggressive manifestations of the centralized unity of state power and on the other, furnish standards by which state and class practice of power may be interrogated, critiqued and condemned. This is one level at which the contradictory reality of state and law may be grasped.

Another level at which this reality presents itself is that of the relative autonomy of the law, understood as adjucdicative power, from the polity and the economy. The relative autonomy of the judiciary is no hypothesis but a social fact. For example, Justice Jagan Mohan Sinha of the Allahabad High Court was able to write a decision unseating a most powerful and popular Prime Minister of India. This was an exceptional verdict, unparalleled in the annals of judicial and political history. This decision provided impetus to the Total Revolution movement; it also generated conditions which led to an audacious arrogance of power in the declaration of Emergency, the resurgent populism which followed its liquidation, the growth of activist judiciary since 1977 and the efflorescence of social action groups. No matter how we choose to analyze the impact of judicial process, on the polity, and of the polity on the judicial process, the Allahabad High Court decision compels us to acknowledge that adjudicative legal order is possessed of a remarkable degree of autonomy. The spectacular development since 1973 of the idea that Parliament's plenary power to change the Constitution by amendments must stop short of violation of the basic identity, basic structure and essential features of the Constitution furnishes yet another unique instance of judicial autonomy at work.

The Indian Supreme Court is the only court in the history of humankind to have asserted, acquired and exercized the power to review constitutional amendments; indeed, at the height of the Emergency the Court struck down the quixotic Thirty-Ninth Amendment which immunized the election of the Prime Minister, among other exalted constitutional karmacharis, from judicial scrutiny. So long as this insistence on constitutional discipline on the hegemonic executive power lasts, the adjudicative legal order ensures expansion of state-free social space for citizens democratic action.

What does the relative autonomy of the adjudicative legal order really mean? In one sentence, it signifies independence within dependence. The judiciary is structured as a state apparatus; it may not be transformed into a revolutionary one. But it may be deployed to develop an insurrectionary jurisprudence, at least from the standpoint of the executive power or an el supremo. And this is what the processes of social action litigation, miscalled public interest litigation, for example, richly demonstrate. They have transformed the Supreme Court of India into a Supreme Court for Indians. And the-transformation was initiated by those who had grasped the meaning of the contradictory reality of the state and the law in India. Today, regardless of many real difficulties, social action litigation has ensured democratization of judicial access, the right to access to justice, though inarticulately present in the text and context of the Constitution, as the most basic of all rights.

If it is premature to celebrate the successes of social action litigation as inaugurating a new human rights jurisprudence in India, it is equally untimely to offer a requiem of it. How is it that this independence in dependence for judicial power as an aspect of state power was allowed to emerge in the first place? The tendency to avoid simple answers because they are simple must be avoided here. And the simple answer was provided by the Communist Manifesto where Marx and Engels wrote, in a much misquoted phrase, that the executive of state is the managing committee of the whole bourgeoisie. Note the word whole. The bourgeoisie as a whole represents a certain kind of unity within disunity. The state, it has been rightly said, does not behave as an omnirational, ideal, collective capitalist; it has to manage intra-elite conflicts, represented by diverse material interests of the fractions of capital.

Autonomous judiciary, howsoever relative, is necessary to mediate intra-class and inter-class conflicts. Relatively independent judiciary is not primarily intended to create state-free spaces for the subaltern classes; it is designed, consciously or otherwise, to mediate conflicting interests within the ruling formation. All this becomes excitingly clear when we recall, for example, that contemporary India presents a peculiar capitalist mix: that aside from capitalism we also find state capitalism and state-regulated capitalism. State capitalism has over time created a whole new category, if not a class, of state bourgeoisie whose interests often conflict with the fractions of capital. This is particularly so in the area of finance capital where the state looms large, through the nationalization of banks and insurance and foreign exchange regulation.

The conflicts are acute and prolonged. It becomes important for the state to have a relatively autonomous judiciary to mediate these conflicts, so that to a certain extent they become distanced from overt politics. It is in the arena of state-regulated capitalism that we find capital fighting the state apparatus: and the fight usually takes place in courts, though of course not only there. And typically the idiom is that of rights. The rights are couched in terms of fundamental rights and rights to natural justice and fair play. Not so explicitly, but through their deep structure, we find at least the following rights against the state claimed by capitalist classes:

- the right to tax planning, a Siamese twin of tax evasion and fraud;
- 'the right to immunity from the processes of law (e.g. successful searches and seizures, and even 'raids');
- the right to most favoured treatment (leading industrialists should be immune from harsh treatment

which should be regularly and mindlessly resorted to when dealing with the exploited classes);

- the right to exploit unorganized labour (migrant, child and female labour);
- the right to exploit consumers;
- the right to gender exploitation (hiring and wage policies affecting women, exploitation of sex in advertisement campaigns even through state owned electronic media);
- the right to pollute (look at the cases before the Supreme Court where .' eminent lawyers, on behalf of industry, argue that water pollution equipment is too costly or that the prosecution is riddled with technical defects, no matter whether the same lawyers contribute to human rights and ecology protection after court hours or on weekends);
- the right to mismanagement (e.g. creation of sick textile mills to be taken over by the state);
- the right to organize political dependencies (through funding of political parties);
- the right to recklessly injure public health (through manipulation or outright opposition to regulatory laws e.g. drug control);
- the right to appropriation of the achievements of pro-poor, social action litigation jurisprudence (e.g., the right to speedy trial generated by Bihar undertrial cases is now sought to be invoked for "smugglers" as well, despite Justice Chinnapa Reddy's recent firm refusal to extend this right to the resourceful);
- the right to conspicuous consumption.

Of course, state-regulated capitalism is not an adversary

of private capitalism; it is an ally which has often to masquerade as an adversary. Very rarely, it appears as an adversary in public discourse. But when it so does, we see the hideous face of state and class power though the law, as in the legalization of black money through the Bearer Bonds Act, and its constitutionalization by the Supreme Court of India, including by some of its most activist justices. We are at an interesting conjuncture of this interaction between state and capital, as the evolving jurisprudence of Fairfax and Bofors has begun to show. The conflict between managers of the Indian state and fractions of capital has now reached full blown proportions. This is clearly shown by the mid-eighties discourse between the lamented Ramnath Goenka and Rajiv Gandhi over the Indian Express raids, partly a reflection of contest between two well known industrial giants. If the freedom of press emerges as a major public issue, it is because the rhetoric of rights helps mask basic instability and disruption within the governing elites.

Thus, the managers of the people conduct the discourse of power inter se through the rhetoric of rights. The struggles of those who are managed must lie in refusing to be the grass when elephants fight, and in, as it were, hijacking the arena for an alternate vision of Indian democracy, state and the law, to convert an intra-class disruption into a resource for inter-class relations. Activists, as ideologues of the people, should try to reap the whirlwind around the Bofors deal, not resting content with a change in players but articulating a demand that the rules of the game, which constitute the game, must be altered fundamentally. Thus, one may struggle for an enunciation of a right to a clean and efficient governance, without which all fundamental rights are meaningless. Citizens must refuse to bear it any more by a struggle against micro-fascism symbolised by routine acts of corruption, which makes impoverishment, staggering human imagination, even more unendurable.

Now, let us look at the new idiom of some of our activists. In their discourse we find the appealing emergence of the idea that if individuals and collectivities are to be empowered, the state must be correspondingly disempowered. Broadly, the notion seems to be that participatory, self reliant and truly democratic development may not occur under the shadow of the state-bureaucracy, police and para-military forces. Social activism can best function as an instrumentality of transformation if there exist expansive state-free areas. Thus, one may resist the proposal , still taking rounds among powers-that be, that rural voluntary agencies be subjected to extensive legislative and regulatory oversight or protest against the scandal of the Kudal Commission, unhappily allowed to perform its repressive functions for long years. This notion of disempowerment makes sense.

Activists do ask that new laws may be made addressing the worst forms of violations of human rights in the civil society, usually associated with the most regressive forms of social behaviour associated with a historic revival of religion, culture and ethnicity. Should there not be stricter law and state action, for example, on sati, dowry murders, sex-selective abortions through the abuse of amniocentesis techniques, nutritional sex discrimination which creates new forms of deferred female infanticide, child abuse, familial violence against women, atrocities against dalits, exploitation of bonded, migrant and contract labour?

The answer is yes. The difficulty with this answer is that it empowers the state, as it were, on the insistent demand of activists themselves. And therefore, an immediate caveat issue: the state must not use "undemocratic" compulsions through Jaw and executive action.

At a public meeting in New Delhi on sati in Rajasthan, the author urged, for example that the state police, or if need be the para-military forces of the Union, should do all they can to nip this evil revival in the bud, as it were. This created a howl of protest since this would empower the state a bit too much. Activists were worried about state terrorism; the discourse on Punjab was immediately invoked! And it was even said that force of the state was not an effective answer to problems of changing cultural styles and values! If you then ask how will activists deal with these manifestations, you are told that they would stage non-violent protest, without a Mohandas (the word "Gandhi" may now no longer be used for him!). When you further ask how such a protest will succeed before tens of thousands of sword-wielding Rajput males, they would say it is the job of the state to protect the free exercise of freedom of speech and association; this means that union para-military forces or state police have a duty to protect the protestors against sati but they have no warrant to uproot fiercely the resurgence of the practice.

Obviously what is state protection for activists is state terrorism against the perpetrators of sati! A similar kind of logic' has pervaded our approach to the eradication of the worst forms of untouchability; in the name of limiting the state through rights and the rule of law we are content to allow a state of affairs when untouchables, forty years after independence, may not draw water from the savarana wells; where the *Chamar,* regardless of the age physical ability and climatic conditions and time of day and night is coerced to drag the carcass away from the village only because he is a

Chamar; where an untouchable may be lynched by the Thakur at his whim and will. And if you ask the same activists whether the deployment of Indian troops in Sri Lanka was justified, some might say it was justified for the protection of the ethnic minorities. An action across the seas stands justified for the very same reasons for which it would be condemned if tried at home!

Let us take just one more instance. Many activists are also abolitionists; they feel, rightly, that the death penalty can never be justified. We feel, again rightly, that bloodthirsty justice is inhumane and that in the long run it does not deter. But let us ask ourselves whether the provision of such a sentence, not at all its indiscriminate application, for calculated dowry murders is necessarily a bad thing? Should we not introduce such a sentence for corporate acts of deliberate, horendous pollution in the top management of the companies which engage in such behaviour only for profits? Imagine if a prosecution for murder was feasible against the top management of Union Carbide India Limited for causing deaths of thousands of people in Bhopal on, and after, the 2-3 December, 1984? Should we ask for special courts and quick procedures, without diminution of safeguards of fair trial, for such cases? The human rights activists response to these questions will be, and has been, marked with the greatest incoherence. Rightly so to the point that we apprehend a state with vast powers. But equally worrying when we surrender our capabilities to inspire fear among those who would indulge in such behaviour. The law as a programme of social transformation, on any reasoned analysis, must evoke credible fear of harsh consequences; to renounce this resource altogether is also to enfeeble the potential of controlling the privileged class deviance, which is far more difficult to combat than the deviance of the impoverished.

Dilemmas Ahead

There are acutely difficult choices to be made and remade concerning the moment, the method, and mood and the message of social intervention. On the moment of intervention itself, there exists interminable theoretical and actual blood-letting. Is there a right moment and an opposite one? Can one say this in advance or only in retrospect? What are the costs of misjudgement and who has to bear these, aside from the activists? Do we have a discourse of moments among activists? What does it have to say, for example, concerning Bhopal? Why were the pre-catastrophe moments not the more suitable ones for intervention? The choice of technology, location of plant, death of workers in prior accidents, extensive expose of the unsafe conditions at the UCIL plant, and victimization of the local trade unions-all these offered moments of intervention. Like the state, why did the activists have to wait for the catastrophe? To take another example, why did women's groups at all levels have to wait from 1979, when some of them protested against a legitimation procession for sati from the Chandni Ghowk to the Boat Club, till 1987? Difficult questions, these; but ones that need to be confronted with ruthless integrity. The questions raise issues of morality, prudence and tactics, each of which need distinct articulation. If those in power can claim an eternity in the province of political attention to burning social problems, are activists justified in also claiming a slice of eternity for their own 'mobilization?' Put another way, should activists be proactive or simply reactive?

The problem of method of intervention turns out to be formidable, too. One set of problems here involve the nature of articulatory style; the other concern the concrete agendum of action. As to the first, does the activist articulate acrimony which summons or gentleness which lulls? Do you call a spade a spade or a bloody shovel? Or both? Do you reinforce tendencies towards dignity of discourse or assault the beastly nonchalance of those who violate others? No matter what choice you make, you incur costs. If you discourse in two voices, there are costs too—costs of credibility on either side. Activists have often to hunt with the hound and run with the hare; an exercise in which they trip, get caught and are often bloodied. There are campaign styles, negotiating styles, aggravation styles and critique styles of discourse. An activist individual or group has to judiciously combine all these and yet avoid the charge of opportunistic politicising. A Himalayan task, this, but crucial. For the managers of the people there are schools of management, public administration and Harvard sponsored, Ford-financed programmes of in-service training for appropriate discourse styles. Activists would, by and large, resist such training for counter-power, even organization of sharing of reflections among them is often quite a difficult enterprise. The problem of articulatory styles is, in essence, the problem of fashioning confrontation as an ally of cooperation, and cooperation as an aid to confrontation in a series of moments through which activism must pass. Articulatory styles must be vehicles of counter-hegemony and at the same time the vehicles of celebration of partial attainments in on ongoing struggles. The problem of an agendum of action includes the moment for intervention but also goes beyond it. Activists must do many things at once: "educate" constituencies, lobby power, resort to law changes), maintain such accomplishments on the ground as a pre-condition for going ahead with tasks disclosed by partial attainments, preserve their cohesive morale and above all survive with integrity as political actors.

In all this, one must realise two additional complexities. For each agenda of explicit social action, there are hidden agenda among activists themselves at enhancing the Utopias, and contributing to the advent of their own millenia. And second, for each activist agendum for action there is the counter-agendum of the state which has to be made either compatible with the objectives of democratic social action or exposed for what it is. This counter-agendum always represents the cunning of capital and the state. It may appear in various guises: as devices for cooptation, at stratagems of consensus on what ought to be done, as generation of false consciousness that the tasks towards which the struggles are directed are about to be accomplished by state action. The promise of the gains of struggle immanent in shifts of political stance, legislative policies and judicial action has to be very critically deciphered all along the way to avoid a fall into the bottomless pit of "reformism" used here in its most pejorative sense. If social activism or democratic social action is a process of learning and unlearning through doing, it will, of course, be natural for an agendum of action to emerge only through action. One must leave the mirage of blue-printing of total change to the technocratic whiz-kids playing endlessly on computer-toys. Activism fosters those kinds of organic knowledges which should not be, ideally, amenable to subjugation by the erudite ones. If, thus, one asks of social activism: should it be engaged in enforcement and implementation of right's willy-nilly, recognized by state power and the law, the answer is 'Yes.' If one further asks: should it also be engaged in promoting the conception of new rights (the right to food, to shelter, to work and livelihood as component rights of the right to life and liberty), the answer is also 'yes.' If you ask, further, whether activists ought to ensure the process of realization of these A new rights, the answer is also in the affirmative.

The three affirmative answers invoke the Indian activists to perform all the twelve labours of Hercules at the same time! If so, how does one empower social activism as a historical process, both through theoretical production of practices and production of theoretical reflection through practice? How do we create conditions for growth and accumulation of experience and knowledge in ways which cumulatively respond to the agenda of activism in India today?

Take the most spectacular example of recent default. The Parliament has recently passed a Legal Services Bill, which totally denatures the radical inspiration of Article 39-A of the Constitution and the labours of inspired leadership by Justices like justice Krishna Iyer, Bhagwati and D.A. Desai. There is not a scrap of expression of outrage by or among the activists. Even Ela Bhatt of SEWA, whose activist credentials brought her to Rajya Sabha as a nominated member, and who has first-hand knowledge of the legal needs of the unorganized, and Justice Bhagwati, an explosively activist justice now in his retirement, have failed, so far to protest at the governmental mockery of legal services, a conception assiduously promoted by him and others. Where are, one may ask, the activist voices protesting at this historic default? If one is not able to generate an impact on one's kindred in activism, how is one to be expected to transform or limit the state? It is, perhaps, pointless to multiply the instances. Activists who indefatigably lament and expose the perfidies of the state and class power are simply unable to achieve ideological and praxiological cohesion which would entitle , them to be recognized as historical tendencies, let alone forces. As driven by factionalism and territoriality which they condemn in state and class power, as ambivalent in their vision of alternate futures as the managers of the state are, as episodically excellent in 'mobilizing' public opinion on spectacular issues but equally devoid of any transformative capabilities as the state managers, activism overall fails to seriously constrain the state. In a sense, through their obsession with the condemnation of state and class power, some activist groups end up introjecting those very characteristics of power they so fulsomely condemn. In this context, the arrogance of power stands reinforced; top bureaucrats and political managers tend to dismiss activism as a very replication of power politics.

Finally, without being exhaustive, activist groups are, not wholly able to convey deep theoretical reflection on human misery to their own constituents. For example, they must willingly do their best for drought relief, shoulder to shoulder with the governing elites. But in between droughts there are encounters where public education campaign on their underlying causes-rapacious capitalist framing; the permanent vested interest of powerful groups in conditions which impoverish; the linkages between and among depletion of plant genetic diversity, the pesticides and fertilized 'revolution'; the nature of international dependency and exploitation, all need to be communicated in terms which will make sense to the small farmer and landless labourer in immediate, existential terms, as opposed to critiques of the development paradigm' and proffering of alternate development. Very few activists in India have the ability to transform erudite knowledges into organic ones and vice versa. If the constituencies of change entrepreneurs begin to become ambivalent, both as regards the state and social activists, blaming the state is an easy, but still an evasive response. The foregoing reflections assume entities called activists" and processes called "activism"; to them have been assigned the historic role of limiting and transforming the state. No longer does one give, in the post-Marx scenario, either epistemological or historical primacy to be working classes; one either abandons them or considers them to be "just one of a number of collective actors formed in the public sphere" engaged in the "production of politics".

Indian National Movement and Human Rights

It is common knowledge that the Indian National Movement was primarily a struggle against British Imperialism. What is however hot so widely known, is that Indian National Movement was more than just a struggle to overthrow the British. It was also a grand project to build a modern India along democratic and civil libertarian lines. The fight against the British was a part of this larger struggle. As the colonial state frequently trampled upon peoples' human rights and civil liberties, the Indian National Movement constantly strove to defend and uphold these values. In fact, overthrow of British imperialism was seen by the leaders of the national movement as a precondition to the development of India along democratic and civil libertarian lines where people would be able to defend their basic rights. This would become amply clear if we compare India's record of civil liberties and human rights with other developing post-colonial societies. Evidently, the human rights that the people of India enjoy, in however limited a measure, is a legacy of our national movement. There were a variety of ways in which the leaders of the Indian National Movement introduced the issue of peoples' human rights into the anti-imperialist struggle. It included making demands from the government, educating the people regarding their rights, conducting struggles around these issues and also demonstrating through practice, whenever they could, their utmost concern for civil liberties and human rights. It has to be emphasized here that ideas of political modernity (democracy, representational government, peoples sovereignty, respect for human rights, freedom of the press among others) were not a gift of the British, contrary to popular belief. These were constantly demanded by the leaders of the national movement and conceded only grudgingly, and partially, by the British government. For instance, from the beginning of the 20th century, Bal Gangadhar Tilak, followed by Gandhi and others, began demanding adult franchise (even though it did not exist in Britain till 1928) but it was not granted to Indians till independence. Till as late as 1935 only three per cent of Indians had the right to vote, But complete adult franchise was firmly put on the agenda. Indian leaders, from the 19th century onwards, constantly criticized the British government for its non-representative character and questioned its, credentials in preparing a constitution for India, Motilal Nehru and Tej Bahadur Sapru went to the extent of preparing a national constitution in 1928. It recommended the declaration of fundamental rights, a parliamentary system of government, adult franchise and an independent judiciary among other things. Even though the Nehru Report, as it came to be known, was rejected by the British government, it inspired the, Indian people and reaffirmed their capacity for governing themselves. From 1930s onwards, leaders like Jawaharlal Nehru began demanding the creation of an elected constituent Assembly which would prepare a constitution for India.

Besides making demands on the British government to enlarge the Space available for an exercise of human rights, the Indian National Movement, from 1920 onwards, actually conducted popular struggles around this issue. It is important to remember that the first all-India mass movement against the British was organized on the question of a violation, by the British, of a crucial aspect of human rights. In 1919, the British government brought forth the notorious Rowlatt Bill (known after its author Sir Sidney A.T. Rowlatt) which would authorize the government to imprison any person without trial and any other legal procedure. This move by the British government was received with unprecedented and fierce opposition by Indian leaders of all shades of opinions. All the Indian members of the Legislative Council - from Srinivasa Shastri to Mohammed Ali Jinnah - opposed the Bill (yet it was passed). The national press was indignant calling it "monstrous" *(New India)*, "a gigantic blunder" *(Amrita Bazar Patrika)*, "repression in exelsus" *(Bombay Chronicle*) and a matter of "shame, indignation and disgust" *(The Hindu* from Madras). An all-India Hartal was organized and the entire country rose in protest against what it considered a blatant violation of human rights. Throughout its life the Indian National Movement upheld human rights as an uncompromisable issue. Yet another way in which the Indian National Movement contributed to the enlargement of space for human rights was by actually practising it when the opportunity came.

The Government of India Act of 1935 provided fully elected popular governments in the provinces. As a result, the Indian National Congress formed a government in seven provinces and successfully practised what it had preached for many years in the past. All the emergency powers exercised by the previous provincial governments were repealed. Ban on illegal political organizations was lifted. All restrictions on the press were removed and securities taken from them were returned. Confiscated arms were returned and forfeited arms licensed were restored. But the most important achievement was the release of thousands of political prisoners who had been languishing in various prisons for many years. During its brief stay of twenty eight months in office, the Congress was able to demonstrate its serious concern for the issue of civil liberties and human rights.

The supreme importance that was accorded to the issues of civil liberties and human rights by our national movement can be easily grasped by a statement of Mahatma Gandhi made in 1922: "We must make good the rights of free speech and free association. We must defend these elementary rights with our lives. Liberty of speech means that it is unassiled even when the speech hurts; liberty of Press can be said to be truly respected when the Press can comment in the severest terms upon and even misrepresent matters. Freedom of association is truly respected when assemblies of people can discuss even revolutionary projects." It is perhaps best to conclude with another of Mahatma Gandhi's statements made in 1939: 'Civil liberty consistent with the observance of non-violence is the first step towards Swaraj. It is the foundation of freedom. There is no room there for dilution or compromise. It is the water of life. I have never heard of water being diluted."

The Disability Rights Movement America

Women's groups protested the city's plans to install public outdoor toilets, but not include any for women. City officials feared the women's larger toilets would attract junkies needing a place to shoot up and homeless people looking for somewhere to sleep. . . . No city, of course, would be crazy enough to build public toilets, but just for men. Yet substitute "wheelchair users" for "women" in the paragraph above to understand what New York City did to infuriate disabled activists at the moment that the Americans with Disabilities Act was being implemented nationwide. When disabled people protested that they were being unlawfully excluded from a public service, they got little sympathy. Typical was a Wall Street Journal editorial that scolded the complainers for putting the narrow self interests of a small number of wheelchair users over the common good of the far greater number of able-bodied people who could use the inaccessible toilets. The journal saw it as an issue of "weighing civil rights against common sense," and came down against the expectation of rights by people in wheelchairs. But to disabled activists, like Frieda Zames of New York's Disabled in Action, the exclusion was as blatant an example of discrimination as if the city had put up toilets and then hung a WHITES ONLY sign on each one. Most galling for Zames was that disabled people were being expected to forfeit, without complaint, their newly won rights to accessibility.

By the time New York unveiled a four-month test of its flew toilets in July 1992, the same month that the last title of the ADA went into effect, the city had placed three large wheelchair-accessible toilets next to three regular ones. But side-by-side toilets took up a lot of space, were twice as expensive to build, and disabled users still complained about the unequal compromise that seemed designed to fail: to use their toilets meant going to a nearby city office during business hours to get a special key card (so that officials could keep out the junkies and homeless). In addition, disabled people got second-class toilets, which, unlike the ones for everyone else, were neither heated nor self-cleaning. As a result of complaints by disabled activists, a worker with a mop was posted outside all day long, a quickly ridiculed use of manpower and money that left the future of accessible toilets in doubt after the test run. To Zames the solution was simple: build one toilet that could be used by all. Anything else, she argued, was separate and unequal. What happens when Congress grants a new group minority rights, but society has little understanding that those rights have been awarded or why they are needed? As the newly recognized minority—disabled people-starts asserting those rights, there are many new breakthroughs for equality. But there are also classes, misunderstandings, even a backlash. The ADA, which promised integration, will have more impact than any civil rights law since the 1964 act that banned discrimination against blacks, women, and ethnic and religious minorities. But disabled people got their rights without dramatic Freedom Rides, church bombings or "I Have a Dream" speeches to stir the conscience of a guilty nation. African-Americans had changed a nation's attitudes and then won civil rights law. But for disabled Americans the reverse was true.

Now disabled people fear that a society that did the right thing-but without the benefit of significant consciousness-raising-has begun to question those rights. Such doubt is raised not just on seemingly small matters, like the right to use a public toilet. Discord is present, too, on the most pressing social issues like reforming health care. Just a few weeks after the full ADA went into effect and the New York toilets went up, the Bush Administration-citing the disability civil rights law-struck down what was being hailed as the nation's boldest effort to redesign health care. Oregon's Medicaid rationing plan sought to resolve the great hypocrisy of American medicine: those with insurance get the world's best medicine, while the uninsured fourteen percent may get nothing. As part of a plan to provide health coverage to its uninsured residents, Oregon wanted to extend Medicaid to an additional one hundred and twenty thousand uncovered poor people.

But to do so would necessitate savings elsewhere in the Medicaid system. Oregon's solution was to ration services. It ranked seven hundred and nine conditions and their treatments on the basis of effectiveness and cost, figured out how much state Medicaid could spend, and then drew a cutoff line at item five hundred eighty seven. Nothing below that would get funded. To put the rationing scheme into effect, Oregon needed formal permission, called a waiver, from federal officials. There were compelling reasons to support rationing. It was a daring experiment at a time when the federal government seemed too timid to solve the problem of providing health care for some 37 million uninsured Americans. But Oregon's plan came with a cruel twist dictated by an era of fiscal limits: it was offering health coverage to more poor people by cutting back the treatment that other even poorer people already received.

Oregon health officials justified this by noting that another kind of rationing already existed. When government said it would pay for the health care of the poorest, but not for that of the slightly less poor, that was, in effect, an implicit method of rationing health care among haves and have nots. Oregon would' try to bring some logic to the system by rationing on the basis of what treatment was most certain to improve someone's life, not on the basis of where one fell on the poverty scale. It was in trying to make decisions about what was worthwhile treatment that Oregon's plan ran into problems with treating disabled people fairly. In early 1992, officials at the Department of Health and Human Services recommended giving the plan a go-ahead and President Bush himself, in his budget plan, had praised the rationing scheme as a "noteworthy" example of state experimentation.

But in March, at a brief Oval Office photo opportunity with officers of the National Right to Life Committee, Bush was urged to stop the Oregon program. Bush, who at first seemed unmoved by the antiabortion group's objections, perked up when the group's vice president, Robert Powell, claimed, "If that plan had been in effect when I was born, I'd be dead." The President listened intently as Powell, who uses crutches and a wheelchair, explained how, when he was just five months old, a malignant tumor had attacked his lungs and spinal cord. Doctors said the cancer was incurable, and the infant lived only because his parents found another doctor (one who used a wheelchair, it turned out) who was willing to aggressively treat the "hopeless" case. Oregon, Powell said, would stop paying to treat such incurable cancers. Bush, who had once struggled to find doctors willing to treat his young daughter dying from leukemia, ordered White House legal counsel Boyden Gray to check Powell's contention that the Oregon plan violated the ADA, The legal opinion that came back supported Powell. Oregon's rankings, Grays office concluded, reflected commonly-held prejudices that a disabled life was a lesser one. The classifications had come on the advice of doctors and medical experts. So it was not surprising, for example, that medical' treatment for traumatic brain injury fell far below the cutoff. Surviving traumatic head injury was something new, and medicine still has little understanding of how to improve the lives of survivors. But people are now living long after such injury.

In making its list, Oregon also had relied upon a telephone survey to gauge people's attitudes about illness and disability. This, the White House argued, had further polluted the rankings with the public's uninformed stereotypes of a disabled life as a sad and pitiable one. The phone survey, the administration concluded, was tied to a significant reranking of at least one hundred and twenty conditions and their treatments. Medical treatment was not covered for amyotrophic lateral sclerosis, or Lou Gehrig's disease, a particularly frightening illness to most people since the degenerative neuromuscular condition was considered fatal. Yet ALS was not a death sentence for everybody. Scientist Stephen Hawking, after all, has lived long and productively, even though AUS has made his life a far more difficult one. At the very least, each person's case had to be considered-separately. To write off everyone with ALS was, in effect, discrimination based on diagnosis. It was to buy into the myth that a disabled life was a tragic one and not worthy of prolonging with medical treatment. There were other examples where Oregon's list conflicted with the ADA. Although Oregon would pay for a liver transplant in the case of liver failure, it would not pay for the transplant if the patient had a history of alcoholism, no matter if that addiction was five, ten, or twenty years in the past But the congressional Office of Technology Assessment criticized this rationing of liver transplants, noting that the operation had a similar rate of success whether a person had a past history of alcoholism or not. (No doctor will give a liver transplant to someone currently abusing alcohol, since that would be a waste of a rare liver donation.) The ADA prohibits discrimination against someone on the basis of past alcoholism or drug abuse. Many of Oregon's decisions had been moved by logic, even if they were flawed with society's automatic devaluing of people on the basis of disability. Saving an extremely premature baby can cost a quarter of a million dollars or more. Prenatal care, which can significantly reduce the chance that a baby will be born prematurely, costs only a few hundred dollars. So Oregon, seeking to emphasize prevention, put crucial prenatal care high on its priority list. But ranked seven hundred eight, next to last, was saving a baby weighing less than eighteen ounces and born before twenty-three weeks gestation. One Oregon official explained to me that the low ranking "is not a problem for our doctors, since they don't try to save babies like that anyway." Indeed, the chances of such a baby surviving are slim, at, by one estimate, about one in ten and even then there is a significant likelihood that the child will grow up disabled. Yet just a few weeks before the Bush Administration's decision, a healthy baby, Zascha Villamar, left a Miami hospital after five months of treatment. She was born after only twenty-two weeks in the womb and she weighed fifteen ounces-a testimony to medicine's ever-growing ability to save younger and smaller babies. Technology and new drugs sometimes could save such premature infant, as long as doctors and governments did not write them off first. Once Washington told Oregon to redesign its rationing experiment, disabled people and their new civil rights law came under swift and pointed attack. "So now we have the architects of the Americans with Disabilities Act deciding that Oregons plan, the product of an arduous political consensus within that state, simply doesn't fit the grand design of their legislated benevolence," the Wall Street Journal grumbled in an editorial. "The Americans with Disabilities Act is beginning to have the look of Big Brother." The New York Times, in an editorial titled "A Bold Medical Plan, Derailed," called the administration's claims of disability bias "unconvincing."

The Oregon decision was a coming-of-age for the ADA. It was an early test that showed the law's vast power to change society and sweep away vestiges of bias. Even most disabled people had not fully realized the enormity of the law's potential. The ADA had been underestimated as just another be-nice-to-the-handicapped law, in part because the two most visible titles of the act required businesses to be accessible to workers and customers. It looked like a law simply to put wheelchair ramps on buildings. Overlooked was the even more significant promise of a third section, which required that all government services, from public toilets to health care, be provided equally. Rights, unlike charity, carried some costs to all: If America was truly committed to providing equality to disabled people, there would be complications and trade-offs, as there had been in the Oregon decision.

The potential for backlash was clear in the gap between the newly militant self-perception of disabled people, and the confused, still stereotypical thinking of the rest of the country. On the eve of the enactment of the ADA, the pitiable poster child and the inspirational "supercrip" remained the defining images of disability. A Louis Harris and Associates survey, released in the fall of 1991, found that 92 percent of Americans said they usually felt admiration when they met people with severe disabilities and 74 percent said they felt pity. Another 47 percent said they reacted with fear "because what happened to the disabled person might happen to them," 16 percent said they felt anger "because disabled people are an inconvenience," and 9 percent said they felt resentment at "the special privileges disabled people receive." But few people, only 18 percent, said they were even aware of the ADA.

Americans had missed the new self-definition of disabled people as a group whose primary issues were ones of discrimination and respect, not health, inspiration, and charity. Even to most disabled people, however, the ADA was a revelation. Even while their world was changing, most had internalized the messages of pity and powerlessness that had permeated their lives. The deliverance of rights with the ADA was a license to get angry, instead of politely asking for help and becoming indebted to the kindhearted. Dr. Richard Edlich had never heard of the ADA until November of 1991 when an official at the University of Virginia, where Edlich teaches medicine, mentioned in passing that the school planned to make its campus accessible in order to comply with the new civil rights law. When asked, Edlich noted that the annual Christmas party was held in an inaccessible location. The university moved it. Then he pointed out that he had been unable to participate in graduation ceremonies since 1987, when he began using a motorized scooter-wheelchair after his multiple sclerosis worsened. The university purchased temporary ramps so that Edlich and other wheelchair riders could join the graduation procession down the Lawn, the majestic quandrangle designed by Thomas Jefferson. University officials simply followed the law. But the experience radicalized Edlich. In the past, like most disabled people, the plastic surgeon had not wanted to "bother" anyone and thought of his full inclusion as an imposition, not as a right. But after the university welcomed him back to its graduation ceremonies, he decided to attend his nephew's graduation at an elite New York City high school. When the headmaster dismissively said Edlich would have to find someone to carry him up the stairs, Edlich filed a complaint under the newly enacted public Accommodations section of the ADA. A Justice Department lawyer flew to New York and the school quickly built a ramp. Back in Charlottesville, Edlich, energized by the way the world was opening up to him, began a survey of his favorite stores and restaurants, and filed more complaints whenever he found a business out of compliance and unwilling to change. It was not that Edlich was bitter or angry, or stood to make any money off his complaints. He simply began asserting his right to full inclusion. The ADA, the doctor says, "has made life a celebration instead of .' being filled with apologies and continually saying -thank you' and 'please help me.'" He had made what he called the "lonely journey" to becoming an activist.

While the cautious were getting militant, the militant were gaining respectability. In Denver, on the day in July that the final title of the ADA went into effect, city officials honored ADAPT. The city erected a plaque to commemorate ADAPT's first protest, in 1978, when nineteen people in wheelchairs sat at an intersection and blocked two city buses for twenty-four hours to demand that wheelchair lifts be added to buses. Only several weeks before ADAPT was hailed in Denver, its members had disrupted a commencement speech by U.S. Health and Human Services Secretary Louis Sullivan, in the type of hostile demonstration that the Bush Administration official had come to expect from contentious ACT-UP protesters demanding more AIDS research. ADAPT insisted on more government spending for personal assistance services and less for nursing homes. A few months later, in October, ADAPT got the promise of support it wanted after its members took over Bill Clinton's presidential campaign headquarters in San Francisco and refused to leave. Clinton dispatched his top rehabilitation official from Arkansas to negotiate with the demonstrators, and a strong statement was issued in Clinton's name backing the new spending emphasis sought by ADAPT. "I believe that every individual has a right to personal care," Clinton said, and proposed using a national service corps as one way to increase the number of personal assistants. Clinton endorsed the disability movement's insistence on the consumer's "maximum control" over the personal assistance they receive and pledged to reconsider federal regulations and funding that create "a presumption in favor of institutionalized care over home and community-based services." Clinton's promise was a sign of the growing respect that politicians paid to disabled voters and the even the most militant of them were treated with seriousness.

Still, even a strong rights law could not make old barriers fall overnight. The Hockenberry Rule-the idea that the ability of disabled people is always underestimated—did not disappear, as journalist John Hockenberry, himself, would find out when he got evicted from a Broadway theater. He had paid $60 for his ticket and had checked in advance that the theater was accessible. But when he showed up, the theater manager refused to help seat him. "You are a fire hazard, sir," the manager complained. Prior to the ADA, theater owners in most parts of the country were free to make such judgments. This time, Hockenberry filed a bias suit against the theater, citing the public accommodations section of the ADA, which had taken effect just two months before his run-in on Broadway.

For Hockenberry, the experience was a "coming out" of sorts. Like most disabled people, he had put up with such insults and discrimination daily. .' Even at National Public Radio's offices, there was never an accessible rest room he could use. But like many disabled people, he had tried to ignore such slights and limits by concentrating on personal achievement. "I thought that what defined me was not disability but background and talent," he explained to journalist Mary Johnson. "The biggest joke played on me-and it's my own damn fault-is that I thought that, by accepting no limits, as my geographic reality enlarged, my sense of limits would go down. And just the opposite has happened."

Hockenberry, who that summer was lured to ABC News, could cover some of the biggest stories around the world. But as a disabled man he was still hostage to the underestimation of others. At the theater, said Hockenberry, "that guy just decided I wasn't going in, and everyone then behaved as though it was impossible to get me in. If you spend a lot of time in the Third World and you come back to the United States you realize the obstacles are just guys standing there, telling you it's impossible. And you know it's not." After a lifetime of being told to make it on his own, Hockenberry admitted, he felt a little uncomfortable about making a claim to rights. Millions of other disabled people were getting angry, too, and like Hockenberry and Edlich were coming to see themselves as a class, united in discrimination and empowered by law. Their expanding ranks would give the disability rights movement soaring power, educate others to their issues, and in the end, create a society more hospitable to all. They are full players now in a civil rights struggle, complete with progress and backlash. But the change in their mind-set is powerful enough to win rights and perhaps eventually convince a nation and the world that people with disabilities want neither pity-ridden paternalism nor overblown admiration. They insist simply on common respect and the opportunity to build bonds to their communities as fully accepted participants in everyday life.

In the next chapter we will describe the role played/ being played by NGOs in the human rights protection.

5

NGOs AND HUMAN RIGHTS PROTECTION

First it is significant to note that the contributions of NGOs and countless individual lawyers, journalists and other activists have helped greatly to further respect for human rights throughout the world. To cite just one example: by 1990, some members of Charter 77 in Czechoslovakia and of Helsinki Watch committees in several nations in Eastern Europe and the former Soviet Union were in power in countries where, just months before, they had been in prison.

Frequently, the fate of those who publicly denounce human rights abuses or work as human rights watchdogs is arrest, abduction, torture and worse.

- According to UN reports, in El Salvador in 1991 death threats were directed at several human rights activists, including the president of the International Association Against Torture.
- In India, the son of the president of the Punjab Human Rights Organization was arrested and executed in 1991.
- At least six human rights lawyers in the Philippines have been murdered in the past four years.
- In 1991 alone, the UN Special Rapporteur on Summary or Arbitrary Executions sent urgent appeals to 49

Governments on some 4,200 cases of death threats levied against persons who sought to cooperate with UN human rights bodies or who sought protection.

To protect the human rights of NGOs and others who, in speaking out on behalf of human rights, become victims of human rights abuses, a working group of the UN Commission on Human Rights is drafting a Declaration on Human Rights Defenders. The document calls for guaranteeing the right to:

- Form, join and participate in human rights NGOs;
- Denounce human rights violations publicly,
- Communicate with international NGOs and intergovernmental organizations;
- Have recourse to effective means of legal redress.

The work of publicizing human rights violations and bringing pressure on offending Governments often falls to NGOs. Their credibility, like that of the United Nations in the field of human rights, stems from the impartial application of universal norms to all Governments.

- At the international level, NGOs such as Amnesty International (winner of the Nobel Prize for Peace for 1977), the International Committee of the Red Cross and Human Rights Watch (with its divisions Africa Watch, Americas Watch, Asia Watch, Helsinki Watch and Middle East Watch) conduct on-site investigations, disseminate detailed reports and wage advocacy campaigns in international and domestic forums.
- Operating with far less public awareness and physical protection than their transnational counterparts are

> domestic human rights organizations, which, where possible, monitor the actions of their respective Governments. Among these groups are the Tutela Archdiocesari Legal Protection Officę of San Salvador (El Salvador), Vicarta de Solidaridad in Chile and the Free Legal Assistance Group of the Philippines.

The success of the human rights movement is best measured by the extent to which some Governments have incorporated human rights concerns into their policy-making. In the United States, the State Department has for more than a decade been required to produce an annual survey of human rights conditions world-wide to help Congress assess how U.S. assistance affects the rights of people in recipient countries. And Amnesty International's 1992 annual report concludes: "Countries whose rulers would not even have paid lip service to human rights a decade ago are now declaring their importance."

The UN Economic and Social Council (ECOSOC) defines anon-governmental organization as "any international organization which is not established by intergovernmental agreement". This broad term encompasses private voluntary organizations, community groups, professional and trade associations, labour unions, academic and scientific organizations and others.

- Thousands of NGOs concentrate on human rights, dealing with human rights in general or with specific rights or issues such as torture or prisoners of conscience.
- Many NGOs focus on other issues but incorporate human rights into their activities. The Latin American Adult Education Centre handles human rights within its wider area of concern.

- Other groups, such as those offering legal assistance to mothers, workers or the poor, indirectly support the advancement of human rights.

NGOs vary in how they are organized. Some are made up solely of volunteers or staff members. Others have restricted membership, such as the International Commission of Jurists, which is made up of 40 eminent jurists from many countries and defends and promotes the role of lawyers and judges in the legal protection of human rights. Some NGOs have members who participate in or contribute financially to the organization's activities. Amnesty International is the largest organization of this kind, with more than 1.1 million members in 150 countries.

Information is by far the most potent weapon in the NGO arsenal. Once NGOs collect and verify information, they transmit it to the United Nations and other international organizations. They also make extensive use of the media to publicize individual cases or general country situations.

- Amnesty International, Human Rights Watch and the International Federation for Human Rights are among the many NGOs which produce surveys, newsletters and other valuable reports on human rights violations throughout the world.
- Promotion— Mainly carried out by NGOs in the legal field, which seek to prevent legal abuses, lobby for laws on human rights protection and work for ratification of international human rights treaties.
- Information campaigns: For the general public and targeted sectors of society such as Governments, lawyers, judges or police. *Human Rights Internet* is an international communications network and clearing-house for human rights information.

- Education: Teaching human rights or encouraging education ministries and universities to incorporate human rights material into their curricula. The World Association for the School as an Instrument of Peace organizes an annual international training session on teaching human rights for teachers in colleges and secondary schools.
- Studies and research: Investigating themes such as administration of justice, links between drug trafficking and human rights or how law functions within indigenous communities.

Article 71 of the UN Charter provides for the participation of NGOs, on a consultative basis, in the work of ECOSOC. Among the 930 NGOs with consultative status are Amnesty International, the International Federation of Red Cross and Red Crescent Societies, the Andean Commission of Jurists and the Regional Council for Human Rights in Asia.

- The United Nations maintains contact with a wide range of NGOs through the Department of Public Information and the Non-Governmental Liaison Service (NGLS), sponsored jointly by several agencies and programmes of the UN system.

NGOs provide information to UN experts who monitor human rights and generally try to influence the decisions of the many UN bodies whose work touches on human rights.

- Participation by NGOs in meetings of the Commission on Human .' Rights has increased from 33 NGOs in 1970 to 62 in 1980 and 150 in 1992.
- The issue of torture was taken up by the United Nations in response to a 1973 NGO campaign aimed at abolishing the practice.

- NGO lobbying helped establish the Working Group on Indigenous Populations and the Working Group on Enforced or Involuntary Disappearances. Says Diego Garcia-Sayan, a member of the latter: "Little would be accomplished without the growing professionalism of human rights groups .... The NGOs present and follow up on information in a reliable, precise and careful manner. Without this painstaking work, the Group would not be able to function as it does .... The Group, along with many intergovernmental organizations, relies basically upon NGOs and not the Governments themselves. The NGOs provide the Group with information, pressure it to act and clamour for results. This is true of all of the United Nations specialized groups."
- According to the Special Rapporteur on Summary and Arbitrary Executions, S. Amos Wako: "NGOs are the source of most of the information and allegations concerning arbitrary and illegal executions received by the Special Rapporteur. This information is indispensable to the effective fulfilment of the mandate of the Special Rapporteur."
- The human rights complaint mechanism known as the "1503 procedure" is kept going almost exclusively by information supplied by NGOs. The procedure authorizes the Sub-Commission on Prevention of Discrimination and Protection of Minorities "to consider all communications ... which appear to reveal a consistent pattern of gross and reliably attested violations of human rights and fundamental freedoms" in a given country.

The consultative status of NGOs permits them to participate (without vote) in the drafting process of UN conventions, declarations and other efforts to set international standards.

- During the drafting of the UN Charter, NGO representatives helped ensure inclusion of articles mentioning human rights, including one to set up a commission for promotion of human rights.
- Some 30 NGOs, among them trade unions and religious, women's and parliamentarian, groups, were instrumental in drafting the Universal Declaration of Human Rights.
- NGOs helped prepare the International Covenant on Civil and Political Rights and the International Covenant on Economic, Social and Cultural Rights, both adopted in 1966.
- The Declaration on the Elimination of Discrimination against Women .' (1967) and the Convention on the Elimination of All Forms of Discrimination against Women (1979) came about as result of substantial input from women's NGOs. In 1976, the Conference of African Women submitted a 25-article draft convention to the UN Commission on the Status of Women, a text which had a significant impact on the final document.
- Amnesty International, the International Commission of Jurists and the International Association of Penal Law helped draft the 1984 UN Convention against Torture. A group led by Defence for Children International helped draft the 1989 UN Convention on the Rights of the Child.

Government ratification of the Conventions they sign often proceeds slowly. Once instruments come into force, government compliance is often lacking. NGOs make their presence felt at both ends of this process.

- In an effort that required ten years, NGOs helped securė the 35 ratifications necessary for the International Covenants on Civil and Political Rights and on Economic, Social and Cultural Rights to enter into force.
- When States parties present their national reports to the United Nations, NGOs provide information on the country concerned to experts entrusted with considering those reports.

NGOs are independent and willing to take risks in areas which Governments and intergovernmental organizations consider too politically sensitive. They have, by their very nature, a freedom of expression, a flexibility of action and a liberty of movement which enable them to complement the role of the United Nations in the promotion and protection of human rights.

According to Garcia-Sayan of the UN Working Group on Disappearances:

> "Anyone who has ever attended a session of the UN Commission on Human Rights has seen the caution-to say the least-with which the government representatives act.... It would seem that there exists a policy of not criticizing neighbouring countries directly or harshly. Strange but notorious silences can be understood simply as indicating geopolitical interests. The 'prosecutors' in these circumstances, that is to say those who hold human rights above other concerns, are the NGOs. They are the fuel and the lubricant which, allow the machine to function and speed the working up."

For precisely these reasons, NGOs are sometimes accused of being anti-government or of undermining public order and the stability of society. Yet it is Governments that commit human rights violations, because human rights are precisely limits on the exercise of official power, and human rights violations are transgressions of such limits. If NGOs are sometimes perceived as being nuisances to Governments, it is because that is their role.

Now we shall come to non-governmental human rights organisations.

Non-Governmental Human Rights Organizations

It is remarkable that development of international norms, institutions and procedures for the protection of human rights has gone hand in hand with the proliferation of non-governmental international organizations (NGO's) working in the human rights fields. On this subject generally, see H, Steiner, Diverse Partners: Non-Governmental Organizations in the Human Rights Movement (1991). As a matter of fact, as with the chicken and the egg, it is difficult to say which came first, Some NGO's played an important role in San Francisco during the drafting of the UN Charter. There they lobbied for the inclusion of human rights provisions in the Charter and for a system that would give NGO's formal institutional affiliation with and standing before UN organs. The result was Article 71 of the UN Charter, which provides that "the Economic and Social Council may make suitable arrangements for consultation with non-governmental organizations which are concerned with matters within its competence."

Article 71 was implemented in due course by ECOSOC. The subject is currently regulated by ECOSOC Resolution 1296 (XLIV) of May 23,1968. It establishes a formal system that/enables qualified NGO's to obtain one of three types of consultative status with the Organization. See Center for Human Rights, United Nations Action in the Field of Human Rights 31-32 (1994). The existence of this system has encouraged the creation of more NGO's, the adoption of similar consultative systems by other international and regional organizations, all of which has produced more NGO's. Today, as a result, there exist a myriad of these groups throughout the world. Some specialize in only one subject, such as human rights, health, or environmental matters; others focus either on more general interests and agendas or on particular issues of a given specialty. Whether or not they have a formal affiliation with an intergovernmental organization, the NGO's resemble domestic pressure groups or lobbies.

Human rights NGO's have played a particularly important role in the evolution of the international system for the protection of human rights and in trying to make it work. Governments which violate human rights are always eager to make sure that the applicable international human rights norms, institutions, and procedures remain weak and ineffective. The human rights NGO's provide a needed counterpoint to these governmental attitudes and deserve much of the credit for the progress that has been made in recent decades.

International Activities

The functions human rights NGO's perform differ depending upon the purpose for which they were established, their resources, the geographic regions in which they operate and the nature of their membership. There are NGO's which are interested in the world-wide promotion of human rights. Others limit their activities to human rights problems in specific regions or sub-regions (for example, Central America,

Africa, Asia) or to specific countries or issues. Amnesty International, the Lawyers Committee for Human Rights, the International League for Human Rights, the International Commission of Jurists, the Watch Committees, to cite but a few well-known NGO's, have world-wide interests. The Andean Commission of Jurists and the Washington Office for Latin America (WOLA), for example, are organizations with regional and sub-regional agendas. The methods NGO's employ in the pursuit of their goals also differ from group to group. Some choose to resort to only one or a limited number of techniques or activities, be it the preparation of reports, the filing of complaints with international organizations, the promotion of international legislation, lobbying before national and international bodies, and soon. Others use all of these tools depending upon the circumstances. Some NGO's limit themselves to the protection of specific groups or to specific concerns. This is true of the Anti-Slavery Society, the Minority Rights Group, or the International Committee of the Red Cross, Others have much broader concerns.

All major human rights NGOs have consultative status of one form or another with the UN, the Council of Europe, the Organization of American States, UNESCO and other regional or specialized intergovernmental organizations. This status permits their representatives, subject to certain conditions and restrictions, to present reports to these organizations, to be heard by their committees and commissions and, in certain cases, to affect the agendas of these bodies.

Many contemporary human rights instruments can be traced to proposals and/or drafts prepared by NGO's. The NGO's have on various occasions succeeded in getting the UN Commission on Human Rights, its Sub-Commission for the Prevention of Discrimination and Protection of Minorities and other UN bodies to focus on specific human rights violations, which they would otherwise not have done. The NGO's also deserve a great deal of credit for the creation by the UN and its Specialized Agencies of institutions and procedures for dealing with human rights violations. This has been accomplished by NGO's through their written and oral interventions in the proceedings of these bodies and by lobbying key representatives and delegations. In recent years, some NGO's have also contributed significantly to the strengthening of the reporting systems that have been established under various human rights treaties. Thus, for example, the International Covenants on Human Rights and the International Convention on the Elimination of all Forms of Racial Discrimination require the States Parties to file periodic reports indicating what action they have taken to comply with their obligations under these treaties. These reports are examined by special committees which these conventions created. As a rule, these committees lack the power to investigate the veracity of the claims made in the reports which the states submit.

They are usually also not empowered to hear witnesses or to request information from sources other than the state representatives, who are heard when their country's report is discussed .' by the committee. On that occasion committee members are permitted to ask the state representatives questions about the contents of their reports. The restraints under which these committees operate make reliable fact-finding difficult. This has prompted a number of NGO's to prepare their own country reports. Their findings are then passed on to any interested committee members prior to its meetings with the representatives of the reporting state. The information supplied by the NGO's enables the members to probe the veracity of the state reports and to get material into the record that does riot appear in the state reports.

Over the past five decades, many intergovernmental organizations have established legal mechanisms that permit individuals, groups and Non-governmental organizations to file human rights complaints. On this subject generally, see Shelton, "The Participation of Nongovernmental Organizations in International Judicial Proceedings," 88 Am. J. Int'l L. 611 (1994). NGO's have invoked these procedures and filed numerous complaints, particularly in cases involving allegations of massive violations of human rights. Here NGO's are often in a much, better position than individuals to gather reliable information and to prepare the necessary legal documentation. NGO's- have filed many complaints with the Inter-American Commission on Human Rights, both under the American Convention and under the OAS Charter-based petition system. Thus, for example, a decision by the Inter-American Commission on Human Rights holding that the U.S. had violated the right to life by permitting the execution of minors originated from a complaint filed by the American Civil Liberties Union and the International Human Rights Law Group. Case No. 9647 (United States), Resolution No. 3/87, Annual Report of the Inter-American Commission on Human Rights 1986-1987, OEA/Ser.L/V/II.71, doc.9, rev. 1, at 147 (1987). This is also true of various cases that have reached the Inter-American Court of Human Rights either in the form of requests for advisory opinions or contentious cases. The Court has permitted NGO's to file amicus curiae briefs in advisory proceedings, and a number of them have done so regularly.

In three contentious cases that were referred to the Inter-American Court by the Inter-American Commission in 1986, the latter invited the lawyers of the NGO's which had originally filed the cases to join its legal team before the Court. These cases are interesting for yet another reason: they demonstrate how national and international NGO's can cooperate in certain circumstances. Here a national NGO-the Honduran Human Rights Commission-first brought the cases to the attention of the Commission. Thereafter the Honduran group asked an international NGO with offices in Washington-Americas Watch-to assist it. The latter's lawyers then stepped in to handle the cases before the Commission. When the Commission referred the cases to the Court, the Commission asked the NGO lawyers to join its .' legal team, which they did.

Human rights NGO's have also pioneered the practice of using distinguished foreign lawyers or judges as observers at trials of individuals who have been charged with or appear to be tried for political offenses. Amnesty International and the International Commission of Jurists try to make frequent use of trial observers in order to ensure due process of law for the accused, for example, the annual reports of Amnesty International. The mere presence at such trials of foreign lawyers acting as trial observers has tended to prevent some abuses; at times it has even produced acquittals. A related practice, utilized with considerable success—particularly by the International Committee of the Red Cross—consists of inspections of prisons and detention centers for political prisoners. The ICRC attempts to ensure that those in detention are treated humanely and that they are provided with medical services and other basic necessities, Other NGO's have carried out important in loco investigations of human rights violations for use by intergovernmental human rights organizations and international tribunals.

National Activities

The policies governments adopt in confronting specific

violations of human rights being committed in other countries are made on the national level. The same is true of the policies that determine what powers governments are willing to confer on international organizations to enable them to deal with such violations. National political considerations also affect governmental decisions whether to ratify human rights treaties or what methods, national or international, should be employed to promote respect for human rights abroad. All of these and related issues must be addressed by a country's human rights foreign policy. Decisions affecting the formulation and execution of these policies are as much subject to various forms of lobbying as are other foreign policy decisions.

Influencing Human Rights Foreign Policy

Human rights NGO's devote a great deal of time and resources to activities designed to influence the human rights policies and diplomacy of various countries. In the United States, for example, human rights NGO's are very active in promoting U.S. ratification of international human rights instruments. They advocate legislation to deny U.S. economic and military assistance to governments that engage in large-scale violations of human rights. They also monitor compliance with that legislation by the Executive Branch. To this end, they present evidence to Congressional committees, publish reports critical of Executive action, launch public information campaigns and institute legal proceedings.

The following description of the activities of one human rights NGO operating in the U.S. provides a good example of the different functions such groups perform:

> Amnesty International U.S.A. has developed an organization of legal,' workers, lawyers, and law students....

The Legal Support Network's activities include: litigation, public education, outreach, work for lawyers who are victims of human rights abuses, research and work for the ratification of human rights treaties.

Similar activities focusing on legal actions are carried-out by other human rights NGO's including, among others, the Lawyers Committee for Human Rights and the International Human Rights Law Group. Informal coalitions and relations between these groups allows them to speak with one voice on important human rights issues when that appears indicated, which gives them considerable political strength. At times they also coordinate their research and lobbying activities to avoid unnecessary duplication and to preserve scarce financial and human resources. Most of these organizations derive their funding from private foundations, membership dues, and fund-raising campaigns. To preserve their political independence and impartiality, which are their strongest assets, a majority of these groups refuse contributions from governmental entities or from sources that might have a political or ideological interest.

Influence of Non-Governmental Organizations

International Non-governmental organizations (NGOs) have proliferated in the latter half of the 20th century. Many of these transnational actors are new to world politics, a province that historically has been dominated by states. In some issue areas, NGOs have acquired significant authority in the eyes of transnational actors. A prime example is the human rights group, Amnesty International which began in 1961 with letter-writing efforts to free individuals imprisoned for the nonviolent expression of opinion. Since then, and especially within the past two decades, Amnesty International has developed the capacity to research, report and analyze global patterns of human rights violations, empowering it to be a source of record in U.N. sessions and national halls of power. Moreover, Amnesty International is only one of a network of international and national NGOs active in human rights. Others include the International Commission of Jurists, the International Committee of the Red Cross and Human Rights Watch, all of which attempt to influence governments by applying general human rights principles to particular situations. Similarly, a growing network of environmental NGOs works to hold governments accountable to international environmental standards. Other NGOs, such as OXFAM, establish economic development projects and administer economic and humanitarian aid with funding from the pockets of private contributors. What these NGOs activities have in common is, while they often challenge governments and sometimes complement government-provided services, they nearly always act in counterpoint with governmental actors.

NGOs operations historically have been dependent upon interstate organizations for the provision of channels of action. However, partly due to the limitations on participation and expression inherent when international arenas are controlled fundamentally by states, these NGOs have also devised new channels of action that allow them more freedom. International NGOs not only cross formal national boundaries - they also have created a direct and independent form of non-governmental diplomacy through networks of their own. The economic, informational and intellectual resources of NGOs have garnered them enough expertise and influence to assume authority in matters that, traditionally, have been solely within the purview of state administration and responsibility. Further many NGOs claim a certain legitimacy for their causes by virtue of popular representation.

Whether or not the influence and independent authority

claimed by NGOs by virtue of their expertise and mandate of popular sovereignty amount to an erosion of formal state sovereignty is both a theoretical and empirical question. While one may riot discuss the conceptual history of sovereignty here, for purposes of this essay it is important to recognize, as has been noted recently, that state practices only murkily reflect formal, diplomatic definitions of - sovereignty, and sovereignty is often highly conditional and socially determined in practice.

Similarly, the relative influence of NGOs is not a static phenomenon, and their impact on state policies has changed and is changing with time. To return to human rights, NGOs have been involved at crucial junctures in strengthening the expectation that states be held accountable for human rights practices in the 20th century, as international and regional human rights norms have been elaborated in response to problematic country cases, and states have been encouraged to create new intergovernmental reporting and monitoring procedures at the formal level. These changes have arisen not so much from enthusiastic state participation as from international popular and diplomatic pressure exerted on governments.

Human rights NGOs, such as Amnesty International, have become skilled at mounting such pressure by feeding information into pertinent public and governmental channels for discussion, on the one hand, and distributing and promoting new human rights instruments, on the other. Further it is often through such activity by NGOs that newly created norms become formalized and develop meaningful impact. This process changes the scope of state sovereignty as it, "reconstitutes the relationship between the state., its citizens and international actors".

Herein, one may consider two cases: the international

role of NGOs concerned with upholding states obligations to protect the human rights of their citizens, and the work of International environmental NGOs. Both issue areas have seen a grounds well of grassroots interest carried to the international level, as well as related growth in interest at the UN and regional governmental levels, arguably in important enough ways to justify the classification Of NGOs as new international actors that represent non-state interests. In pressing for environmental issues when states lack the necessary resources or commitment for pursuing a comprehensive vision of environmental conservation, environmental NGOs are motivated by some of the same humanitarian principles as are human rights NGOs.

Additionally, both types of NGOs foster the creation and maintenance of an international public consensus on principle of human rights and the environment that tends to impel responsive states to adhere to new legal and behavioral norms of practice related to these issues. To date, however, the degree to which the two have emphasized participation in formal governmental arenas, as well as the creation of independent networks outside governmental channels, has differed. While human rights NGOs place a strong emphasis on respect for legal norms of human rights and thus look to intergovernmental channels for effective action, environmental NGOs have introduced an added dimension of modern NGOs activity by being even less dependent on state channels of action. How and why do such NGOs have an effect on states? NGOs in the issue areas under consideration represent a focused, but potentially broadly appealing, set of ideas, information and values.

The commitment of NGOs to particular principles such as human rights or the environment enables them to mobilize a highly motivated international public membership. Their members provide the financial and volunteer resources needed to gather extensive information and expertise. Commitment to a very focused set of concerns, in contrast to the obligations of states to respond to a greater range of demands, allows NGOs to gain leverage on selected policy issues. This can be advantageous internationally, where human rights and environmental NGOs challenge state sovereignty through the very attributes that make them different from states: narrow issue focus, intense and principled commitment and relatively high levels of information, expertise and, sometimes, resources to commit to issues.

Human Rights and the Environment

Certain public goods such as communications, trade and environmental protection traditionally have been regulated by states at the domestic level. International exchange of goods and information also demands that states cooperate to establish mutually recognized regulatory standards in matters such as trade, monetary standards, communication and technology. As the legal, economic and ethical implications of such regulatory regimes cross borders, the issues themselves become internationalized, often coming into conflict with the goals of particular states.

A growing literature on international governance documents the growth of international regimes that organize state practices in particular issue areas. Regimes are conceived of as tools for states' pursuit of self-interest, created and maintained in response to international demand for rules governing mutually beneficial international transactions.' The concept of regimes, therefore, is fundamentally state-centric, although it can be inferred that non-governmental organizations also would cluster around international regime-based institutions, to exert influence on particular issues. Although the regimes concept has been applied to human rights, the authoritative moral element in their enforcement is overlooked by the more state-centered theories of international governance. Human rights norms impose a duty on states to respect human dignity, both internationally and through the treatment of their citizens. Compared with the well-established sovereignty principle, codified in the Universal Declaration of Human Rights adopted by the U.N. in 1948, this duty to protect human dignity is a relatively new principle of international law." Human rights obligations potentially limit state policy choices in a categorical way, so that in practice, international demands that human rights obligations be fulfilled conflict with the older international principle of non-interference in domestic affairs Thus, the moral component of human rights concerns, the idea that human rights should be a part of state practice under all circumstances, is at odds with a conventional interest-based explanation of regimes. In the environmental field, the principles advocated by NGOs include humanitarian and conservationist concerns for the well-being of humans and the rest of nature.

As with human rights protection, the potential conflict between international demands for environmental conservation and a state's claim to the right to control the resources within its borders touches directly upon state sovereignty. For example, the international community demands the preservation of Brazil's rainforest on the grounds that the rainforest is an international public good, while Brazil maintains that its right to exploit the rainforest for economic purposes overrides any international moral claim. While the construction of any type of international regime can entail, to some extent, state concessions of sovereignty, environmental and human rights NGOs pose a particular challenge to states by calling for the universal application of certain ethical principles related to state conduct. Respect for human rights and environmental principles, however, requires not just verbal deference but concrete technical and procedural implementation as well. This often carries costly political and economic consequences for states reluctant to force changes either on themselves or on one another for fear of setting a precedent of intervention. For these reasons, states are likely to neglect the implementation of more restrictive standards of conduct unless pressed by third parties, and NGOs and private citizens, rather than states, have served as prominent conduits of pressure and influence on these issues.

Elements of NGOs Influence

It is pertinent to note that NGOs influence has grown in recent years precisely because they are different from states. First, NGOs focus on single issues or sets of issues to the exclusion of others, while states must perform many functions, with national security as a top priority. The organizational mandate of Amnesty International, for example, commits it to an exclusive focus on promoting the Universal Declaration of Human Rights and related international legal instruments. Environmental groups as well, despite the complexity environmental issue linkages, have limited policy concerns compared to states. Second, in taking up principle-based issues, NGOs commit themselves to causes that state's priorities frequently subordinate to other foreign policy interests or ignore entirely. But international NGOs can draw on the activism of local memberships at the state level, in order to bring domestic public opinion into play.

The involvement of domestic actors allows NGOs to bring pressure on states internally, based on domestic representation and legitimacy, as well as internationally, based on humanitarian principles and generalized public opinion. There is also evidence that most states care how they are regarded by others, suggesting that international pressure alone can affect state action under certain conditions."

However, international NGOs are likely to be less successful in their attempts at influence if they cannot establish links with domestic actors. This problem is evident with regard to governments that repress domestic representation and civil protest or are too weak to be responsive to public demands. Third, in contrast to states, the commitment of NGOs to their issues is intense. State and intergovernmental agencies deal with varied and competing policy concerns, while NGOs specialize on one or a few issues. This is not to say that NGOs do not have to balance their own priorities, but their scope is narrower and their membership is less ideologically diverse than the issues and citizenry to which states are accountable. As a result, NGOs can apply their resources of volunteer memberships and paid staff in a manner that is more focused than the attention and resources that state representatives may be able to devote to the same issues.

In the next chapter, we shall discuss the rights of women and their protection and the role played by NGOs in this direction.

6

NGOs and Women's Rights

> "Possibly man could live twice as long if he didn't spend the first half of his life acquiring habits that shorten the other half."
>
> —*Mary L. Wright*

Human rights and women's groups have long recognized that human rights need a broad constituency. Non-Governmental Organizations (NGOs) and other sectors of civil society have thus played a vital role in informing and educating women in terms of their rights; exposing violations of women's human rights; and campaigning for legislative and other changes at the national, regional and international levels. The campaign to identify women's rights as human rights can be traced back to the non-governmental movement and its efforts to place the improvement of the status of women firmly in the United Nations framework. These early efforts by, women's groups, non-governmental organizations, researchers, women's movements and individual activists led to the establishment and strengthening of links which would go on to prove a powerful force at both national and international levels. Recent, important initiatives by the non-governmental community in relation to the human rights of women include the following:

- The worldwide campaign by women's groups placed the human rights of women and violence against women squarely on the agenda of the 1993 World Conference on Human Rights;
- The campaign for a strengthening of United Nations mechanisms to address the issue of violence against women including through the establishment of a Special Rapporteur on Violence Against Women;
- The initiative by women's rights advocates to ensure that human rights provided the basic framework of the Platform for Action which was adopted by the 1995 Fourth World Conference on Women; and
- Campaigns to expose and document rape of women as a war crime in both Rwanda and the former Yugoslavia

Non-governmental organizations (NGOs) and the United Nations are natural partners in the struggle for all human rights. The United Nations has long recognized that NGOs have a freedom of movement and a flexibility of action which allow them to identify critical issues and to develop and apply appropriate responses. The relationship between the United Nations and those groups which are working for the realization of women's human rights must be nurtured and strengthened. This will require the development of new and creative means for cooperation and collaboration.

Towards Strengthening the Human Rights of Women

No doubt, while great achievements have been made for the human rights of women since the adoption of the Universal Declaration, it is clear that much remains to be done. The traditional marginalization of women's human rights is an accurate reflection of the subordinate position which women continue to occupy in many parts of the world. International human rights law and the mechanisms which have been established to enforce that law provide one important weapon in the struggle for human rights. The strengthening of this system - and of its regional, national and grass roots counterparts - is a priority and a responsibility of the United Nations, individual States and all sectors of civil society. The 50th Anniversary of the Universal Declaration provided a very good opportunity to focus on the development of concrete initiatives to further women's rights.

Main Thrusts

- NGOs Campaigning for the effective integration of gender into the international human rights system;
- Campaigning for the unconditional, universal ratification of the Convention on the Elimination of All Forms of Discrimination Against Women; for the removal of substantive reservations-, and for the strengthening of its implementation machinery (including the adoption of an optional protocol which will allow for the consideration of complaints from individuals);
- Developing innovative activities at all levels to increase women's awareness of their human rights, of the mechanisms which are available to protect and enforce those rights and of the various methods of advocacy which can enable women to gain greater access to economic and political opportunities.
- Advocating human development programmes which explicitly recognize and advance universal principles of equality and non-discrimination 'and which embrace education, improved reproductive health and more credit for women;
- Strengthening of the partnership between national and international women's and human rights NGOs as well as between all such NGOs and the United Nations system. This partnership should ensure that

> the human rights of women remain firmly fixed on the national and international agenda and that accurate information about the state of the world's women is collected, analysed and disseminated.

In 1998 the Office of the High Commissioner for Human Rights contacted a number of institutions, agencies and women's organizations from all regions of the world with a request that they provide information on their activities for the promotion and protection of women's human rights in the framework of the 50th Anniversary of the Universal Declaration.

United Nations Development Fund for Women (UNIFEM)

The commemorative activities of the 50th Anniversary of the Universal Declaration of Human Rights provide the framework within which UNIFEM highlight the achievements of women over the past 50 years. The high level panel focused on:

(a) Reviewing the progress made in implementing international agreements regarding the human rights of women;

(b) Eliciting a public re-statement of the international community's commitment to ensure the full realization of the human rights of women;

(c) Strengthening a global partnership towards the elimination of violence and discrimination against women.

The Role of NGOs

The most important Recommendation of the World Conference on Human Rights held at Vienna, Austria from 14 to 25 June 1993 was that "Human Rights, Democracy, Rule of Law and development be included in the curriculum of all educational institutions". It was on January 1,1995 that the United Nations declared the UN Decade for Human Rights Education. It is heartening to note that in the same year, the Asian Institute for Human Rights Education was established at Bhopal. The AIHRE has forged ahead with the formulation of curriculum and preparation of sample lessons with the collaboration and cooperation of SCERT, Madhya Pradesh and DIET, Bhopal. The Conference of 1995 (WCCI) could come out with a declaration endorsing these attempts. The Regional Conference of WCCI held at Palayamkottai, Tamil Nadu has gone a step further in promoting Human Rights Education jointly with a sister organisation IAEWP (International Association of Educators for World Peace). We have in India a National Commission on Human Rights and several state level commissions. But how far these have succeeded in ensuring human rights to our citizens? Human Rights violations are taking place in most places. How many are brought to sight and grievances redressed? Only a few atrocities against women are on the increase. Child labour is another area. Rights of the girl child are not secure. The aged are neglected. Corruption is on the increase at all levels. Even people at the helm of affairs are booked, at least after their powerful days. People amass money through foul measures. The rich are becoming richer and the poor, poorer. Human Rights are there in paper, but in actual practice they are very much neglected. So commission and laws are not enough. Awareness should be created among the people.

Citizens should become law-abiding. None should get exemption based on political, communal or money power. From the lowest class onwards children should study human rights, values, democracy and practice them. Even if it is not in the curriculum or text book, every teacher and educator also should try to understand and make use of the hidden curriculum. This will naturally lead to the establishment of a society, state and world order dedicated to peace, progress and prosperity. IAEWP is one such NGO which tries at International and local levels to build up a warless society, where we-feeling is dominant. Educators at all levels are the best persons to inculcate human rights education theory and practice among the future citizens. Our formal system alone cannot attempt or succeed in this endeavour. The non-formal sector has to play an active and ever increasing role in conscientising the masses. Herein comes the role of NGOs. Name-sake interventions are not enough. Rapid Action Forces are to be formed along the lines of social action groups (Activists) to counter human rights violations/ not through confrontation and conflict, but through creating awareness and ensuring wilful participation and adjustment.

People's Council for Social Justice (PCSJ) is one such working in India (specially in Kerala). They are educating the masses and organising Neethimelas, outside the courts. Family courts are also in operation... But many are afraid of approaching these courts and commissions. What is needed first is to inform the public of such organisations, their role and functioning. Folk art forms and modern media have to be folly and effectively utilised to create awareness among the people on human rights, democracy and development. Education and development are the two sides of the same coin. One has to lead to the other. But is it happening? People look upto others for achieving their goals and stating their needs and urges. Prioritizing development activities (especially local) is the first step to be undertaken. Kerala has launched such an attempt in the preparation of IX Plan proposals. From the rural village/ward upward, the exercise is in this direction of establishing and maintaining human rights. From the lowest level of self-government upwards, efforts should be made to involve every citizen in the nation-building work. We, teachers and teacher educators have to be in the forefront of such an attempt.

The UN Decade has started in January, 1995 and will go upto December 2005. If we are to achieve something tangible, we do not have any more time to spare on thinking or preparatory work. More than 15 years have elapsed after the formal launching of the decade. It appears that not much has been planned or implemented so far. So it is upto the Centre and State government, Educational Institutions at all levels and NGOs (big and small) to have a round table, prepare an action" plan and implement one's share, wholeheartedly.

Today in India, in many fields we are lagging behind. Even we have nearly half of our population embedded with illiteracy, poverty unemployment, etc. We are trying to make education a right for all. Values are eroding. Western influence is affecting our youth in many ways. Our unique culture is being spoiled. How to overcome these? The only way out is human rights education direct and indirect for all using formal and non-formal approaches. Multimedia approaches should also be used to preserve our Indianness, the heritage which our forefathers have builtup. The role of the UN should also be subjected to careful analysis and necessary changes have to be effected (including increase of permanent membership in the security council). Declarations are not enough. They have to be carefully translated into action. We educators have to pledge to bring about such desired changes and work hard in that direction. GOS's and NGO's have a role in such areas. We should stop accusing each other. What is needed .'is cooperation and collaboration.

The concern for human rights and fundamental freedom has assumed a global dimension and is of vital significance to the world community. Human Rights intrinsically and pervasively impact the quality and fulfilment of life of societies in all nations and ensure the prevalence of freedom, justice, peace and order in the world. "The task of the protection and promotion of Human Rights is a complex one and requires the co-operation of all sections of society, political parties, nongovernmental organizations, lawyers, judges, public servants, teachers, police, media persons, and others. I appeal to all of you to observe human rights in your homes, at the work place, in your neighbourhood and everywhere. The goal is to create a culture of Human Rights across the length and breadth of the country". There are certain minimal rights which have come to be accepted as basic freedoms of the individual.

These rights are broadly classified into civil and political rights on the one hand and economic, social and cultural rights on the other hand and these are indivisible and interdependent. The aftermath of World War-II which caused unprecedented misery, death and destruction made the conscience of the world think of the ways and means to remove the violations of human rights and dignity practised by some nations.

This concern culminated in the Universal Declaration of Human Rights on 10th Dec. 1948 by the General Assembly of the United Nations. It sets forth the fundamental liberties and rights common to all people on earth. Since, the declaration, colonial people have been liberated, several conventions adopted and a United Nations High Commission for Human Rights established. The preamble to the Declaration records that recognition of the inherent dignity and of the equal and the inalienable rights of all members of the human family is the foundation of freedom, justice and peace in the world and their disregard results in barbarous acts which outrage the conscience of mankind. Therefore, human rights should be protected by the Rule of Law. The U.N. Declaration comprises of 30 Articles. To protect and implement these Articles there are other connotations of great importance, namely, the recognition for the international instruments adopted by UN, ILO, UNESCO and others and alongwith their recognition, also the adherence to them. But the question remains, are we fully conscious of the ethical truth contained in the Articles of the HR Declaration? Do we recognize in our way of life and behaviour the implication of the fact that human rights belong within the common heritage of humanity? These rights reveal a purity of purpose. They demand urgent implementation.

Today the society is more or less violence striven. Concern with human rights can not stop with the enunciation alone. There is need for more positive and operational steps. In order to carry the work of promotion of HR's various nongovernmental organisations, have started the work in every part of the world. NGOs are the voice of the people of the world. It is gratifying to note that inspite of sharp differences among themselves, the NGOs managed during the Vienna Summit to reach an agreement among themselves for their joint proposals. NGOs have made their impact on the civil society of Asia, Africa and Latin America in the preparatory conferences in Tunis, San Jose, Bangkok and the Asian Conference. Now the people in general no longer leave their problems to Government alone to see the violence and injustice but depend on the NGOs. NGOs have a share in the responsibility of greater accountability to their own and their future generations.

The United Nations Charter

The charter of the United Nations makes reference to human rights and fundamental freedoms in a number of clauses. In the preamble, the people of United Nations express their determination "to reaffirm faith in fundamental human rights, in the dignity and worth of human person, in the equal rights of men and women and of nations large and small". The United Nations can only live upto the expectations which are raised by its charter and collective efforts are made by all of its organs as also by other organs of international and national society and Governments, inter-governmental and non-governmental agencies and organizations of the world and alongwith them the individuals share the responsibility of joining in a common human rights efforts.

Human Rights Organizations

In the initial stages, for achieving the goal the International Human Rights Organizations were founded by League of Nations and United Nations viz.; London-based Anti Slavery Society for Human Rights in 1938, the International Committee for Red Cross in 1963, the French League for Human Rights in 1898, the larger number of NGOs at national, regional and local level emerged after 1970. Some of the significant NGOs are People's Union for Civil Liberties (PUCL) in 1974, the People's Union for Democratic Rights (PUDR) in 1976 and Centre for Democracy (CFD). These organisations have established their expert activity by investigating and undertaking on the spot studies and by publishing their observations. The activities and functions of the NGOs must be through their perception and action and the NGOs deserve to be recognized in the perspective of social, cultural and economical rights as the Fundamental Human Rights. Justice P.N. Bhagwati has rightly observed: "we can escape from this paradox and break the vicious circle by organizing the poor." Thus, the activists and the NGOs have greater opportunities to work but of course with greater professionalism to face greater challenge.

Prospective Functions

It can be safely assumed that the Non-governmental organizations can play a very main role. The important functions may include:

1. Collection of information about the violation of HRs and monitoring the same.
2. Education.
3. Legislation.
4. Preventing HR abuses and rendering humanitarian help to the victims.
5. Solidarity.
6. Working in the areas of social right.

In fact, there is a very minor point of contention. NGOs in India suffer from non-cooperation, i.e., the consumers of NGOs help nurture a feeling of hostility. Thus NGOs undergo a very tough time in convincing the people that their attitude is good and that they will help the deprived class.

Though NGOs have become a household name due to mushroom growth of NGOs, formed by vested interests, their credibility becomes dubious. For credible recognition dedicated NGO personnel must have Identity proofs so that may be instrumental in promoting human rights awareness programme at grassroot level.

7

NGOs' Influence

"The mark of the immature man is that he wants to die nobly for a cause, while the mark of the mature man is that he wants to live humbl for one."

—*William Stekel*

To begin with first we introduce you to channels of NGOs influence.

Today, NGOs face a choice of operating within arenas that are not necessarily mutually exclusive. The first is the intergovernmental realm. Intergovernmental organizations (IGOs), such as the United Nations, the Council of Europe and the Organization of American States, are the fora in which international legal norms are created, and NGOs seeking influence at this level must use such channels. However, because of their growing expertise and involvement in international issues, NGOs have earned a measure of authentic autonomy from states even within intergovernmental organizations. For example, human rights NGOs regularly lobby diplomats at the United Nations who, in most cases, are not experts in human rights or international law. To develop proposals and shepherd them through the complex U.N. system requires experience and skill that take time to acquire. Further, although diplomats formally receive instructions from their governments, information also flows the other way, with the result that the lobbying efforts of informed NGO staff can have a significant influence on shaping government positions. Over time, NGOs are likely to possess more extensive knowledge and a more comprehensive view on their issue than any given diplomat. Overall, the neutrality of NGOs faithfulness to principle, relative to particular state interests, when combined with the authority of their issue expertise, gives NGOs the potential for autonomous influence within intergovernmental arenas. A second realm of activity is not directly related to intergovernmental fora. With increasingly dense networks of communications and informational exchange in the 20th century, international NGOs now also pursue concerns with other NGOs in self-created international arenas. In this respect, the interaction of NGOs might be said to form a nascent international civil society, which is independent of government policy making paths but brings individuals and grassroots groups together for informational exchange and political action. In these self-created arenas, where the agenda is controlled by the NGOs rather than states, there are fewer constraints on NGOs expression.

The two channels of influence, intergovernmental and independent, correspond to two possible conceptions of NGOs. The first is the conception of the NGOs as a third-party advocate within intergovernmental arenas. The second is the conception of the NGOs as an organizational agent of social action outside traditional channels, or "the institutionalization of new populist movements."

In intergovernmental arenas, NGOs seem most threatening to states when they are most like them, that is, when they appear to be allied with identifiable state interests. A classic charge governments use to discredit NGOs is that they are front groups linked to particular nationalistic or ideological positions.. Such Criticism is often lodged against Amnesty International, for example. A collection of government and editorial responses to the group's work published in the 1980s shows a remarkable balance of accusations from both sides, of Cold War ideology. In reaction to Amnesty International's 1976 campaign against torture in Uruguay, a Uruguayan newspaper editorial wrote, "Amnesty International has adopted virtually a unilateral position against Western countries and has remained almost totally silent on the subject of atrocities committed in the communist world." On the other hand, an excerpt from the Soviet newspaper Izvestia accused Amnesty International of being a tool of the West: "Even during its early years Amnesty International was in the keep of the imperialist secret services, first and foremost by the Americans, whose interests it serves?"

Historically, NGOs in the United Nations have represented humanitarian concerns. When NGOs were invited to consult with the U.S. delegation at the drafting of the U.N. Charter, their presence was understood to serve the interests of the U.S. government as much as those of the NGOs Consultants. The NGOs presence, nevertheless, enabled them to secure human rights language in the U.N., charter and continued direct access to the United Nations through the Economic and Social Council (ECOSOC). The establishment of formal NGOs consultative status in ECOSOC on 21 June 1946 was a calculated concession to U.S. NGOs, one which they used to advance human rights principles at the international level. NGOs with consultative status in ECOSOC are organizations "representative of major population segments ... involved with the economic and social life" of the areas they represent, "having special competence in a few of the

Council's areas of activity," or able to contribute usefully to the Council's work in some way." An inevitable tension arises, however, when NGOs seek to change the behavior of states through activity related to intergovernmental arenas, over which states exercise formal control. Ultimately, NGOs involved in domestic and international consultative and advocacy efforts are formally subordinated to state and intergovernmental administrative practices. The procedural tools available to NGOs through consultative status preparation of reports, filing of complaints, promotion of international legislation and lobbying before national and international bodies - give NGOs limited procedural power relative to states. NGOs do not vote in ECOSOC, and they only observe proceedings in the General Assembly. When the U.N. Commission on Human Rights was set up, NGOs were "restricted, in formal terms, to stiff, cameo appearances." Indeed, until the late 1970s, "convention and habit ensured" that human rights NGOs would express their concerns in the United Nations " with circumlocutions, euphemisms, and evasions" -conventional diplomatic language, reined in by state practice. Compared with states, NGOs may be limited in terms of formal participation within intergovernmental organizations (IGOs), but larger NGOs have evolved to rival state representatives in their effectiveness on certain issues.

NGOs are motivated to make intergovernmental provisions for humanitarian concerns effective, and they can provide services that supplement intergovernmental resources as well as counterbalance the reluctance of intergovernmental bodies to monitor politically sensitive domestic state practices. NGOs acquire a substantive and historical expertise that may be unmatched even by government agencies. In the Human Rights Committee, the body that supervises compliance with the International Covenant on Civil and Political Rights, NGOs "supply information so that the members are better informed in posing questions to governmental representatives when they present their reports." The expertise supplied by NGOs extends to consultation on the drafting of particular texts formally advanced by states in intergovernmental discussions.

Besides informational resources and expertise, NGOs tap into financial and volunteer resources that, as states grow stingy with resources devoted to international cooperation, can rival IGO budgets. While budgets and staffing levels may be constrained for intergovernmental organizations, NGOs can draw on their memberships for resources. Amnesty International's staff size and budget now stack up favorably against the proportion of U.N. resources dedicated to human rights concerns. The head of the U.N. Centre for Human Rights in Geneva commented that "at present, less than one percent of the United Nations budget and less than 0.75 percent of its staff are dedicated to human rights .... We have less money and less resources than Amnesty International, and we are the arm of the United Nations for human rights. This is clearly ridiculous." A further indication of the low priority that states give to issues supported by NGOs is the consistent lag in staffing and funding for the administrative unit of the U.N. Committee on NGOs within ECOSOC.

A 1992 General Assembly resolution passed in response to a report by the U.N. Secretary-General noted that, in contrast to the numerical increase of NGOs in consultative status and the increasing importance of their contributions to ECOSOC proceedings, "resources have remained at the same level since 1947, when the Unit was established." The availability and size of NGOs resources devoted to human rights, therefore, when compared with intergovernmental resources devoted to the issue, can be a source of advantage for NGOs, even in state-governed arenas. Still, in many cases, exerting NGOs influence at the international level depends upon placing issues on the intergovernmental agenda, which requires securing cooperation from states and relying on their membership to take advantage of state representational mechanisms.

NGOs may direct members willing to approach their own foreign policy-making bodies on behalf of the NGOs, thereby effecting a two-tiered form of NGOs influence: expert lobbying at the intergovernmental level, backed up by political pressure generated by citizen demand and awareness at home. Popular opinion thus plays a role in allowing NGOs the influence both nationally and internationally to capitalize on their memberships' purchase on representation before particular governments.

International and domestic NGOs can have great impact on government positions, in part because it is now "increasingly difficult for governments to stem the flow of information from local groups to international 'umbrella' human rights groups and international governmental monitoring bodies." This sharing of information is a key aspect in the growth of NGOs influence, for NGOs activity increasingly takes place outside of formal intergovernmental channels. NGOs are important members of issue networks, comprised by "a set of organizations, bound by shared values and by dense exchanges of information and services, working internationally on an issue."

Notably, in exemplary cases, NGOs complement each other's areas of expertise as they pursue a common goal. In a typical example in the area of human rights, a group of statisticians has formed a Committee on Scientific Freedom and Human Rights under the aegis of the American Statistical Association (ASA). The committee publishes an on-line informational newsletter that encourages its members to participate in the Amnesty .International letter-writing network, Urgent Action. In this way, the statistician's group, piggybacks on Amnesty International's area of expertise. In addition, by coordinating a pool of professional statisticians prepared to volunteer internationally for human rights monitoring projects, and by publishing a textbook on data analysis and human rights, the ASA committee offers another form of expertise in its reliance on already established professional networks to offer specialized services." In fact, these newly dense networks of communications and informational exchange give international NGOs the option to choose between pursuing their own goals within international governmental arenas, recognizing that their autonomy will likely be limited or subordinated to state goals, and pursuing concerns with other NGOs in self-created international fora with fewer constraints on expression. Some do both, but the vision moving some newer NGOs dictates a link between methods and goals that eschews conventional politics and thus, State-mediated politics. This vision is that of the NGOs taking shape as "institutionalized representation of new populist movements."

Indeed, while the focus here so far has been on the direct influence of NGOs in interactions with states, NGOs have also created their own system of activity and influence separate from the governmental sphere, referred to below as "parallel NGOs activity." In this section I rely on recent studies of the environmental movement in Latin America to illustrate features of citizen-based exchange sponsored by NGOs in contrast to influence mediated by governments. The environmental movement is one in which a variety of approaches, including parallel NGOs activity, has proliferated. Environmental groups at the national level in Brazil, for example, have approached environmentalism as a transformative social movement, emphasizing cultural politics (e.g., communicative activities aimed at reinterpreting politics by identifying and transforming what are understood to be social structures of domination) over formal political opportunities (e.g., influence attempts aimed at affecting policies and legislation through government channels and representative mechanisms)."

The Brazilian environmental groups have taken a broad view of environmental Activism, forming alliances with non-environmental groups to address "green" concerns in varying social arenas and rarely mobilizing solely around specific environmental policy problems." By contrast, Venezuelan groups have concentrated on more narrowly defined political opportunities such as government-sponsored conferences to achieve influence on environmental issues, often in response to immediate threats. They too, however, began to supplement that activity with broader public appeals, such as use of the mass media to influence public opinion toward the end of the 1980s. Brazilian environmentalists, accustomed to a grassroots approach to environmental activism at the domestic level, transferred this philosophy to the international level in 1992.

Eager to facilitate interaction among NGOs, Brazilian activists sponsored a special assembly for NGOs held concurrently with the 1992 United Nations Conference on Environment and Development (the "Earth Summit"). Rather than being an organizing tool to achieve maximum influence at the intergovernmental conference, the parallel conference, dubbed the Global Forum, was intended to provide a more open venue for the exchange of information among NGOs.

Many participants, according to Hochstetler, had come to believe that "official treaties and government declarations were less important than similar citizen commitments."

Some groups, however, did plan to pursue both strategies. The parallel venue was designed to attract the participation of a variety of groups, since NGOs with conventional intergovernmental orientations had access to participation in the Global Forum concurrently. As for the official U.N. conference, NGOs lobbied successfully for relaxed criteria regarding formal NGOs participation at Rio and in meetings leading up to the conference. Thus, NGOs participation in the official conference was not limited to those with ECOSOC consultative status, and a broader range of NGOs were able to participate. The parallel approach benefitted both the Brazilian environmentalists, with their interest in social transformation, and groups with more pragmatic philosophies. The Brazilians set up the parallel conference as a potential launching pad for a global citizens' movement on the environment. This led them to approach the meetings as a prototype for what might be called a global civil society. To some extent, their idealism was rewarded.

In the international encounters prompted by the Earth Summit, Brazilian groups were buoyed by the willingness of NGOs from the North to discuss structural issues, such as North-South relations, that governments were unwilling to address. In contrast, Venezuelan environmentalists, accustomed to working closely with their own governmental representatives, saw the parallel conference as a forum in which to "advance the agenda of the South."

The Venezuelan activists' rationale was that their counterparts in the North could function as progressive influences among northern governments, advancing public opinion that sound international environmental policy should also address the developmental needs of the South." Both attitudes indicate that conferences like the Earth Summit provide significant opportunities for greater organization and linkage between international and domestic NGOs, whether the NGOs view the political opportunities available to them through a state-centric lens or in broader socio-cultural terms.

The parallel approach of the Brazilian domestic movement in the 1980s meant that the environmental groups in Brazil were not the primary channels for international funding and interest in the preservation of the Amazon river basin. It has been found that, throughout the 1980s, the holistic cultural emphasis of Brazilian environmentalists led them to focus on macro-level political and economic structures and to de-emphasize causes and solutions rooted in specific policies." International environmental lobbies, on the other hand, favored applying pressure to change specific policies. In consequence, international sponsorship of efforts to preserve the Amazon basin harmonized more easily with non-environmental domestic political actors such as rubber tapper groups and indigenous activists, who also employed policy-specific tactics." With some exceptions, the ostensibly non-environmental groups that have participated in conservation efforts are "much more systematically integrated into international environmental networks than into their own national environmental movement."

The flow of international funding to the more project-oriented environmental groups is a trend that has been identified throughout Latin America." Specific environmental projects that fall under the rubric of sustainable development and are administered by regional or national NGOs, tend to attract a socially diverse, domestic membership. Thus, they are perceived as a safer avenue for international funding than older NGOs that were less guided by project-oriented ideologies This suggests that the very shape of environmentalism, especially in developing countries, is *molded* by international funding trends. The typical stages in funding for Latin American environmental NGOs have been described as starting with money from international sources that favor grassroots action, then moving on to larger grants from private and governmental sponsors who favour sustainable development projects and large-scale environmental stewardship. Based on these trends, a change in how domestic NGOs define their projects is evident. Similar forces appear to be at work regarding government environmental policy, as World Bank funding guidelines emphasize environmental sustainability for development projects. Here, lines between the governmental and the non-governmental grow blurry as NGOs assist with the administration of national projects. For example, a World Bank loan to Mexico in 1992 required collaboration between the Mexican government and Mexican environmental NGOs." A further example is the Brazilian government's protest that, despite its territorial sovereignty over the Amazonian rainforest, it cannot bear the costs of conservation on its own." The Brazilian government has maintained that if Brazil is to refrain from exploiting rainforest resources, it requires assistance from the international community in implementing conservation and development programs. Thus, the modern NGOs has potential to increase its influence over the policy-making agenda in intergovernmental arena. The intergovernmental policy-making arena is likely to remain a central point for coordinating action on international issues such as human rights and the environment, but the NGOs contribution to formal international arenas can turn them into organizational avenues for citizens as well as states on pressing global issues. To a certain extent the prospects for increased authority of NGOs are positively linked to similar prospects for IGOs. Therefore, the shrinking of state resources devoted to IGOs, or the reluctance of states to participate in multilateral policy making can be expected to have a-negative impact on overall NGOs influence as well as on intergovernmental structures in the long run. NGOs activity in parallel arenas also indirectly contributes to intergovernmental activity by helping to coordinate the positions of large international NGOs with domestic indigenous or culturally specific understandings of issues, such as human rights, the environment development. NGOs accustomed to consulting with governments may then carry such considerations into their intergovernmental work. While NGOs' intergovernmental influence on human rights is earned by taking up causes states ignore or contravene and by mastering the intricacies of diplomacy to apply intergovernmental authority to humanitarian concerns, the challenge for human rights NGOs in actually changing state domestic practices remains daunting. It has been argued that repressive states can tolerate high levels of diplomatic and economic isolation for long periods of time.

In this respect, the interchange between international NGOs and domestic groups becomes vital to NGO effectiveness, It is difficult for domestic NGOs to thrive under repressive governments, but international contact can foster their physical as well as political survival in a hostile environment. Domestic NGOs, for their part, help to provide information and lobbying efforts in support of NGO objectives at national and international levels. The challenge for human rights NGOs is not so much to develop international allegiances that compete with loyalty to the state as it is to increase popular demand that states respect principles of human dignity as a matter of practice. The independent potential for NGO accomplishments outside of the intergovernmental realm, such as the use of transformative, citizen-based politics in the environmental movement, is more difficult to assess, in part because the history is brief. The Brazilian case suggests that domestic efforts to create other than state-centric, culturally based modes of activism on the environment are now at a disadvantage, in terms of recruiting international resources to their cause.' However, it is possible to say that the interpretive activities of transformative movements, taking place alongside efforts focused on changing specific state practices, have the potential to strengthen ties between less developed countries and the broader NGO networks, many of whose resources come primarily from participants in affluent countries. In this respect the case of environmental NGOs seems to mirror that of human rights: Their memberships are motivated more readily by perceptible threats rather than pursuit of a comprehensive agenda rooted in structural change. Funding sources as well, favor projects promising early and observable results. The seeming dichotomy between the principled and the pragmatic, evidenced in the international response to Brazilian environmental activism, suggests the potential for conflicts over NGOs roles in the future. While investment in humanitarian values or moral principles virtually predicates dissatisfaction with the slowly grinding intergovernmental processes, funders' demands for effective practical remedies even when NGOs try to invoke broader considerations may lead to the neglect of the root causes of global problems. Still, as their capacities expand internationally, NGOs will likely be held by their members and by outsiders to progressively higher standards of effectiveness. The pressure on NGOs to pursue intergovernmental influence may hot always balance easily with their need to inform and be informed by local experience. Once intergovernmental recognition has been gained, international NGOs face the challenge of maintaining their hard-won expertise and respect, while preserving the focus and responsiveness to particular values that motivated their original entry into international politics.

NGO Perspective for Exchange and Dissemination

It outlines the relationships between human rights and information handling from the viewpoint of non-governmental organizations. It stresses the need to further develop a decentralized network for exchange and dissemination of information. Information, has been defined in different ways by social scientists, physicals, mathematicians and, of course, information scientists. According to the *Encyclopedia Britannica* (1986), "In information theory, information is thought of as a choice of one message from a set of possible messages". A more playful description is that "information is the difference that makes a difference". Reproduction techniques, diversification of media (audiovisual, electronic) and increased circulation speed, have all contributed to a situation where information is now potentially more available to more people. Information as a discipline derives from that an importance which justifies all attention that human rights workers can give to it by collecting, processing and disseminating information. However, information is not an aim by itself. Information obtains its value by being used, for action and research contributing to the protection and promotion of human rights. Various developments have taken place over the last decennia which indicate the increasing importance of human rights information handling:

- The concept of human rights is expanding, and nowadays not only includes the more traditional civil and political rights as well as economic, social and cultural rights Various issues are seen from a human rights perspective. Many organizations propose to extend the concept to include also the "peoples" or "solidarity" rights pertaining to groups rather than individuals such as the right to development, the right to peace and the right to a clean environment.

- The number of non-governmental organizations has grown strongly worldwide, many of them are concerned with the protection and promotion of human rights. This includes groups linked to churches, trade unions, professional associations, educational, cultural and political organizations. Most groups work at the local level and focus on particular issues, while others are more clearly oriented towards international problems. All have recognized the need to work in an effective way, which includes systematic information handling.
- There is a potential (but unevenly distributed) abundance of information because the growing number of organizations are publishing an increasing number of documents. The material published includes brochures, newsletters, press releases, appeals for urgent actions, analyses of human rights situations, reports of conferences and fact-finding missions. Organizations derided to systematically collect and process information also for longer-term purposes, for example providing evidence of violations of human rights to tribunal courts, in countries where a dictatorship was replaced by a civilian regime. Much of this material is published in-house, with the use of typewriters and personal computers with word processing and desk-top publishing programs. This type of documents constitute the most up to

date human rights information, and is often referred to as "grey" or "fugitive literature", although the term "non-conventional literature" sounds more positive. It is often reproduced in an inexpensive way, and disseminated to members of the organization, researchers, activists and like-minded groups.

- Over the last decennia, there has been an enormous growth of information technologies, including telecommunications and computer technologies. This has meant that information can be easier retrieved and handled, for example within databases, and can be faster communicated, for example through telefaxes and electronic mail. While originally the use of such technologies, was limited to large companies and government departments, information technology has become considerably cheaper and more user-friendly, making it also accessible to non-governmental organizations in developing countries.
- In the seventies, there was a debate on the possibility to establish a centralized clearing house on human rights information, which for technical reasons would have to be based in the West. The idea was that there should ideally been one place from where a reliable assessment of the human rights situation in different countries would be quickly available. However much such a simple, direct access was and still is needed, the idea was flawed in two major respects. Firstly, it underestimated the problems inherent in agreeing on what is the scope of 'human rights' and what constitutes reliable information. Secondly It mixed up the question of access (such as references to what exists) with the provision of the documents (information) itself. Hence, its emphasis on the work of centres based in the industrialized North.

> Fortunately, there has been a strong proliferation of human rights groups in the South over the last decade. These groups are now much more able to decide themselves, on basis of their own needs, how they want to handle their information.

Remarkably, the NGOs have understood that issues related to information handling are not in first instance technological questions, but rather political and economic issues, because access to information is access to power. Most NGOs are relatively small and have limited resources, also for information handling. One single organization is not able to process all existing information which it may require at one moment or another. Therefore, access to information Las become a central issue. Organizations are trying to increase their capabilities to obtain and disseminate the right information at the right time to the right people.

The access can be improved by setting up a documentation centre in which the information is easily accessible. Such a documentation centre should be a dynamic unit serving the action oriented functions of the organization, rather than being a traditional library. There are different types of documentation centres: some collect fugitive material about specific subjects or countries, while others specialize in primary information about human rights violations.

The first question to be answered when establishing a documentation centre is what is the scope of the collection in relation to the users which it wants to serve? It is better to have it small and well-defined collection which is accessible rather than a large number of documents without scope and difficult to retrieve. Requirements for a documentation centre include a classification system, a cataloging system (with a description of the document in a standard format), and a systematic and consistent way of using terminology in abstracting and indexing.

Decisions also have to be made with regard to access to the collection, possibility of data exchange, circulation of material, security measures to be taken etc. A major decision is whether the collection is to be recorded manually or in a computerized database. The advantage of computerization is that it creates almost endless possibilities for processing and reprocessing, creating and recreating data for varying needs and conjunctures. Over the last years, personal computers have become more easily available and cheapen also in developing countries, it is important to realize that the computer is only a tool which can facilitate work, but that human beings remain responsible for handling the data. Information needs to be used and shared rather than hoarded. It is up to each organization to decide itself, on basis of its own mandate and self-interest, with whom it wants to exchange which type of information.

> If organizations are willing to share information, this can best be done within a decentralized network, in which the participating groups:
>
> - are conscious about the role and importance of information handling and exchange;
> - have or obtain the competence necessary for systematic information handling;
> - agree upon the standards to be used for the exchange;
> - initially accumulate information through their own means;
> - know about the efforts of other organizations, and build up relations of collaboration and trust in the quality of each other's work;
> - workout a division of labour among themselves, in which each organization handles information within its area of relative expertise, and duplication of labour is being narrowed down.

The Need for Standardization

Considerable attention has to be given to the development of compatible, effective and appropriate tools to facilitate the recording and exchange of information. Standard formats are intended to ensure compatibility, allowing exchange of data which have been recorded manually or within different types of computerized systems. However, experience has shown that harmonization of standards for information handling is of great value even without actual exchange of data. The users (often the same organizations that produce information) can become familiar with certain screens and methods, the information workers can develop routines and typing efforts can be diminished, and above all it becomes feasible to train information workers from different organizations in the same area and issue training modules for a larger number of people. Economy of scale applies also in the non-profit sector. When the HURIDOCS network was established in 1982, a main task envisaged was the development of standard formats for documents which would fit the requirements of human rights organizations. The bibliographical standard Formats, published in 1985, are primarily standards for communication - and it is possible to make adjustments for internal use, as long as organizations remain able to exchange data according to the formats. HURIDOCS decided to develop in first instance standard formats for the recording and exchange of bibliographical information (i.e. the elementary description of the main features of documents, such as books, articles, reports). These standards were developed on basis of formats used in traditional libraries, but were simplified in order to facilitate use by smaller NGOs involved in documentation for action. Many non-governmental organizations in developing countries are mainly collecting primary information about violations of human rights ("events"). At their request,

HURIDOCS set up a Task Force to develop formats also for this type of information. Organizations based in the "South" have been brought together to share and compare their experiences with regard to recording information on types of violations of human rights (such as torture, disappearances, arbitrary killings). A preliminary meeting of persons concerned with this Issue took place in New Delhi, In March 1988. Since then, the Task Force held two more meetings (in Manila and Utrecht) and made considerable progress in the development of formats for different aspects of human rights violations. The aim is to develop formats which could be applied worldwide while allowing for flexibility because of the different requirements of different types of organizations. The Task Force worked out separate, but inter linked formats for events, victims, sources, perpetrators and interventions, It has tried to facilitate the use of the Formats by relatively new or small organizations by also developing a "Short Format". At present, a preliminary version of the Standard Formats is available for testing. Various organizations which are handling information by computer have requested HURIDOCS to provide the necessary software.

Therefore, HURIDOCS has also developed computerized versions of the bibliographic standard formats (Bibsys for Dbase, Model for Micro-Isis) as well as the 'events' formats (in Chile a computerised version of the events standard formats is being put together). Once programmed and documented HURIDOCS makes them part of public domain software.

Perspectives for the Coming Years

The full potential of existing information may be utilized only in a system which permits precise, speedy and convenient access to the existing body of human rights information to all participants. Non-governmental human rights organizations in all countries need to strengthen their competence, so that they will be better able to handle and share information with like-minded groups in a decentralized network, in which each group concentrates on its area of relative expertise. At the national level, there are different models for exchanging human rights information. One possibility is that the NGOs exchange information on bilateral basis, Another possibility is to establish a clearing house or resource centre, to which all participating organizations provide their public documents (statements, reports, newsletters etc.). This resource centre would be open to the participating organizations as well as to the public, and would also produce a regular overview of new documents emanating from the NGO network as well as from others. At the global level, no such arrangement function yet, but is being built up informally among some documentation centres. By promoting common tools, HURIDOCS tries to ensure that there is at least the possibility to establish a division of labour and/or a common database, if the groups concerned decide to do so. However, the existing technical possibilities for exchanging data have only been used partially. The division of labour needs to be further specified, so that it is clear which organizations are taking care of which types of documents. Organizations based in the South should be stronger involved in such consultations. Technical requirements for a decentralized network include standards for describing and recording materials (described above), a communication standard and a common subject indexing language. The communication standard involves agreement with regard to technical matters such as types of diskettes or speed of modems for exchange through electronic mail. Apart front the transfer of data, communication in general between the people in various organizations needs to be faster and more efficient. This can be achieved by using an electronic mail system to which various like-minded organizations have access. Many organizations in the HURIDOCS network are using the Geonet and Peacenet communication hosts (and there are other socalled 'small host' serving the electronic communication needs of grass roots organizations), but the use of e-mail needs to be further extended. Indexing is crucial for efficient retrieval of references and documents. Unto now it has not been possible to develop a global thesaurus on human rights because of varied geographical and thematical scope of human rights organizations worldwide. There are valuable thesaurus covering specific regions (Central America) or subjects (refugees) as wells a thesaurus covering human rights terms rather than terms related to violations. It has been argued that a core list of human rights terminology should be developed, as while organizations working in particular areas could in addition develop their own terminology reflecting their specific requirements. A more structural question is the form in which the exchange of information is to be organized. Organizations can exchange data (printouts, diskettes) on a bilateral basis. Another possibility is to produce bibliographies on specific topics and/or regular accession lists. One might even go further and consider whether the establishment of an accumulated database under a data producers collective should be encouraged/There are considerable differences between a centralized documentation centre/clearing house trying to collect the whole range of human rights information, and an accumulated database to which various centres within a decentralized network contribute according to their specializations and on basis of an agreed-upon division of labour. The last structure leaves it open to the participating organizations t® continue their own work and stay in touch with their own users, while at the same time having access to data prepared by other organizations. Various regulations need to be developed with regard to the methods of indexing, access to the accumulated database by participating organizations and outside users, financial conditions etc.

It is an area which HURIDOCS has not yet fully explored due to pressure of work, but it has become clear that the network should address these issues.

Training

Documentation staff needs to be trained in order to enhance its capacities to carry out systematic work. Many documentalists within NGOs do not have a librarianship background, and those who are professional librarians realize that their work often requires qualifications additional to their education. Various organizations are exchanging interns involved in documentation work, on a bilateral basis or in collaboration with internship programmes. HURIDOCS has worked out an elaborate training program, and conducted training courses and workshops indifferent parts of the world. HURIDOCS does not concentrate on training people working in computerized environments. It aims to train participants on how to use the technology they want, while remaining in control of the process themselves. HURIDOCS has organized various workshops and training courses which focus on strengthening the information handling capacity of human rights organizations. From 7 November to 16 December 1988, a first, global training course "Human Rights Information Handling in Developing Countries" was held in Manila, the Philippines. This six-week course was attended by 25 participants, from human rights documentation centres in various developing countries. Local courses were held for and in collaboration with human rights groups in Sri Lanka,

Thailand and Pakistan, to mention only those in Asia. HURIDOCS intends to organize more such courses, the next one being planned for Nepal in January 1991.

HURIDOCS will continue its training program, with annual courses for the different regions and local courses. At the same time, there will be an internship program for documentalists of smaller or recently established NGOs who could profit from the knowledge and insight of more experienced organizations. Decisions are needed on whether courses should continue to have a strong focus on human rights documentation work, or if they should be oriented more to office management in general, including word processing, accounting systems, desktop publishing etc. More clarity is also needed on the different levels of course (basic skills, advanced level). At the same time, HURIDOCS is establishing a resource pool of trainers from the South which are able to conduct training courses abroad, in order to strengthen the decentralized character of the network, although HURIDOCS has been able to put more South-South cooperation into practice than most others in the last years. This has also consequences for the way in which the network is organized. Over the coming years, a structure may be envisaged in which each region would be governed by a regional council which would have a certain degree of independence while coordinating its activities with similar structures in the other regions. There is a need to establish regional units within the different regions in the South: Latin America, Asia and Africa. Such units could coordinate regional Task Forces, organize workshops and training courses within the region etc. regional units would be relatively independent of the Continuation Committee.

An eventual transfer of the HURIDOCS Secretariat to the South is also to be considered, but would not seem to impose .itself in urgent terms as increasingly the work is carried out at the national and regional level and HURIDOCS is not a documentation or information centre. The issues mentioned above require further discussions, within the participating organizations, at regional meetings and training courses and at the HURIDOCS General Assembly. Human rights organizations in developing countries are the main source of human rights information, They should increase their insight into the importance of information handling for the protection of human rights, be it in their own immediate environment or at a wider regional or international level. Also their experience and knowledge is required to better arrange for improved access to information. The potential of information technology for the improvement of human rights will only be realized if policies and practices are supported by the NGOs which form the basis of the worldwide human rights movement.

8

NGOs and Mechanism of Commission on Human Rights

The first procedure set up by the Commission on Human Rights was the confidential 1503 procedure named after the resolution of ECOSOC under which it was set up. In the case of gross and massive violations of human rights and fundamental liberties, any victim and any organisation has the right to submit a communication to the Secretariat of the United Nations. Hundreds of thousands of complaints are thus submitted every year to the Centre, for Human Rights in Geneva and are first considered by the Sub-Commission. Five experts who are elected every year meet during two weeks before the session (July) and decide on the cases to be transmitted to the Sub-Commission, the five experts then examine those cases brought to their attention (August) and decide which cases will he transmitted to the Commission. In January of the following year, the working group on communications of the Commission meets. This group is composed of five states, selected every year. They prepare the recommendations for the Commission on all cases which have been submitted to them by the Sub-Commission. Finally, during its private session (March), the Commission takes decisions concerning the cases brought to its attention. The introduction of this procedure kin the work of the United Nations constituted at the time of considerable progress. For the first time, states were directly accountable to this world organisation with regard to their human rights record, even if they did not subscribe to a specific international obligation. However, as time went by, the confidential procedure lost its attractiveness. Firstly, the procedure is lengthy. The Sub-Commission only considers a case, a copy of which has been transmitted by the UN Secretariat to the government concerned at least three months before the session of the Sub-Commission. Moreover, the entire procedure is confidential, which has led many member states of the Commission to vote according to their interests, contrary to their public statements. The confidential procedure is however not useless. Almost 300,000 communications were submitted to the UN Centre for Human Rights in 1989, and in many cases, the work undertaken within the framework of the confidential procedure led to improvements in the situation.

Public Procedures

The drawbacks of the confidential procedure are no doubt the reason why most of the NGOs prefer to use the public procedures of the Commission: These procedures have been introduced since the beginning of the 1980's, The Commission nominated Special Rapporteurs and Representatives, experts and working groups entrusted to study certain themes and certain situations and to submit a report with recommendations to each annual session. The principal procedures include the following:

— *Working Group on Enforced Disappearances:* the working group is composed of five experts (one from each region). It is chaired by Mr. Ivan Tosevski (Yugoslavia), it meets three times a year and receives direct testimonies from witnesses and victims. Its annual report presents country by country statistics.

- *Special Rapporteur on Summary or Arbitrary Executions* (Mr. Amos Wako, Kenya): receives information and complaints concerning cases of extra-judicial killings.
- *Special Rapporteur on Torture* (Prof. Peter Kooijmans, Netherlands); receives information and complaints on cases of torture and inhuman treatment.

The working group on disappearances and the special rapporteurs on torture and summary executions have undertaken several field visits. Their missions cannot take place without invitation from the government concerned, which limits their scope of action. However, it is the pressure of NGOs and from Member States of the Commission which often lead a government to invite one of these special rapporteurs or a delegation of the working group (if only to avoid a condemnation by the Commission). These three procedures also include a mechanism for urgent action enabling the working group and the two rapporteurs to contact the authorities of the country concerned without delay, asking for explanations.

- *Special Rapporteur on Religious Intolerance* (Mr. Angelo meets in New York and Geneva. Vidal d'Alrneida Ribeiro, Protugal).
- *Special Rapporteur on Mercenaries* (Mr. Enrique Berhales Ballestreros, Peru)
- *Special Rapporteur on the Sale of Children* (Mr. Vittit Muntarbhorn, Thailand)
- *Group of Experts on Southern Africa*
- *Group of Experts on Israeli practices in the Occupied Territories*

- *Special Rapporteur on the situation in Afghanistan* (Mr. Felix Ermacora, Austria)
- *Special Rapporteur on Iran* (Mr. Galindo Pohl, El Salvador)
- *Special Representative on El Salvador* (Mr. Josd Antonio Pastor Ridruego, Spain)
- *Special Representative on Guatemala* (Mr. Christian Tomuschat, Germany)
- *Expert on Haiti* (Mr. Philippe Texier, France)
- *Expert on Burma* (in confidential procedure, Mrs Sadako Ogata, Japan)
- *Expert on Equatorial Guinea* (Mr. Fernando Volio Jimenez, Costa Rica).

All these experts can receive communications from governmental and non-governmental sources. As one can imagine, states are cautious and rarely denounce other states. Thus most of the information concerning violations, and which provides the basis for the analysis by experts, comes from NGOs. It is clear that none of the procedures of the Commission would operate without the contribution of NGOs.

The Treaty Bodies

Several International Conventions adopted by the United Nations have created independent bodies of experts entrusted to supervise the implementation of international instruments. These concern the following bodies:

- *the Human Rights Committee* (set up in 1977 to oversee the implementation of the Covenant on Civil and Political Rights). This Committee is composed of 18 members. It meets in New York and Geneva.

- the Committee on Economic, Social and Cultural Rights, for the Covenant on Economic, Social and Cultural Rights (18 members, session in Geneva). This Committee is a body of ECOSOC.
- the *Committee for the Elimination of Racial Discrimination* (CERD, 1970), for the International Convention on the Elimination of All Forms of Racial Discrimination (18 members, sessions in Geneva).
- the *Group of Three,* in application of the International Convention on the Suppression and Punishment of the Crime of Apartheid (three members of the Commission elected every year by the President, sessions in Geneva).
- *the Committee on the Elimination of All Forms of Discrimination against Women* (1982), on the Convention on the Elimination of all Forms of discrimination against Women (23 experts, sessions in Vienna and New York).
- *the Committee against Tbrture* (1987), for the Convention against Torture (10 experts, sessions in Geneva).

These six committees receive and consider the periodic reports of states parties to these conventions, In their reports, the states should provide an overview of their problems and the measures introduced with a view to the implementation of the Convention.

Moreover, these committees are entrusted with the preparation of commentaries concerning the interpretation of the various provisions of the Conventions. Finally, three Committees can receive individual complaints (after exhaustion of all internal remedies) only if this additional provision has been expressly accepted. These include the Human Rights Committee (for the states having ratified the first additional protocol), the Committee for the elimination of Racial discrimination and the Committee against Torture." In the very short term, two other Committees will be created - on the rights of the child (now that the Convention on the Rights of the Child has entered into force) and a Committee on migrant workers (Convention which is in the process of being adopted by the UN General Assembly).

The Rights of NGOs

Before all these committees, the rights of NGOs are more restricted than within the UN Commission and its Sub-Commission since NGOs generally do not have the right to take the floor. The reports and documents submitted by the NGOs to members of these committees (whether officially or by dissemination of information in the corridors) are however an important element in the discussions of the experts when they consider reports submitted by the States parties. Notwithstanding the procedures concerning individual, complaints, all sessions of these committees are public. Nevertheless, the work.of the treaty bodies is very technical and fairly inaccessible to NGOs.

Diversity of the Procedures: These six treaty bodies do not always have the same authority, the provisions of these conventions being very different in this regard. The same rights are sometimes protected in different in this regard. The same rights are sometimes protected in different terms by several conventions, which leads to duplication and confusion, The same holds true for the procedures envisaged: certain committees can receive inter-state complaints, others individual complaints, and yet others are not endowed with such provisions It is thus not easy to rationalise the system.

Problems of Functioning: Certain committees are funded, in whole or in part, by the states parties to the convention concerned. Delays in payments being numerous, the meetings of the committee must be cancelled, thereby leading to further delays in the consideration of reports already submitted. Furthermore, a large number of states are late in the submission of their reports. Presently, several A hundreds reports due to be submitted by states have not yet been received, Finally, during the session of the Committee, the experts, who are not remunerated, have to review hundreds of pages on situations which they are not always familiar with, and the Secretariat of the committee is too restricted to be able to prepare the work.

Access to Information: The national NGOs directly concerned often lack the opportunity to react in time, the reports prepared by their state being rendered public only at the last moment, and then only in the United Nations premises. A large number of periodic reports are never published in the country itself. The same holds true for the comments made by the experts on the states reports. It is sometimes even difficult for NGOs active in Geneva to obtain information in advance, pertaining in particular to state reports to be considered at the following session of a particular committee. Access to information is an insurmountable obstacle for the NGOs of developing countries. This is why only a restricted number of NGOs can actually contribute to the work of the treaty bodies. NGOs such as Amnesty International and the Quakers are present at all the sessions of the committees and play an active role in the preparation of commentaries, The Lawyers' Committee for Human Rights based in New York has over several years published reports on the human rights situation in those countries whose reports were to be considered at the Human Rights Committee or the CERD. Dozens of representatives worked on this project. Other NGOs Intervene in a more targeted fashion by submitting such or such a report to a body. The International League for Human Rights based in New York has in this way disseminated its report on Vietnam, and "Article 19" from London has regularly commented on state reports, as has done the International Federation for Human Rights from Paris and the International Commission of Jurists from Geneva, etc. During the third session held in Geneva from I to 5 October 1990, the Chairpersons of the treaty bodies stressed that the treaty bodies should have access to all sources of Information.

They underlined the importance of information submitted by NGOs. To ensure that the participation of NGOs becomes a reality, the United Nations needs first to improve its services, in particular with regard to the dissemination of information to the public.

Maintaining the Existing Mechanisms: The NGOs thus become the indispensable partners of the United Nations for the implementation of its human rights programme. While being a strong negotiating power in the United Nations system, they must also from time to time use all the means at their disposal to preserve and maintain the supervisory mechanisms. However, the maintenance of the international procedures do not function on their own. Most of the special procedures of the Commission on Human Rights depend on an annual mandate which has to be renewed every year. In other terms, at any of the sessions of the Commission, any of it's procedures could be terminated. The supervisory mechanisms in the countries are the most fragile. Following an opening up of its democratic process in one country under consideration, diplomatic circles are immediately inclined to renounce on the supervisory mechanism whose maintenance would by a denial by the authorities who have taken the first steps in the right direction. However, a democratic process does not always go hand in hand with an improvement of the human rights situation. The most tragic example is Guatemala. Over the past five years, the Commission has no longer condemned this country despite information disseminated and action taken by over 50 NGOs with regard to serious allegations of human rights violations. The Commission approaches the problem by providing advisory services, that is to say technical assistance which many observers consider useless. At the beginning of 1990 a similar debate was initiated with regard to the mandate of the Special Rapporteur on Chile. President Aylwin who had been recently elected has obtained the confidence of the Commission whereas a number of NGOs raised concern with reference to the unresolved cases ot disappearances and summary executions, the problem of impunity and political prisoners.

Indeed, the dictatorship has come to an end and the brutal repression has ceased in Chile, but the majority of human rights issues are still not solved. Following the liberation of Nelson Mandela and other South African black leaders, several member states initiated a similar debate concerning South Africa, but for the moment the supervisory mechanisms and the pressure on the government of South Africa maintained. The thematic mechanisms are also the object of vivid debates, especially on the part of states called into question in the annual reports submitted to the Commission. It is thus encouraging that the Commission decided in 1989 to renew for a period of two years the mandates of the five thematic rapporteurs (enforced disappearances, summary executions, torture, religious intolerance, mercenaries). In order to become truly indispensable, these mechanisms should have mandates ranging from three to four years. Also included on the list of thematic studies should be the mandate of the Special Rapporteur on the sale of children. The existing mechanisms can also be threatened by the bad functioning of certain United Nations bodies.

This was exemplified by the cancellation of the 1986 session ot the Sub-Commission. The financial difficulties of the United Nations led the UN Secretariat to introduce a series of economic measures. Entrusted to suggest measures affecting the human rights programme, the Director of the Centre for Human Rights, Mr. Kun Herndl, simply proposed to cancel the annual session of the Sub-Commission without even taking the trouble to consult or inform the experts. In view of the feelings of several governments with regard to the Sub-Commission concerning its initiatives on certain sensitive issues, a majority soon adopted this proposal. However, the cancellation of the session of the Sub-Commission also led to the interruption, for one year, of the confidential procedure (no examination took place of tens of thousands of individual complaints), and .' to the cancellation of the session of the working group on indigenous populations and that on slavery and slavery-like indigenous populations and that on slavery and slavery-like practices. And in the proposal of the UN Director for Human Rights, nomination was made of these dramatic consequences. Several NGOs, some governments and experts opposed this decision, but nothing would have happened had the NGO community in Geneva not reacted The initiative was taken by the Director of the Anti-Slavery Society, Peter Davies, who proposed to hold an alternative session and began to collect funds. The proposal of Peter Davies was adopted by the NGO Special Committee on Human Rights which convened an International Seminar on the theme "Human Rights and the United Nations", whose preparation was entrusted to the International Service for Human Rights, a Geneva-based service organisation. The meeting was organised in a few weeks. Following the refusal of the United Nations to provide a conference room, the Director General of the International Labour Organisation ILO invited the delegates. The seminar was held at the headquarters of the ILO in Geneva from 8 to 10 September 1986 with the participation of 15 members of the Sub-Commission, 13 international experts, 53 NGOs, 47 governments and 7 international institutions.

The organisers took over the costs of travel and expenses of 28 experts, and issued the daily press releases as is done during the usual session of the United Nations Sub-Commission. The international seminar had many repercussions in the UN system. During the seminar, the 15 members of the Sub-Commission realising that they had the quorum met in private session, thereby provoking anxiety on the part of the Director of the Centre for Human Rights. The participants of the seminar adopted conclusions and recommendations which were submitted to the UN General Assembly, to ECOSOC and the Commission on Human Rights. The NGOs managed to substitute this failing UN organisation. Their drafting capacity, their organisational skills and constructive proposals astounded many observers. In the future, delegates of the world organisation will think twice before deciding to cancel essential bodies in the UN mechanism for the protection of human rights.

Prespectives and Challenges for the 21st Century

Since the signature of the United Nations Charter on 26 June 1945 in San Francisco, the activities of the United Nations in the field of human rights protection have been considerable. This is due, in large part, to the action of NGOs which, in 45 years have been able to concretise the role which those involved in the creation of the United Nations had decided to entrust them with. A role relaying the action of this world organisation and public opinion, a role of information and actual analyses of problems with which individuals and peoples are faced with, a position of spokespersons for victims and those who tire excluded. It is now important to preserve and to reinforce that which has been acquired. In order to achieve this, NGOs should seriously take into consideration the criticism directed at them and the evolution of the situation in the world. This consideration is essential if they are to better define their priorities and field of action in the years to come.

He who wants to sell his products needs to know the market. Non-governmental actors have sometimes a tendency to forget that the United Nations is just the sum of its parts, i.e. states. At all the stages of the UN procedures, it is governments and their representatives who decide, and their interests do not always coincide with those of nations and peoples. This corresponds to the very nature of the United Nations Organisation. Action should be derived from this reality rather than from a utopic concept of the United Nations. The NGOs must thus develop forms of cooperation with governments. For the proposal of one NGO to be adopted by the United Nations, one must find among the participating governments to the various bodies, those who will support the proposal and submit it to others. At each stage of the process, one must also find a majority. Governments are thus potential partners and not targets. NGOs must achieve an equilibrium between, on the one hand, the indispensable denunciation of crimes committed by several governments, and on the other hand, the necessity to find support among the governments. The exercise is not easy. The cooperation with governments is also important with regard to putting an end to human rights violations. The publicity afforded to reports presented by NGOs incites governments to increasingly respond to allegations. The leading organisations such as Amnesty International have developed working methods which entail an exchange of views with the accused governments. During the United Nations meetings, many NGOs have learned not to leave the room immediately after an intervention and to discuss the issues with the representatives of the country concerned. In this regard, the task is daunting, since one has to be two to initiate a dialogue. And several particularly repressive country and multiply the obstacles to their action within international organisations. Several NGOs have regular meetings with governmental delegations of all the regional groups. This is particularly the case of the "Quakers" which have increased their exchanges with diplomats. As a result, their proposals receive more easily attention in all the regional groups. Informal meetings of some NGOs and diplomats from all regions are also organised by the International Service. But these are fledging initiatives which need to be developed in the coming years. The inauguration in Geneva of the South Centre will largely contribute to the increase of such exchanges. Former secretariat of the "South Commission", the South Centre is now the secretariat of G-15 which regroups the Heads of State of 15 developing countries.

Criticisms of NGOs

The debate on the interventions of NGOs is particularly vivid during the V sessions of the Commission and its Sub-Commission, that is to say, when NGOs make use of their right to intervene during the debates. These concern in particular oral NGO interventions which are more the object of protest since they are more publicized in the media.

A number of criticism are directed at the intervention of witnesses. In their oral interventions at the UN Commission and Sub-Commission, several NGOs regularly appeal to the members of their organisation who were victims or witnesses of serious human rights violations. When they are presented without animosity and without too much emotion, these reports have a considerable impact on the debates: a personal experience is an indisputable reality and the concise facts thus exposed must be discussed. In such situations, certain states seek to discredit these witnesses in order to avoid having to respond to the accusations. The witness is thus portrayed as belonging to a subversive group whose alleged aim is to overthrow the government, or to achieve independence from the central authority. A large number of governments have problems with guerilla groups or autonomous movements. Such an argument therefore can lead many delegates to be careful. This is all the more so in many authoritarian regimes, raising the issue of human rights is indeed a political act and provides support (even indirectly) to opposition groups.

Notwithstanding the squabbles and protests after certain NGO *sppechers,* serious criticisms have been formulated these last few years with reference to the disregard some NGOs have to the rules, or even the provocative elements of certain interventions. These criticisms are concurrent with the threat to limit the oral interventions of NGOs during the debates. The proposals discussed during the session are sufficiently preoccupying to present these here in greater detail. To understand the essence of the problem, it must be remembered that each NGO has its own specific character, works in a given field, recruits its members and runs its affairs entirely as it sees fit. NGOs with consultative status range from professional and trade-union associations to religious and cultural organizations, is, veterans groups and research centres. The NGO world is one of diversity, and its diversity is a great asset. It is therefore natural for NGOs to hold a variety of views on questions before the Commission. For example, Jewish organizations, themselves often quite dissimilar to one another, are, not likely to agree with Arab organization-; over the Palestine issue. Among Arab organizations, there is one NGO which regularly stands behind the Iraqi government with which others tend to find fault. The organizations representing indigenous populations are even more heterogeneous. The common ground of all NGOs is their will to promote and contribute to United Nations action in the economic and social domains. They do so, each in their own way, according to their perception of matters subject to their own freely established rules and regulations. NGOs are proud of their independence. There are no hierarchical authorities to dictate what they must do, not even CONGO. And that is as it should be. Moreover, as we have seen already, NGOs are also scapegoats. Some Governments try to discredit them. Just as predictable is the way NGOs are blamed for more and more of the Commission's problems, usually about two weeks into the session, as discussion grows tedious and confused. Is debate running behind schedule? It's because there are too many NGOs. Is the Commission being politicized? The fault of the NGOs.... One therefore must put these criticisms into perspective. More worrying, however, is the general irritation with NGOs that has begun to surface. The phenomenon had already been observed after the 45th session, with harsh criticisms being leveled by States who were regarded as staunch supporters of NGOs. During the 1990 session of the Commission on Human Rights, a great many Member States moved on from criticism to threats, The working document submitted to the Working Group on the enhancement of the Commission by the Non-Aligned Movement contained a whole section on NGOs. The proposal was not approved. All the same, those countries which took up the cause of the

NGOs all stressed that some steps would have to be taken. They cited the growing number of NGOs have prepared joint statements in order to avoid repetition and to put concrete initiatives before the Commission to promote greater respect for human rights, Joint statements have been prepared on a variety of themes (the rights of the child, the right to development, the Advisory Services) and situations (China, East Timor, Eritrea, Guatemala, Tibet, etc.). For all their diversity, NGOs have been able to speak with one voice on several occasions. However, joint statements do not offer a panacea and should not become standard practice, for that would divest them of their value and mask the very diversity which makes NGOs so rich. There is thus an effort at self-discipline on the part of NGOs yet this effort is voluntary. This implies that there are also organisations which do not see a necessity of such in effort or overstep their limits by not respecting the rules. These few NGOs do not realise that by not listening to the suggestions of the other NGOs, they provide member states with the perfect excuse to limit the rights of all NGOs. These first initiatives taken by the Non-Aligned group during the 1990 session of the Commission on Human Rights and the official debate in the western group on NGOs indicate that in the years to come, measures will indeed be taken by the United Nations. These measures are likely to affect all NGOs and may very well prove restrictive. In this regard, would it not be better for the NGOs to take the initiative? Within the existing framework of CONGO, they could for example prepare a code of conduct preaching self-discipline. This code would be submitted to each NGO for consideration, which may or may not be taken into account.

9

Human Rights Organisations in Developing Countries

In order to understand human rights activism in the developing world, one needs to take a closer look at the people involved in human rights organizations. Three main categories have been involved: intellectuals, professionals, and activists. Prominent among the professionals have been members of the legal elite - leaders of the legal profession, former member of the judiciary and prominent legal academics. Their involvement has been of a more conventional kind, helping provide legal services and legal representation to indigents, or to those whose civil and political rights have been violated, or in "test cases" and "public interest litigation." Their approach has been mainly to work within the existing law, using existing legal processes to enforce human rights or to help bring about incremental development of the content of specific human rights. Their has been the conventional liberal approach to human rights which presumes that compliance with rights is the societal norm and rights which presumes that compliance with rights is the societal norm and rights enforcement is only necessary in a few deviant cases. But in most Third (developing) World societies, this presumption does not hold true and an alternative breed of human rights activist emerges seeking to arouse public awareness of gross and widespread violations of human rights (especially, but not exclusively, economic, social and cultural rights) and seeking assertion of those rights through both legal and extra-legal methods, including protests and direct action. This category of activists is not content with working within the existing legal order but is intent on helping reform such order as part of process of securing social change and structural transformations. The influence of these human rights activists upon the professionals and intellectuals has led to their gradual reorientation and professional resocialization. Thus, professional and intellectuals in the Third World have attempted to reach out to human rights activists through a variety of intellectual and professional movements:

1. *The Regional Studies and Development Studies Movement* in many Third World countries has helped reorient lawyers and social scientists to special problems of development and underdevelopment and to the human rights implications of such process. This has helped forge a new sense of identity and solidarity around "Third World issues" and has helped sensitize them to processes of impoverishment, exploitation, exclusion, and dependency and to tile roles of human rights theory and activism in fighting against such processes. Concepts of dependencia, integration into the global capitalist system, and transnationalization have been thus brought into human rights thought and action.
2. *The Critical Studies Movement* has called attention to deep-rooted pathologies that exist in law and the legal profession in most Third World countries. The Movement has been iconoclastic: debunking legal sacred cows and myths by calling attention to the

wide gap that exists between the law on the books and the law in action; between law and justice the movement has worked towards securing fundamental changes in the legal system to make it more accessible, more indigenous, more just (by fostering notions of redistributive justice) and more supportive of social change.

3. *The Alternatives Movement has* challenged the "development models" adopted by Third World countries -models emphasizing modernization, industrialization, economic growth (without conscious policies of redistribution), and integration into the global capitalist system. The movement stimulate human rights activism in support of the victims (e.g., indigenous people, displaced people) of development policies and projects and has also stimulated activism centered around formulating and implementing policies and programs of "alternative development" which are built and the adoption of alternatives to Western consumer-oriented life-styles. This movement has brought interdisciplinary perspectives and skills into human rights thought and activism in the Third World and a fresh "alternative" set of values. It has helped foster the perception that, "law is too serious a matter to be left entirely to lawyers; for the issue of human rights is not merely a legal one but a potent political and social issue," It has also helped stimulate the process of deprofessionalization of law through "bare-foot lawyers" and "community dispute-settlement mechanisms".

4. *Participatory Action research.* By far the greatest impact of an intellectual movement on human rights in the Third World has been the movement towards

participatory action research. The concept of participatory action research (PAR) originated in Latin America but soon gained acceptance in Asia and Africa. PAR emphasizes the importance of participatory development of knowledge, action strategies and human rights through close interaction with grassroots communities. PAR has fundamentally changed human rights thinking and activism in the "Third World by broadening the base of human rights actors to include those who are victims of human rights violations.

Human rights activists in the Third World have also increasingly reached out to intellectuals and professionals as a result of a number of action strategies they have adopted. Originally, most social activists adopted an attitude of "legal nilhilism"; the less contact with the legal system (particularly the criminal justice system) as their work on grassroots conscientization and organization gathered momentum. They soon began to shed such an attitude. Contact between activists and intellectuals and professionals increased within the context of specific action strategies which necessitated new forms of association and organization:

1. *Campaigns:* such as the Infant formula Campaign
2. *Coalition:* such as the International Coalition for Justice in Bhopal.
3. *Solidarity and Protest Organizations:* such as Greenpeace.
4. Lobby *Groups:* such as the Asia Pacific Forum for Women, Law and Development.
5. *Regional Networks:* such as the Asian Regional council on Human rights.
6. *Social Movements:* such as the consumer movement,

the women's movement and the environmental movement.

To sum up, intellectual movements, social movements, and pragmatic-action strategies and campaigns have brought the main human rights actors in the third World - victims, activists, intellectuals, and professionals together in a variety of situations of infraction. As a result, human rights organization in the third World have become more interdisciplinary in nature and more V broad-based in composition. They have also become harder to identify and define. A few Third World NGOs wear the label of human rights. But the .' vast majority of Third World NGOs, concerned primarily with education, or development, or delivery of support and services, have adopted human rights into their agendas and programs of action. A broad definition of human rights organization in the Third World would have to include all these "non-specialist" NGOs which are undertaking significant human rights activities.

Typologies of Third World Human Rights Organizations

It would not be possible, desirable, or sensible to attempt to construct a single, comprehensive, all-encompassing typology of Third world human rights organization. Rather, one might suggest the many ways that loose typologies might be drawn.

1. *Governmental /Nongovernmental /Intergovernmental.* While the majority of human rights organizations in the third World are nongovernmental, their has been the recent trend (especially in countries like the Philippines, which are undergoing a process of re-democratization) to establish governmental human rights commissions.

2. *International /Regional /National /Local.* In Asia, where the governments have firmly rejected any regional intergovernmental human rights organization, a number of regional nongovernmental organization have sprang up.
3. According to Membership, In Asia, a distinction is usually drawn between people-based organizations (PBOs) and participatory organization of the rural poor (PORPs) on the one hand which are primary-level organizations (e.g. of small farmers, fisherfolk), and support groups which render services to PBOs and which are referred to as secondary-level organizations. Human rights organizations could also be classified on the basis of membership drawn on professional lines.
4. *According to Victim-Group Served.* Some human rights organizations serve only single target groups, e.g. women, children, indigenous people. Others serve a variety of victim groups.
5. *According to Functions.* Distinctions are being made between human rights organizations performing, mobilizational roles, advocacy group; documentation center; forum; coalition; or campaign are used to describe a range of human rights organizations in the Third World. Most of them tend to be multifunctional or, at least bi-functional.
6. *According to Category of Human Rights specialization* this Western categorization of groups focusing on civil and political rights and those focusing on economic, social, and cultural rights, is not much used in the Third World where organizations tend to focus on both categories of rights. However, because of the gravity of problem in some countries, human rights

organizations have emerged focusing on particular sets of rights such as those relating to ethnicity.

Many third World human rights organizations did not start as explicit human rights organizations at all and may have been emergency-aid organizations, philanthropic, developmental, or environmental organizations. This fact is often reflected in the roles and functions they play once they begin to address a specifically human rights-oriented agenda. Third World human rights organizations are not a mirror image of their first World counterparts. Nevertheless, it is possible and usefull to study Third world human rights organizations in terms of the conventional roles of human rights activism.

1. *Promotion.* Many third World human rights organizations do embark on typical human rights promotion activities employing locally appropriate devices such as comic books, folk theatre or folk music, poster competitions, etc. But often, the promotional work forms part of a rights awareness program that is fostering rights assertiveness as a means towards conscientization, mobilization, and organization for direct action.
2. *Standard setting,* third World human rights organization are increasingly recognizing the importance of participating in standard- setting work, both at, the international level (e.g. in relation to the right to development, or the convention on the Rights of the Child) as well as at the national level (e.g. in the Philippines to develop comprehensive national codes on agrarian reform and on fisheries' resources).
3. *Monitoring.* Third World human rights groups have

been actively monitoring implementation of national legislation (e.g. dealing with women's rights and child labour in India) and are beginning to be concerned with international human rights law (e.g. by bringing complaints before the Sub-Commission on rights of Minorities and Indigenous People).

4. *Enforcement.* Impressive strides have been made here by third World human rights groups in assisting enforcement of rights through the courts (e.g. by adoption of metalegal tactics in the Philippines).
5. *Lobbying for Law Reform.* There has been a flurry of activity here especially in countries like the Philippines where parliamentary, legislative processes have been restored after a long lapse of time.

In addition to these conventional roles, human rights organizations in the third World have also played unique roles which result from their human rights activism originating in community and victim-group mobilization and organization. Thus they have acted to:

(1) Help create, grassroots organizations and help their organizational development. They have helped organize people to make better use of their own local productive resources, to create new resources and services, to promote equity and alleviate poverty, to influence government actions towards the same objectives and to establish new institutional frameworks that will durably sustain humane people-powered development.

(2) Help act as an intermediary between local government and community organizations.

(3) Help, where circumstances warrant, raise funding and direct it to local community organizations.

(4) Help develop capacity for and strengthen community based resource management with an emphasis on participation, equality and equity. Human rights organization working in neglected rural areas have helped set up local production-related organization such as water-user societies, pastoral-grazing associations, credit, production or consumer cooperatives, food processing cooperatives, farm equipment purchase or lease associations, tree grower associations, fishermen cooperatives, etc. At first glance, these activities seem far removed from human rights work. But these kinds of organizations have proved critical instrumentalities, not only for participatory local development but also for grassroots realization of human rights, At times these organizations have averted serious denials of human rights which would have resulted had their efforts not prevented ecological degradation imperiling the very survival of the most depressed sections of the local community.

(5) Help create not only the means for community organizing but also for community self-defense.

(6) Help assert community rights and raise community awareness and expectations,

(7) Help protect activists against reprisals from high-handed administrators.

Thus, human rights organization in the Third World have had to constantly undergo a process of self-development. There has been a need for constant reflection based on praxis to reconceptualize human rights concepts and theory, There has also been a need for a professional unlearning and relearning process accompanied by the development of genuine professional humility. So far as lawyers are concerned, there has been a need for new kinds of law-trained people to act as:

— community workers who help to organize and participate in collective efforts of people to identify their legal problems and appropriate strategies;

— advocates of collective demands and group interests both in courts and in administrative, legislative and other institutions.

— community educators helping to develop community knowledge of law and legal paraprofessionals within the community whose knowledge and skills are geared to community needs.

— critics of proposed or existing legislation and administrative actions which impinge on the rights and interests of, impoverished groups;

— law reformers asserting the claims of rural communities for changes in legislation and state structures; and

— jurists seekings to develop new jurisprudential concepts needed, for example, to articulate new rights which will help to empower the poor in their struggles against impoverishment.

Third World Human Rights Organizations: The Need for Linkages, Networking and External Support

It has been a paradox that the greater their success and achievements, the greater has been the need for support for human rights organizations in the third World. Below, we briefly identify some of these needs. To elaborate upon such needs would he presumptuous. That task would be better left to a consultation with the human rights organizations themselves. There is, of course, a perennial and chronic need of funding. This need will be addressed later in this paper. Other, and often more important, needs include:

1. *Defense:* There is a crucial need to devise effective mechanisms at national and international levels, for the defense and protection of human rights activists, community groups and people's organizations which face reprisals because they are seeking to assert rights and secure remedies. Recent events in Malaysia and Singapore underscore the need for urgency for developing Amnesty International-type counterparts to protect Third World human rights activists - especially those working at grassroots level. There is also a need to develop national and regional mechanism to deal with an allied problem, As human rights NGOs become more successful, some governments seek to close the political space for their continued operation by enacting a variety legislative and policy measures which increase regulation and restrict the activities of NGOs. There are usually accompanied by attempts to coopt, fragment, and divide the NGO community. Recognizing this danger, several Asian human rights organizations have recently formed a Coalition to resist. While the Coalition is still in its infancy, its work will be of interest far beyond the region,

2. *Solidarity:* Third World human rights NGOs have little opportunity for south-south exchange of experience and for solidarity building. Such opportunities are beginning to be created for development NGOs but usually permitting only limited exchange on only a regional basis. This world human rights activism has reached a level to

well justify A the setting up of mechanisms for exchange across the regions of the Third world,

3. *Information sharing* : Much of what has been said regarding needs for solidarity apply equally here, too. Existing systems for human rights documentation are indeed a valuable first step. But mechanisms also need to be devised to facilitate person-to-person exchanges and information sharing. The same could also apply to human resources development, for example, with regard to barefoot lawyers.
4. *Linkages with International Human Rights System;* It is increasingly being felt by Third World human rights organizations that they are now ready to press for enforcement of human rights, not only in national fora but also in the variety of interaction, leading to the development of more enduring linkages, between Third World human rights activists and the international human rights law community. Such interaction would doubtless prove mutually enriching and lead to more effective enforcement of human rights roles and functions they play once they begin to address a specifically human rights-oriented agenda. Third world human rights organizations are not a mirror image of their first World counterparts. Nevertheless, it is possible and usefull to study Third world human rights organizations in terms of the conventional roles of human rights activism.
   1. *Promotion.* Many third world human rights organizations do embark on typical human rights promotion activities employing locally appropriate devices such as comic books, folk theatre or folk music, poster competitions, etc. But often, the promotional work forms parat

of a rights awareness, program that is fostering rights assertiveness as a means towards conscientization, mobilization, and organization for direct action.

2. *Standard setting,* third World human rights organization are increasingly recognizing the importance of participating in standard-setting work, both at the international level (e.g. in relation to the right to development, or the convention on the Rights of the Child) as well as at the national level (e.g. in the Philippines to develop comprehensive national codes on agrarian reform and on fisheries' resources).
3. *Monitoring.* Third World human rights groups have been actively monitoring implementation of national legislation (e.g. dealing with women's rights and child labor in India) and are beginning to be concerned with international human rights law (e.g. by bringing complaints before the Sub-Commission on rights of Minorities and Indigenous People).
4. *Enforcement.* Impressive strides have been made here by third World human rights groups in assisting enforcement of rights through the courts (e.g. by adoption of metalegal tactics in the Philippines).
5. *Lobbying for Law Reform.* There has been a flurry of activity here, especially in countries like the Philippines where parliamentary, legislative processes have been restored after a long lapse of time.

In addition to these conventional roles, human rights

organizations in the third World have also played unique roles which result from their human rights activism originating in community and victim-group mobilization and organization thus they have acted to:

(1) *Help* create grassroots organizations and help their organizational development. They have helped organize people to make better use of their own local productive resources, to create new resources and services, to promote equity and alleviate poverty, to influence government actions towards the same objectives and to establish new institutional frameworks that will durably sustain humane people-powered development,

(2) *Help* act as an intermediary between local government and community organizations.

(3) *Help,* where circumstances warrant, raise funding and direct it to local community organizations.

(4) *Help* develop capacity for and strengthen community based resource management with an emphasis on participation, equality and equity. Human rights organization working in neglected rural areas have helped set up local production-related organization such as water-user societies, pastoral-grazing associations, credit, production or consumer cooperatives, food processing cooperatives, farm equipment purchase or lease associations, tree grower associations, fishermen cooperatives, etc. At first glance, these activities seem far removed from human rights work. But these kinds of organizations have proved critical instrumentalities, not only for participatory local development but also for grassroots realization of human rights. At times these organizations have averted serious denials of human

rights which would have resulted had their efforts not prevented ecological degradation imperiling the very survival of the most depressed sections of the local community.

(5) *Help* create not only the means for community organizing but also for community self-defense.

(6) *Help* assert community rights and raise community awareness and expectations.

(7) *Help* protect activists against reprisals from high-handed administrators.

Thus, human rights organization in the Third World have had to constantly undergo a process of self-development. There has been a need for constant reflection based on praxis to reconceptualize human rights concepts and theory. There has also been a need for a professional unlearning and relearning process accompanied by the development of genuine professional

5. *Organizational Development:* For many Third Word human organizations, and other NGOs twin profound processes are presently at work: an inner-oriented one by which NGOs are striving to overcome structural weaknesses, dispersion, amorphousness within their own house, and a concomitant outer oriented process by which NGOs are learning to contribute more effectively to the broader, societal goals they pursue. They are facing a need for expansion in coverage and comprehensiveness (i.e. extensive development) as well as for strengthening the many fragile and ephemeral NGOs that risk disappearing without a trace (i.e. extensive development). There is a need for strengthening internal, organizational structures, fortifying their decision-making and

reproductive processes. There are problems of need for scale-up and replication to achieve greater impact. There is a need for better and ongoing participatory evaluation. Sensitively provided support that enables access to modest resources (financial and human), coupled with autonomous and participatory interaction and consultation, will go a long way towards meeting these needs.

6. *Research for Better Comprehension and Analysis.* There is need, only partly met, for greater reflection, self-appraisal and critique of the Third World human rights movement. The need is for research at conceptual, theoretical, and action levels. This research must largely be undertaken as a participatory process and the findings of the research need expression and dissemination through new channels to complement existing ones. The fruits of such introspection may well benefit human rights organizations not only in the Third World, but everywhere.

The specific mechanisms through which the above needs for external support can be addressed will need to be evolved through a partnership of equals and not by donor benevolence alone. Equally important is the need to devise effective participatory mechanisms whereby Third World human rights NGOs can make an effective impact upon the policy-making processes of government and development assistance agencies - be they bilateral or multilateral.

Third World Human Rights Organizations Funding

Third World NGOs have done some hard thinking regarding problems and dilemmas involved in funding, especially where funding is sought from an external source. They have identified opportunity costs, credibility costs, flexibility costs, flexibility costs, and vulnerability costs that might result from funding. They have grappled with the struggle for self-reliance and .' autonomy on the one hand, and access to an adequate resource base on the other. They have experimented with a variety of funding mechanisms such as grants, endowments, and revolving funds. They have experimented with income generation which carries its own strengths and limitations. International NGOs have played a crucial role in raising private funds and channeling them to developing countries but there have been problems of NGO independence, geographical allocation of resources, interference in the NGOs own agenda, priorities and approach; and of NGO accountability. Third world NGOs have helped work out for themselves some of the problems inevitable in a donor/recipient relationship and have even begun to articulate the elements that help build up a good relationship: demand-led, honesty, commitment to values and goals, relevance, flexibility, confidentiality, partnership, long-term collaboration." They have even been able to soften donor insistence upon "projectizing" activities and have earned recognition of the principle that not only project but also processes are deserving of donor support.

Thus, over the years, Third World NGOs and donor agencies have been working seriously towards fashioning a truly rewarding "partnership of equals." This partnership is presently in great peril with governments in countries like Indonesia and India placing severe constraints upon the NGOs freedom to receive foreign funding. These restraints have also been accompanied by a variety of other restrictive or corporative measures which place in jeopardy the effective survival of NGOs as autonomous and independent entities. The NGOs are fighting back against their own governments "repressive policies:" At this juncture, their most vital need for external support is precisely support in their present struggle for survival. Donors can, and shod, exert influence over recipient governments to ensure that the latter maintain public policy and legislative frameworks that safeguard the role of NGOs - a role they have fought so hard and so long to get recognized. Similarly, donor agencies must be vigilant to ensure that NGOs win their struggle not only against repression but also against cooptation. The current flood of rhetoric from governmental and international agencies alike, looking to NGOs to perform a variety of functions and play a variety of roles that governmental agencies themselves cannot, must be viewed with healthy scepticism as a potentially cooptative ploy.

Relationships Among Human Rights NGOs

Institutional Relationships

By and large, Third World human rights NGOs have tended to shy away from institutional relationships with one another. Attempts to coordinate have (often rightly) been received as attempts to control. NGOs cherish their autonomy, identity, and independence and there foe are willing to accept at most, loose coordination within a membership organization (e.g. Thailand, Philippines). Other factors militating against formal institutional relationships involve "turf"; competition for scarce or limited resources; ethnic; religious, or other cultural diversity; different perceptions of mandate ranging from narrow civil libertarian to broad empowerment focused. Different perceptions of mandate and different philosophies of human rights or of human rights activism also keep human rights NGOs (e.g. Amnesty International And, to a lesser degree, the International Commission of Jurists) have their own national chapters and these link together in their own international institutional form. But between countries, even at a regional level, there are few instances of institutional relationships between human rights NGOs but instead there tends·to be regional human rights NGOs formed. Fresh problems arise in the relationship between Third World human rights NGOs and regional and international human rights NGOs especially in respect of division of labor.

Functional Relationships

Third World human rights NGOs are much more successful in their functional relationships. They have often come together in action campaigns, They have worked together on training programs, on fact-finding missions and on election monitoring. Such situations do not endanger each NGOs independent identity, hence functional relationships have proved much more effective than institutional relationships. Although there is much talk of the human rights community, at both national and international levels, there is much plurality within such community if indeed there be one rather than several distinct communities. Similarly, the phrase "human rights movement" is often used prematurely even in situations where there has been an upsurge in the volume of human rights activity but not yet the emergence of a movement.

Thus, third World human rights organizations have brought fresh approaches both theoretical and strategic, to human rights activism. On the theoretical plane they have focused attention not only on human rights but also on inhuman wrongs; not only on human rights but also on the right to be human. They have sought to address human rights violations resulting both from governmental lawlessness as well as human rights situations where vindication of right is essential for continued survival. Yet they have struggled to establish not only the right to survive but also the right to survive with dignity and equity. They have grappled with the violence, both of human rights violators as well as the violence out of which human rights are born. They have worked to generate not only a jurisprudence of rights but also to generate ruth, indication and shame regarding human rights violations. They are constantly struggling to keep human rights truly for all. They deserve fullest external solidarity and support in their times of crises.

As of now the division of world's nation-states in First, Second and Third world has become obsolete, now to types are there—Developed and Developing. In this chapter we have given glimpses of human rights' position in the Developing (Third) world countries.

In the next chapter we will elucidate the picture of NGOs' role in human rights protection.

10

Role of NGOs in Human Rights Activism

Non-Governmental Organizations (NGOs) have made their contribution to this process of standard setting especially within the UN Commission on Human Rights and its Sub-Commission, where NGO experts are welcomed in the working groups which draft these documents. For examples the chairman of the working group drafting the proposed Convention on the Right of the Child has publicly thanked the NGOs for their contribution to its work.

In some cases the initiative for new legal instruments has been instigated by NGO action. Thus UN Declaration against torture was stimulated by the work of NGOs, and in particular of Amnesty International. This in turn led to the Swedish initiative for a UN Convention on this subject and the representatives of NGOs with particular knowledges of torture practices were able to make a significant contribution to the drafting of that convention. Virtually all of these documents elaborate in greater detail the rights proclaimed in the Universal Declaration, and many of them establish a system of reports by State Parties which are examined by a committee of independent experts, who question representatives of State Parties about their reports and then make a public report to the General Assembly of the United Nations. Again, these committees monitoring the performance of State Parties to conventions are heavily dependent upon the written contributions of NGOs. The reports of the State' Parties understandably concentrate upon their positive achievements. It is left to the NGOs with knowledge of the subject to supply to the committee members a brief which will enable them to probe more deeply in their questioning of the State Parties representatives. Sometimes this contribution of the NGOs is officially recognized. In *most* cases it is informal, but nonetheless vital for the effective work of the committees. In the same way the Non-Governmental Organization make numerous interventions, both written and oral, in the sections of the U.N. Commission on Human Rights and its Sub-Commission, drawing attention to violations of human rights in different countries of the world.

As in the 1988 meeting of the Commission some States complained that the NGOs were taking up too much time of the Commission.

This was answered by the delegate of the United States as follows:

> My government would like to underscore its strong support for the efforts of non-governmental organizations in assisting the United Nations and member-States in discharging their responsibilities in the human rights field. The non-Governmental organizations focus public attention on abuses which need correction and issues which must be resolved. They assist those whose human rights and fundamental freedoms have been abused, who are often poor and illiterate, in seeking redress . . . the best of the non-governmental organizations have developed great expertise and have jealously guarded their impartiality

> and credibility without the presence and sometimes the passion of representatives of non-governmental organizations, the Sub Commission would be a poor, and poorly-informed place, as would be this Commission. Other legal instruments are Declarations of the General Assembly or the Economic and Social Council of the UN on particular subjects. They carry weight as legal texts, setting out guidelines, but not having the same obligatory effect as conventions and other treaty documents.

There is a provision in Article 10 of the Universal Declaration that everyone is entitled to a fair trial by an independent and impartial tribunal in the determination of his rights and duties. All governments claim that their judges are completely independent. Unfortunately, in all many countries the independence of judges is eroded by corruption or governmental pressures. Frequently their terms of service are such that there are many ways in which subtle but effective pressures can be brought to bear on them. Ten years ago, with a view to trying to improve this situation our organization established in Geneva its Center for the Independence of judges and lawyers. At the initiative of this Center the Sub-Commission of the UN Human Rights Commission decided to make a study on this subject. We then organized two international seminars with judges and lawyers from all regions of the world who drew up a set of principles for protecting the independence of judges. These were then submitted to the Sub-Commission where the Rapporteur embodied them in an Annexure to his report. The next stage was a conference convened at Montreal by the Chief Justice of Quebec, a wider representation of judges and lawyers, at which these documents were the main working papers. The conference produced a more detailed and authoritative draft, which was in turn submitted to the UN Committee on Crime Prevention and Control in Vienna.

They produced a draft which was submitted to the 1985 UN Congress on Crime Prevention and Control held in Milan and attended by most of the countries in the world. The Secretary of our Center and a representative of the Canadian Government worked hard in lobbying delegations and negotiating amendments to the text to make it acceptable to the delegates. The result of all this was that the Congress approved unanimously a declaration of 16 principles on the Independence of the Judiciary, containing in general terms nearly all the basic safeguard, and protections proposed in the earlier documents. This text was then submitted to the General Assembly of the UN where it received unanimous approval. In this way it became the first and only international instrument making clear what is meant by the independence of judges and what procedures and conditions of work are required to make it a reality. This document is now a most valuable tool, being pressure upon governments to alter their procedures so as to comply with the principles which they have approved in the General Assembly. These examples illustrate how NGOs can contribute to the slow but vitally important task of 'standard setting' as it is called in the United Nations.

The same process goes on at the regional level in the Council of Europe, the Organization of American State and now the Organization of African States. For example, the International Commission of Jurists and the Swiss Committee against Torture submitted to the Council of Europe a Draft Convention for the prevention of torture by means of regular visits to places of detention in the State Parties. This has now been adopted and signed by all the States of the Council of Europe and is likely to come into force this year. The possibility of a similar Convention in America is being explored. The International Commission of Jurists has recently submitted a document containing recommendations for the

Rules of Procedures of the new African Commission on Human Rights under the African Charter. Virtually all its recommendations have been adopted. One may ask what is the use of all these documents if the rights in the Universal Declaration are being abused throughout the would. The answer is that this body of international law can be an effective tool for persuading governments to introduce reforms in their laws and practices. To illustrate, some years ago a Japanese lawyer called Totsuka came to see us to ask if we could help him and some colleagues of his to persuade the Japanese Government to amend their Mental Health Law. Before the war, the law was that the families were responsible for looking after the mentally ill. It was, and to a large extent still is, an ignorant popular belief that mental illness is hereditary. The result was that the families hid away, even chained-up in the basement, their mentally ill, for if it became known that they had a mentally ill member of their family, their sons and daughters could never get married. After the World War II, the Government passed a law permitting, any doctor, not necessarily with any knowledge of psychiatry, to establish a mental hospital with a considerable continuing government grant. It only required two such doctors of the hospital to say that a person required treatment in a mental hospital, and the consent of the family, for that person to be locked up indefinitely as an involuntary patient. There was no right of appeal to a court, or tribunal, and no access to a lawyer. The average time they spent in hospital was 8 years. With modern psychiatry a patient should not, normally, require more than a few months treatment. As a result of this law, private mental hospitals became a remarkable growth industry. Last year there were 330,000 involuntary patients in Japan with modern psychiatric methods. These should not have been more than 50,000 at most. A group of Japanese lawyers and psychiatrists tried to *get* the law changed.

The opposition supported them but the vested interests of the private hospitals, the families of the mentally ill, and the drug industry was such that the Government would not move. So Totsuka, asked us to raise the matter at the international level. We published an article describing some shocking cases in these hospitals. In one large hospital over 200 patients in a period of 3 years died unexplained deaths. We then raised the matter at the UN Sub-Commission on Human Rights. We wrote to the Prime Minister and to the Minister of Health, but there was no response. We then approached the Foreign Ministry and pointed out that this system was a violation of the Covenant on Civil and Political Rights to which Japan is a party.

Article 9 of the Covenant says: . . . The Foreign Ministry in Japan, as in other countries, is very concerned about the image and reputation of its country abroad. The result was that they persuaded a newly appointed Minister of Health and his officials that changes were needed and the Government agreed to reform the law. We sent to Japan a mission comprised of two internationally renowned psychiatrists and a judge of a mental health appeal court in the United States, to examine the system of the Japanese mental hospitals. They made a report with a large number of detailed recommendations. Last year the Government introduced a new law amending the previous law and meeting quite a number of these recommendations. The Government has recognized that this is a first step and say that they will review the working of their new law in five years time. We have recently sent another mission to Japan with the same experts to see what impact the new law has made upon the practice in mental hospitals in Japan, and to make recommendations. The mission was received courteously by Government representatives at national and prefectural levels, and by private hospitals. This is perhaps an exceptional case, but it does illustrate how the international conventions and other legal instruments can be a useful tool.

Most governments, when attacked for their human rights violations protest paragraph 7 of the Charter which says that the Charter does not authorize the United Nations to interfere in matters which are essentially within the domestic jurisdiction of any State. The answer to that can be illustrated by another episode. Under the dictatorship of the Colonels in Greece we received reports that six lawyers had been arrested and were being tortured. We sent a high-powered mission of very distinguished lawyers from the United States and Canada to inquire into this matter and try to secure their release. The government refused to see them, but they were convinced by the evidence they received that the allegations were well-founded. Before leaving they held a press conference, followed by another in New York on their return, which resulted in front page reports in the press. Six weeks later the lawyers were released. A year or two later I was in the US State Department and asked whether they thought our mission had been helpful. Their answer was very positive. They explained that they were able to say to the Greek Government, "We do not want to interfere in your internal affairs, but when your activities provoke such a reaction from distinguished lawyers, it becomes an internal affair for us and affects our relations with you". We have no doubt that it was the US Government pressure that led to the release of the lawyers.

We had a similar experience later concerning the termination of the massive disappearances in Argentina under the dictatorship. Numerous NGOs had reported on them in detail, but the Government dismissed the reports as communist inspired propaganda. However, as a result of the NGO reports the Inter-American Commission on Human

Rights sent a mission to Argentina, which came to the same conclusions and published a very strong and well-documented report condemning the disappearances. In response to this inter-governmental pressure the Government eventually gave way and at first reduced, and then ceased, the practice. These cases illustrate the fact that the work of NGOs is often at its most effective when it leads to governmental or inter-governmental action.

It is pertinent to note that another result of this massive body of human rights instruments is its side-effects. Largely as a result of the so-called Charter policy in the United States, linking human rights performance with development aid (a policy which in fact was started by the US Congress before Charter became President), all governments have been obliged to take human rights into account in their foreign policy. Many of them have special sections in their foreign, ministries, staffed with people well versed in human rights. In some countries they have inter-departmental committees to coordinate policies and ensure that new legislation or policies do not violate human rights obligations. Bad as may be the record in some countries, there -will within each government be those who are pressing quietly for more respect for human rights, and they make use of the international documents in doing so.

In fact, Human rights law has become a whole new branch of international law. There are professors who specialize in this field, and faculties of law introduces courses in international human rights law. The number of human rights NGOs, and their expertise, has greatly increased, at both universal and regional levels. Their role has been widely recognized and they are now able to take a much greater part in the work of the United Nations and other inter-governmental bodies. In short, human rights have become an important political issue which governments and parliamentarians cannot ignore. For most people in the West the words 'violations of human rights' conjure up violations of civil and political rights, arbitrary arrests and detentions, political prisoners, torture of suspects, police or soldiers beating up or throwing tear gas or even firing at students and other demonstrators, military dictatorships, one party states, apartheid and other forms of discrimination, press censorship, etc. This is understandable. Such things shock the conscience of mankind, and we see them daily in our newspapers or on our television screens. But the people from the so-called-Third World, especially the rural poor who make up the majority of most States in Africa and Latin America, the principle violations, of their rights are lack of food, housing, health and hygiene, education, employment, and an adequate standard of living when these reach even more massive proportions than usual due to some natural disaster, we are then reminded by the media of their plights. But the thousands who die every day from the want of their economic, social and cultural rights cease to be 'news'.

Until recently, there have been very few international lawyers seriously interested in economic, social and cultural rights. Many of them dismiss the Covenant on Economic, Social and Cultural Rights and other legal texts as being soft law. This is because, with some exceptions, they do not confer rights on the individual which are enforceable in a court of law. Consequently these lawyers think they are merely high-sounding goals, and that it is for governments to decide for, themselves to what extent they will apply resources to promote these rights. In the field of civil and political rights there are international judicial bodies like the European and Latin American Courts of Human Rights and, in the United Nations there are monitoring committees of independent experts dealing with individual complaints and gradually building up a substantial body of case law or jurisprudence' as the French call it. It is only recently that a serious procedure has come into existence for monitoring and entering into discussion with governments on their performance in carrying on their obligations in the field of economic, social and cultural rights. The convention on these rights provides for State Parties to prepare reports on the measures they have adopted and the progress made in achieving observes of the rights. These reports are examined by a Committee of the Economic and Social Council of the United Nations. For several years this Committee, which met in New York, was composed of representatives of States, supposedly expert in this field. In practice, they were virtually all diplomat from the mission in New York with little or no expertise on the subject. The result was virtually nil due both to ignorance and to the reluctance of diplomats to attack each other as they had set up of persons with real expertise. As they serve in their individual capacities, they speak much more frankly.

Like all such bodies in the UN they tend to work on the basis of consensus. Unfortunately in the first year they made little progress as they were obstructed by a Soviet delegate who was a relic of the Brezhnev era and had never heard of glasnost and perestroika. Fortunately, news of this reached Moscow and he was persuaded to resign. At this year's meeting much progress was made in devising procedures which will make their work meaningful. The obligations of governments under the Covenant on Economic, Social and Cultural Rights do not fall only on the developing countries.

Article 2 of the covenant says that each State Party undertakes to take steps 'individually and through international assistance and operation, especially economic and technical, to the maximum of its available resources, with a view to achieving progressively the full realization of the .' rights recognized in the present Covenant' (emphasis added). Article 55 of the Charter of the United Nations says that 'with a view to the creation of conditions of stability and well-being which are necessary for peaceful and friendly relations among nations... the United Nations shall promote higher standards of living, full employment and conditions of economic, social progress and development; and solutions of international economic, social, health and related problems and international, cultural and educational co-operation.

The United Nations and its specialized agencies have no existence apart from their member States, so these obligations fall upon each of so-called developed countries to cooperate to the maximum of its available resource in helping peoples in the developing countries to achieve their economic, social and cultural rights. It is to be hoped that the new ECOSOC Committee will bring pressure to bear on the developed countries to increase their contributions to the maximum of their available resources. The specialized agencies have an extremely important role in securing achievement of economic, social and cultural rights, in particular the ILO, WHO, UNESCO, UNICEF, FAO and, though not strictly a specialized agency, the UNDP. The ILO is outstanding for its detailed and numerous conventions and for the procedures it has developed for examining complaints and pressuring governments for better performance in the labour field. This is largely due to its tripatite structure, one third being nongovernmental trade union representatives. UNESCO has a Committee which can receive and examine complaints against governments, but its record is not very impressive. The other agencies have no such procedures. Indeed the very term human rights has until recently been taboo in the

WHO, for fear that it will arouse the hostility of those Third World nations which sometimes regard human rights as a stick in the hands of the Western powers to beat them with. The reason for change of attitude of the WHO is that they have realized that they need the cooperation of human rights organizations to help poorest people that the cruel discrimination against AIDS victims is a serious violation of their human rights, as well as being an obstacle to obtaining the cooperation of victims which is essential to control the spread of the disease.

The International Commission of Jurists attaches great importance to economic, social and cultural right. As far back as 1959, at its first Third World Congress, held in New Delhi, it proclaimed the dynamic concept of the rule of law, in which it stated that lawyers, in addition to promoting and defending civil and political fight, should use their skills and knowledge to help the disadvantaged to secure their economic and social fights. Inspired by the work of some human rights activists in South Asia and in South-East Asia, we have in recent years been holding international seminars in Africa, Asia and Latin America on the subject of 'Legal Services for the Rural Poor.' We realized that human rights, and particularly the legal aspect of human rights was entirely unknown to the rural poor, who are the majority of the Third World's population. Often illiterate, they know nothing of lawyers or the law it is probably as an instrument of their oppression. Equally, the lawyers tend to know little or nothing about the problems of the rural poor, and the way they are oppressed and cheated out of their land and other rights. So what we have been trying to do is to interest lawyers, and the faculties of law and of social science in the universities, to study these problems and to bring legal assistance to people at village level.

In fact, this is not the ordinary legal aid, which is mainly limited to providing lawyers to defend the poor when charged with serious criminal offenses. When a rich man consults his lawyers, what he wants is to be informed about his rights and obligations, to be told how to claim those rights and, where necessary, to have the lawyer negotiate on his behalf. As a last resort, and only when there is no other solution, he wants his lawyer to take proceedings before a court. It is these services that the poor lack and that lawyers should find ways to provide. What we urge them to do is to train students of law or social sciences or newly qualified lawyers to go out to rural areas to do this work. Some call them para-legal, and they need not necessarily be lawyers. Sometimes people doing development work take on this work part-time. They must, of course, be trained in the law on matters affecting the rural poor, such as the land law, family and divorce law and inheritance law. There are two rights in particular which are a sine qua non of any self-reliant development, that is development where the people can solve their own problems with the minimum of assistance from outside. The two rights are freedom of expression and freedom of association. Without these there will be no fundamental change in their situation and no true development.

The para-legals must first find out what the problems are, then explain the position in law, and then encourage the people to combine together in the spirit of self-reliant development to assert their rights, if necessary with the help of lawyer in the town. We urge these young lawyers, sometimes called para-legal, to work with grassroots development organizations. They will obviously have more chance of success if they have the help of people working for development in the rural areas, who have the cultural differences which so often result in distrust of lawyers from the towns. Recently we had in Jakarta of lawyers who have been doing this work for several years in the countries of South-East Asia.

This was the first time they had met to share their experiences, identify the obstacles to their work, and devise ways to overcome these obstacles. It transpired that what they need most is support from the law faculties, so as to train and recruit more young lawyers for this work, and from the Bar Associations to get the support, where needed, of senior lawyers. Perhaps the leading theorist in this work is an Indian Lawyer, Clearance Dias, who works world-wide from the office in New York of his organization, the International Center for Law in Development. He expounds on what he calls the 'empowerment' of the rural poor. It is apposite to end by quoting him:

> "Human Rights", he says "Can play a significant role in the empowerment of the impoverished. The oppressed can become more self-reliant through an understanding of their rights and indeed the right to organize and rights of association are vital to impoverished groups seeking to mobilize and organize themselves and thus develop countervailing power. Moreover, such impoverished groups become more empowered as they develop their capacities to assert rights through collective action. As awareness of rights helps diminish dependency and builds up confident self-reliance when have-nots' appreciate that they are entitled to resources as a matter of entitlement and no just benign charity. Moreover, rights safeguarding the dignity of the human being are of considerable psychological importance in the struggle to break out of the culture of dependency and to establish self-esteem and a sense of self-worth.

Obviously, Human rights can play significant role in

securing the accountability of those who wield power and control resources essential to the satisfaction of basic human needs. Rights to secure mandamus or prohibition are important checks on abuse of power. Right of access to information, rights to a public hearing and freedom of speech and of the press are crucial in checking governmental lawlessness and abuse of discretion or powers by bureaucratic and government officials. Human Rights are also important as a means for securing participation. "Perhaps, more importantly, human rights represent a vital expression of values."

Initiatives in India

Upto 1990, the Human Rights Commission in India was not proper and regulated. It was only for the year 1990 first time National Commission for Women Act 1990, was enacted and National Commission for Women was established. Secondly, National Commission for Minorities Act, 1992, was passed and Minorities Commission was established. National Commission for women is initially meant for safeguarding the interest of Ladies, while the Minorities Commission is concerned with the plights of Minorities only. National Commission of Scheduled Castes and Scheduled Tribes has been established to look into the grievances of Scheduled Castes and Scheduled Tribes throughout India. It is a definite fact that upto 1990, there was no specific authority to look after the general interest of society and the human rights of masses. It was only in the year 1993, Protection of Human Rights Act was enacted which has and thereafter National Human Rights Commission has done a lot, doing a lot and shall definitely do a lot for the causes of human rights.

Coming first to National Commission for Women. National Commission for Women is a statutory and autonomous body, constituted by the Government of India.

The Commission since its inception is very much perturbed by the growing instance of long pendency of cases in various courts of the nation. V. Mohini Giri was the Chairman and Padma Seth was a member alongwith Sri Saddiq Jilani a legal consultant. Definitely, the constitution of National Women's Commission towards women is remarkable as and when any problem pertaining to ladies is brought to the knowledge of national women's commission. Currently Dr. Girija Vyas is the Chairperson of the Commission. It starts its functioning and always proper relief has been delivered to the needy ladies. The contribution of the National Commission for women may be counted under three major heads, (i) Parivarik Mahila Lok Adalat, (ii) Mahila Jail Adalat, and (iii) to generally supervise the interest of ladies in society and to take appropriate steps. The National Commission for women strongly felt the need of strict implementation of the Legal Services Authorities Act, 1987 by which the legal aid boards were empowered to organize Lok Adalats for the speedy disposal of cases.

The new has coined a new and innovative idea of organizing "Parivarik (Mahila) Lok Adalat" for the speedy deposal of cases relating to family. Emphasis on amicable settlement of disputes is an important aspect of the Parivarik (Mahila) Lok Adalat's ideology. To this end the process of conciliation is applied strictly in the adjudication of disputes. Simplicity of procedure and flexibility of functioning are the two essential features of Parivarik (Mahila) Lok Adalats, which are not encumbered by elaborate rules and civil or criminal procedure or the laws of evidence. Parties are heard in a normal and informal manner.

With the above objectives in view, the commission sent letters to the Chief Justices of High Courts requesting them to advise the State Legal Aid and Advise Boards to cooperate with the National Commission for Women in organizing Parivarik (Mahila) Lok Adalats. The Chief Justices were also requested to advise the District and Sessions Judges who are also the chairpersons of the District Legal Aid and Advise Boards, to actively help the NGOs (Non-Governmental Organizations) to organize the Parivarik (Mahila) Lok Adalat. The National Commission for Women thus invites Non-Governmental Organizations to send their proposals. In response to its call the Commission has received positive response from the people belonging to all walks of life in support of the Parivarik (Mahila) Lok Adalats in a successful manner. As of now from and Andaman & Nacobar Islands to Cochin in the South, the NCW has sponsored over 110 such Parivarik (Mahila) Lok Adalats in which approximately 7000 cases were handled and nearly 2000 cases were disposed of by the Adalats.

Remarkably, the cases dealt in Parivarik Mahila Lok Adalat fell into the following categories:

(i) Maintenance to wife, children and parents U/s 125 Cr.P.C.
(ii) Matrimonial disputes.
(iii) M.V. Accident cases.
(iv) Restitution of conjugal rites.
(v) Reconciliation between parties.
(vi) Divorce.
(vii) Custody of children,
(viii) Cases u/ss 498-A & 406 IPC.
(ix) Proper rights to women.
(x) Bigamy.
(xi) Labour laws.
(xii) Mahila Jail Adalat.

It is significant to mention that Custodial Justice for women has been one of the activities of the National Commission for Women. One of the functions specifically assigned to the Commission, Custodial Justice for women has been one of the activities of the National Commission for women. One of the function specifically assigned to the Commission of the National Commission for Women Act, 1990 is to "inspect or cause to be inspected jail, demand home, women's institution or other place of custody where women are kept as prisoners or otherwise, and take up with the concerned authorities for remedial action if found necessary". Visit to Jails were undertaken by the Chairperson and as well as the Members from time to time. The experience of such visits have revealed the appalling conditions under which the prisoners in general and women detente in particular are languishing for years. It is a sad reality that nearly 70% of the female jail population constitute under trial prisoners. The Commission has taken a serious note of the reality and gave urgent attention to the fact that there were so many undertrial women languishing in jails for years for offenses and the sentences for which would have been much less if they were convicted in time. Besides this there were many women under trials charged with petty offenses for which they should not have been in jails at all. Most worrying is the fact that in the case of women life convicts who are having minor children at the time of conviction, the children grow alongwith the mothers inside the four walls of the prison without any fault of their own. The Commission feels that this is legally unsound and a clear violation of the Fundamental Rights guaranteed under the constitution of India. Furthermore basing on the above analogy in response to the public interest petitions filed by NGOs and other activities the apex court has passed orders to release such kind of persons.

In the light of the above facts the National Commission for Women has rightly felt the need of organizing Mahila Jail Adalats for the speedy disposal of cases related to women. To this end the commission is seeking the cooperation and support of judiciary, Home Ministry and other Organizations concerned for organizing Jail Adalats on the lines of Parivarik (Mahila) Lok Adalats. Apart from all these statutory duties, National Commission for Women cautiously safeguards the interest of ladies and when it comes to the notice of the commission that when there is a violation of women's rights, stern actions have been taken by the National Commission for women. The demand of 30% reservation among M.Ps and M.L.A.s is a bye-product of this commission. Even in the general election of Parliament, 1998, the Commission has issued an ultimatum to all political- parties either to safeguard the interest of ladies or otherwise face their agony. It has been further made clear by the commission that the commission shall support that party or person. That party, which has put a competent lady as a candidate to the election. Every-day in the news paper, you always find that commission is doing a lot for the respect of the ladies.

National Commission of the Minorities has been established under National Commission of Minorities Act, 1992. Presently, Sardar Buta Singh is the chairman of these commissions. Likewise chairman of the National Commission of Minorities has also revealed various lacunaes and defects for the policies of upliftment of minorities and several occasions it has tried its best that all minorities should be treated at par with other citizens. The most important commission for the human rights nowadays is National Human Rights Commission. The importance of this commission has now been realized by all Government Agencies, authorities and by all private individuals.

Let us now consider first Annual report which has covered upto March 1994.

I. The proposal for a Commission was originally contained in a Human Rights Commissions Bill which was introduced in the Lok Sabha on 14th May 1993. However, the powers, functions and manner of functioning of the proposed Commission, as contained in that Bill," were extensively criticized, most notably when that Bill was considered by the Parliamentary Standing Committee on Home Affairs. The Ordinance of 28 September 1993 was drafted in the light of the comments made on the original Bill, as was the resubmitted Bill, which was presented to parliament on 25 November 1993 to replace the Ordinance, The Statement of Objects and Reasons of the November Bill made clear the purposes of the Act subsequently adopted. While noting that India was a party to the International Covenant on Civil and Political Rights and the International Covenant on Economic, Social and Cultural Rights, both of which were adopted by the United Nations General Assembly on 16 December 1966, and that the rights embodied in those Covenants stood substantially protected by the constitution of India, . the statement observed that there had been "growing concern in the country and abroad about issue relating to human rights." Having regard to this, and to changing social realities and emerging trends in the nature of crime and violence. It had been considered essential to review the existing laws and procedures and the system of administration with a view 'to bringing about greater efficiency and transparency. The Bill received Presidential assent on 8 January 1994.

The vacancy thus caused is to be filled. In accordance with Section 3(4) of the Act, Shri R.V. Pillai joined the Commission as its Secretary-General and Chief Executive Officer on 20 October 1993 with the rank of a Secretary to the Government of India. In accordance with Section 8 of the Act, the Central Government has notified the salaries and allowances payable to the Chairperson and Members of the Commission as also the terms and conditions of their service. In exercise of the powers conferred on it by Section 10(2) of the Act, the Commission has issued regulations governing the procedures to be followed in the conduct of its business.

Functions of the National Human Rights Commission

It would be helpful here to recapitulate the considerable scope and range of the functions envisaged for the Commission under Section 1.2 of the Act, "All or any" of which are to be performed by it. These functions are to:

(a) inquire, suo *motu* or on a petition presented to it by a victim or any person on his behalf, into complaint of:

  (i) violation of human rights or abatement thereof, or

  (ii) negligence in the prevention of such violation, by a public servant;

(b) intervene in any proceeding involving any allegation of violation of human rights pending before a court with the approval of such court;

(c) visit, under intimation to the State Government, any jail or any other institution under the control of the State Government, where persons are detained or lodged for purposes of treatment, reformation or protection to study the living conditions of the inmates and make recommendations thereon;

(d) review the safeguards provided by or under the constitution or any law for the time being in force for the protection of human rights and recommend measures for their effective implementation;

(e) review the factors, including acts of terrorism that inhibit the enjoyment of human rights and recommend appropriate remedial measures;

(f) study treaties and other international instruments on human rights and make recommendations for their effective implementation;

(g) undertake and promote research in the field of human rights;

(h) spread human rights literacy among various sections of society and promote awareness of the safeguards available for the protection of these rights through publications, the media, seminars and other available means;

(i) encourage the efforts of non-governmental organizations and institutions working in the field of human rights; and such other functions as it may consider necessary for the promotion of human rights.

11

NGOs and Civil Society

In civil society NGOs have been playing significant role in generating awareness about various issues in society and undertaking development activities for the amelioration and betterment of the deprived sections of the society. These roles they are performing globally. In India they have exerted a considerable influence on society through contributing to socio-economic development of people particularly the weakened sections. In the area of protecting to human rights they have also played a significant role, The following paragraph describes the role of NGOs in influencing international convention:

> The role of the NGO group in the drafting of the (1989) Convention on the Rights of the Child, has been described as being without parallel in the history of drafting international instruments'. Its imprint, claims Price Cohen 'can be found in almost every article'. Even so the NGOs failed in their effort to raise the minimum age for recruitment into armed forces and participation in hostilities to 18 years. However, the NGOs (in particular Radda Barnen and the Friends World Committee Consultation) refused to accept this failure as final and persuaded the Committee on the rights of the Child (the expert body set up to oversee the implementation of the Convention) to take up the issue. The result is a further standard setting

exercise; the drafting of an optional protocol to the Convention to remedy this deficiency. In which underage recruitment occurs. Some indication, of the extent to which on this working level NGOs are taken into partnership with governments,, is given by the fact that at the 1994 Working Group drafting the optional protocol, the proposal to give the Committee on the Rights of the Child greater powers appeared. In draft headed 'Poland (Quakers' Art. 7 amended) and was referred to throughout as the Polish/ Quaker proposal'. Not surprisingly, the Draft Report of the Working Group shows strong evidence of NGO input". (Brett, 1995;101) In the case of human-rights vis-a-vis NGO it may be noted that one of the oldest NGO, i.e. the Red Cross, has been in the forefront of protecting and taking care of human right in war zones almost for a century. However in 1948, a number of NGOs have been playing significant role upholding human rights. NGO's role got a significant boost to the World Conference on Human Rights held at Vienna in 1993. In India there are now a large number of NGOs which have been trying to protect human rights. The most prominent of them are Peoples Union for Democratic Rights and Peoples Union of Civil Rights. Apart from these organisations, there are others which try to struggle for protecting human rights by propagating, advocating, campaigning and creating awareness among people about human rights. In different states of India, for example, in West Bengal, Punjab and Andhra Pradesh there are now a number of human rights organizations which continuously monitor and create awareness about human rights situation. Apart from these, there are NGOs which, thought not directly involved in human rights violation but indirectly assist in promoting human rights in society. Today India has largest numbers of NGOs and trade unions in the world. A considerable number of these organisations working in different spheres to promote human rights by creating awareness about human

> rights and changing peoples material situations which often provides fuel the violation of human rights. Today Ammesty International also plays a considerable role in voicing concern and highlighting human rights violation cases in India. In brief, NGOs in India have been playing a most important role in promoting knowledge of human right, identifying problems in the protection and enjoyment of human rights and seek changes in legislation and practice that further their protection and enjoyment.

In the first half of the twentieth century, at the close of the World War I, international concern for human rights found expression in certain provisions of the Covenant of the League of Nations. Similarly, according to the Charter of the United Nations, one of the purposes of the United Nations (UN) is "to achieve international co-operation in promoting and encouraging respect for human rights and for fundamental freedom." The UN Charter specifies the obligations with regard to human rights which each member state assumes at the time it ratifies that instrument, and details how the Organisation seeks to ensure the realisation of those obligations. The Universal Declaration of Human Rights adopted in 1948, defines more specifically the "human rights and fundamental freedoms" mentioned in the UN Charter. These include civil and political rights such as the right to life, liberty and security of person, the right to take part in the government of one's country, and the rights to freedom of thought, conscience, religion, expression and opinion, and economic, social and cultural rights such as the rights to work, to education and to participate in the cultural life of one's community.

Notwithstanding the serious international concern for human rights, according to the rough estimates of the UN Centre for Human Rights, at least half of the world's people still suffer from some serious violation or deprivation of their basic economic, social, cultural, political and civil rights. These violations range from torture, execution, rape, arbitrary detention, violence and disappearances, to extreme poverty, slavery, child abuse, famine and undernourishment, and lack of access to clean water, sanitation, and health care. Nevertheless, international community is fully determined to prevent every type of violation of human rights. In this connection, it must be mentioned that the role of national governments in the realisation of human rights is particularly important. Human rights involve relationships among individuals, and between individuals and the state. Therefore, the practical task of protecting and promoting human rights is primarily a national one, for Which each state must be responsible. At the national level, rights can be best protected through adequate legislation, an independent judiciary, the enactment and enforcement of democratic institutions. When states ratify a human rights instrument, they either incorporate its provisions directly into their domestic legislation or undertake to comply in other ways with the obligations contained therein. Therefore, universal human rights standards and norms today find the expression in the domestic laws of most countries. Often, however, the fact that a law exists to protect certain rights is not enough if these laws do not also provide for all of the legal powers and institutions necessary to ensure their effective realisation.

It has, therefore, become increasingly apparent that the effective enjoyment of human rights calls for the establishment of national infrastructures for their protection and promotion. Official human rights institutions have been set up by many countries in recent years. While the task of such institutions may vary considerably from country to country, they share a common purpose and for this reason are collectively referred to as national institution for the protection and promotion of human fights.

National Institutions and Human Rights

In 1978, the Commission on Human Rights decided to organise a Seminar on National and Local Institutions to draft guidelines for the structure and functioning of such bodies. Accordingly, the Seminar on National and Local Institutions for the Promotion and Protection of Human Rights was held in Geneva from 18 to 29 September 1978 during which a series of guidelines was approved. These guidelines suggested that the functions of national institutions should be:

(a) To act as source of human rights information for the Government and people of the country;
(b) To assist in educating public opinion and promoting awareness and respect for human rights;
(c) To consider, deliberate upon, and make recommendations regarding any particular state of affairs that may exist nationally and that the government may wish to refer to them;
(d) To advise on any questions regarding human rights matters referred to them by the Government;
(e) To study and keep under review the status of legislation, judicial decisions and administrative arrangements for the promotion of human rights, and to prepare and submit reports on these matters to the appropriate authorities.
(f) To perform any other functions which the Government may wish to assign to them in connection with the duties of that state under those international agreements in the field of human rights to which it is party.

In regard to the structure of such institutions, the guideline recommended that they should:

(a) Be so designed as to reflect in their composition, wide cross-sections .' of the nation, thereby bringing all parts of that population into the decision-making process in regard to human rights;

(b) Function regularly, and that immediate access to them should be available to any member of the public or any public authority;

(c) In appropriate cases, have local or regional advisory organs to assist them in discharging their functions.

The guidelines were subsequently endorsed by the UN Commission on Human Rights and by the General Assembly. The Commission invited all member states to take appropriate steps for the establishment, where they did not already exist of national institutions for the protection and promotion of human rights, and requested the Secretary General to submit a detailed report on existing institutions.

Global Trends: Establishment of Human Rights Commissions

In line with these guidelines, in many countries, special commissions have been established to ensure that the laws and regulations concerning the protection of human rights are effectively applied. Most commissions function independently from other organs of governments, although they may be required to report to the legislature on a regular basis. In keeping with their independent nature, commissions are generally composed of a variety of members from diverse background but each with a particular interest, expertise or experience in the field of human rights. Each country may have its specific requirements for restrictions for the selection members, such as quotas on the number of representatives or candidates from different professional

.categories, political parties, or localities. Human Rights Commissions are concerned primarily with the protection of nationals against discrimination and with the protection of civil and other human rights. The precise function and powers of a particular commission will be defined in the legislative act or decree under which it is established. These laws or decrees will also serve to define the Commission's jurisdiction by specifying the range of discriminatory or violative conduct that it is empowered to investigate. Some commissions concern themselves with alleged violation of any rights recognised in the constitution. Others may be able to consider cases of discrimination on abroad range of grounds including race, colour, religion, sex, national or ethnic origin disability, social conditions, sexual orientation, political convictions and ancestry.

One of the most important functions vested in a human rights commission is to receive and investigate complaints from individuals (and occasionally from groups) alleging human rights abuses committed in violation of existing national law. In order to properly carry out its tasks, the commission will usually be capable of obtaining evidence relating to the matter under investigation. Even if only used rarely, this power is important in that it guards against the possibility of frustration through lack of co-operation on the part of the person or body complained against. While there are considerable differences in the procedures followed by various human rights commissions in the investigation and resolution of complaints, many rely on conciliation in the investigation and resolution. In the process of conciliation, the commission will attempt to bring the two parties together in order to achieve a mutually satisfactory outcome. If conciliation fails to resolve the dispute, the commission may be able to resort to arbitration in which it will, after a hearing, issue a determination. It is not usual for a human rights commission to be granted authority to impose a legally binding outcome on parties to a complaint. However, this does not mean that the settlement or appropriate remedial steps recommended by the Commission can be ignored. In some cases a special tribunal will hear and determine issues outstanding from an unresolved complaint. If no special tribunal has been established, the commission may be able to transfer unresolved complaint to the normal courts for a final and binding determination. Another important function of a human rights commission is to systematically review the government's human rights policy in order to detect shortcomings in human rights observance and to suggest ways of improving it. Human rights commissions may also monitor the State's compliance with its own and with international human rights laws and if necessary, recommend changes. The ability of a commission to initiate enquiries on its own behalf is an important measure of its overall strength and probably effectiveness. This is particularly true in regard to situations which involve persons or groups who do not have the financial or social resources to lodge individual complaints. The realisation of human rights cannot be achieved solely through legislation and administrative arrangements. In recognition of this fact, commissions are often entrusted with the important responsibility of improving community awareness of human rights. Promoting and educating about human rights may involve informing the public about the commission's own functions and purposes; provoking discussions about various important questions in the field of human rights; organising seminars; holding counselling services and meetings; as well as producing and disseminating human rights publications.

NGOs and Human Rights

In the international crusade against human rights

violations, the role of NGOs can hardly be over emphasised. As a matter of fact, the development of international norms, institutions and procedures for the promotion and protection of human rights has gone hand in hand with the proliferation of Non-Governmental International Organisations working in the field of human rights, NGOs played an important role during the drafting of the United Nations (UN) Charter as they lobbyed for the inclusion of human rights provisions in the Charter and for a system that would give NGOs a formal institutional affiliation with and standing before the UN organs. The result was the incorporation of Article 71 of the UN Charter which provides that "the Economic and Social Council may make suitable A arrangements for consultation with non-governmental organisations which are concerned with matters within its competence.

Article 71 was implemented in due course by the Economic and Social Council (ECOSOC) and it established a formal system that enables qualified NGOs to obtain consultative status with the ECOSOC. Since then, the human rights NGOs have played a very important role in the evolution of international system for the promotion and protection of human rights and in trying to make it work.

The Vienna Declaration on the Role of NGOs

The World Conference on Human Rights held at Vienna in Austria in 1993 has also recognised the significant role of the NGOs in the promotion and protection of human rights. In its Resolution No. 38, the Declaration says:

> The World Conference on Human Rights recognises the important role of Non-Governmental Organisations in the promotion of all human rights and in humanitarian activities at the national, regional and international levels. The World Conference on Human Rights appreciated their contribution to

> increasing public awareness of human rights issues, to the conduct of education, training and research in this field, and to the promotion and protection of all human rights and fundamental freedoms. While recognising that the primary responsibility for standard setting lies with States, the conference also appreciates the contribution of non -governmental organisations to this process. In this respect, the World Conference on Human Rights emphasises the importance of continued dialogue and co-operation between Governmental and Non-Governmental Organisations.

The World Conference has further urged the NGOs to intensify their efforts in co-operating and co-ordinating their activities against the human rights violations in general and against the evils like racism and racial discrimination in particular. Recognising the human rights of women and of the girl-child as an inalienable, integral and indivisible part of Universal -Declaration of Human Rights, the World Conference has urged the NGOs to intensify their efforts for the promotion and protection of human rights of women and the girl child.

The World Conference on Human Rights has also recommended that NGOs and other grass-roots organisations active in development and/or human rights should be enabled to play a major role on the national and international levels in the debate, activities and implementation relating to the right to development and, in co-operation with governments, in all relevant aspects of development co-operation.

Finally, the World Conference on Human Rights has recognised the important role played by NGOs in the effective implementation "of all human rights instruments and, in particular, the Convention on the Rights of the Child.

Protecting Human Rights Defenders and Human Rights NGOs

Are there any as yet untried strategies and tactics for extending protection to besieged human rights activists and organizations - is a serious and a complex question.

It is a serious question because we are not dealing here with abstract academic discourse; we are dealing with people's lives, with their freedom, and with their physical and mental integrity. We are also dealing with the survival of organizations which operate as an essential break on the juggernaut of state power. It is, perhaps, sufficient to note that the human rights of the average citizen are in far greater jeopardy when civil rights lawyers are killed with impunity; the threat to the unknown labourer rises dramatically when trade union leaders are disappeared, and peasants or indigenous fighting for land rights are more likely to be brutalized when their spokespersons are arrested and tortured. Human rights organizations, which monitor human rights violations, are vital to the attainment and maintenance of a political order in which the power elite is compelled to uphold the rule of law, to keep the political process open, to tolerate freedom of expression, and to respect the fundamental rights enshrined in the International Bill of Rights.

The question of devising new strategies and tactics for protecting those on the frontlines of the human rights struggle is complex because, before one can attempt to tackle it, it is necessary to try and answer at least four preliminary questions.

Human Rights Activist

Unlike card carrying party members, licenced professionals, or baptized Catholics, there is no particular membership, schooling, or initiation ceremony that marks an individual as a human rights worker, advocate or defender (as the activist is variously referred to). The human rights activist may be defined as an individual who has made a major commitment to, and openly and visibly taken up, the defense and promotion of the human rights of others. The activist is most easily identifiable when he or she is an officer or staff member of a recognized human rights organization. The Salvadorans, Herbert Ernesto Anaya, brutally slain in October 1987 while he was General Coordinator of the El Salvador Human Rights Commission and Dr. Segundo Montes, Director of the Institute for Human Rights of the Central American University Mose Simeon Canas", executed as ruthlessly two years later (in November 1989), were human right defenders. So too are Raja Shehadah, co-founder of the West Banks's Al-Haq (Law in the Service of Man) and his fieldworker. Shawan Jabarin, who spent a year in administrative detention for his monitoring.

But the term human rights defender encompasses a far greater and more diverse population, It includes lawyers, (sometimes not identified with a specific human rights NGO), who take on human rights cases, defend political prisoners, or publicly challenge repressive legislation. Kenyan lawyers, Gibson Kamau Kuria and Kiraitu Murungi, both recently forced into exile to escape arrest or a worse fate, are examples. Thongpai Thongpao, in Thailand, who for many years was almost the only Thai lawyer prepared to provide free legal assistance to political prisoners; the late Jose Diokno, who founded FLAG (the Free Legal Assistance Group of the Civil Liberties Union of the Philippines); or Emilio Mignone of CELS (the Center for Legal and Social Studies) of Argentina, are all examples, One should note perhaps, that lawyers, disproportionate to their number, have been in the forefront of the human rights struggle, whether acting alone, through bar associations, or in leadership roles in human rights organizations.

Human rights defenders also include journalists and writers who use their pens to expose violations. The New York-based Committee to Protect Journalists publishes an annual report on members of the press who have been censored, harassed, threatened, imprisoned, tortured or killed for daring to speak truth to power. Editors, publishers, poets, novelists and song writers may fall within this category. Some here may remember that Chilean guitarist and song writer, Victor Jara, was seen as such a threat to the junta that, in the Soccer Stadium in Santiago, the military broke each of his fingers one by one before killing him. A special category of defenders are those who have come together to form groups of the families of political prisoners, detained, disappeared or executed people: the Mothers of the Plaza de Mayo in Argentina provided the model of this type of association. Others which subsequently formed include the Grandmothers of the Plaza de Mayo, the CO-MADRES of El Salvador, FIND and KAPATID in the Philippines, and the GAM (Group of Mutual Assistance) in Guatemala. Latin Americans subsequently created a federation - FEDEFAM - of the groups of relatives to provide a measure of coordination and support among them. The leaders of such groups - which have often been the first or, at times, the sole voice of protest in exceedingly repressive situations, have been particularly vulnerable to suffer the same as their loved ones on whose behalf they organized.

Human rights defenders include a large number of persons from diverse professions and sectors of society. They include, for example, medical doctors who have refused to collaborate with, and have publicly denounced the complicity of doctors in the administration of torture or psychiatric abuse. Today defenders includes forensic doctors prepared to perform autopsies on persons who are alleged to have died under torture or to exhume mass graves in the hope of identifying bodies of the disappeared; and geneticists trying to match missing children with their grandparents. It includes prestigious scientists: the title Andre Sakharov, exited to Gorki for refusing to remain silent in the face of Soviet abuses, and Chinese astro-physicist Fang India, who used his prestige support the pro-democracy movement are only the best known of such scientists. Religious leaden have been prominent as human rights defenders, sometimes heading up human rights organizations (as with Sister Mariani Dimarnan of Task Force Detainees of the Philippines, Adolfo Perez Esquivel of the Service for Justice and Peace, or Luis Perez Aguirre of SERPAJ-Uruguay) and sometimes simply using the pulpit, as did the martyred Archbishop Romero. In Tibet, Burma and Vietnam, monks have been in the forefront of protests against tyranny. Trade unionists, peasant leaders, student leaders, the leaders of indigenous groups, activists from women's movements, children's rights activists, anti-apartheid leaders-all these may fall within the circle encompassed by the word "defender" if they are championing the human rights of others and trying to hold power structures accountable for infringement of internationally recognized human rights standards.

Non-Governmental Human Rights Organizations

A human rights NGO is a private association and which devotes significant resources to the promotion and protection of human rights, which is independent of both government and all political groups which seek direct political power, and which does not itself seek such power. This is not to deny that the human rights struggle is, in essence, a highly political struggle, It would be naive to assume that one can hold governments accountable to human rights norms with purely moral argument, especially in situations of intense conflict. Total autonomy and independence may be an ideal which is aspired to-as with Amnesty International-thought achieved more or less imperfectly, since an organization's membership base, funding, and ideology inevitably influence its political posture. However, the foundation stone of human rights monitoring is political non-partisanship. The legitimacy and the credibility of it human rights organization rests in large part on the objectivity of its fact-finding and the Integrity with which it applies international human rights standards. A group that allies itself with government or opposition, seeks political power and office for itself, or subordinates human rights concerns to other political objectives— no matter how noble—has moved beyond the compass of human rights work. Having said this, it is important to realize that, it is the ideals of the human rights movement that have gained greater and greater legitimacy, and as these ideals have increasingly become identified in the late 1980s with the struggle for democratic processes. A broad spectrum of organizations - including political parties, professional associations, trade unions, religious bodies, ethnic organizations, and a wide array of private interest groups - have become engaged in human rights debates, issues and struggles. Some of these organizations have established special human rights committees; others have written human rights planks into larger platforms or agendas. Any one of these groups may be an important actor in the human rights arena as, of course, are governmental and inter-governmental organizations with specific human rights mandates. All contribute to the political pluralism that is a counterpoise to the centralizing tendencies of the modern state.

Any of these groups may become a significant ally for a human rights organization in a particular battle, What distinguishes a human rights NGO from other political actors is that the latter are, typically, seeking to protect the rights of only their own members or constituents; a human rights group seek to secure the rights for all members of the society. A political group seeks to advance its own particular interests or programs; a human rights groups seeks to keep the political process open to all legitimate societal forces. Governments have used a wide range of tactics and strategies in an effort to suppress human rights organizations and their leaders. These have ranged from the detention and incarceration of activists in prisons and psychiatric institutions, usually without trial or in kangaroo trials; disappearances or extra-legal executions through the surrogates of death squads, paramilitary and vigilantes; death threats; labeling such groups as subversive and denying them the right to register or banning them after they have been established; censoring what they can say or what the media can say about them, denying them access to newsprint or the broadcast media; harassing them with legal proceedings, with unwarranted searches and seizures, and oppressive surveillance of the activists or members of their families; cutting off their access to domestic and especially foreign funding; interferring with their mail and depriving them of their passports - the list is limited only by the imagination of the oppressors. The human rights movement as we know it today is approximately 20 years old. Although its origins reach back to the last century, it is essentially a post World War II movement, and it is really in the 1970s that it took on its present characteristics: viz. a movement made up of independent national, regional and international NGOs which seek to hold governments accountable to internationally defined standards of human rights. It is a highly diverse movement that has now spread into every continent and comprises thousands of organizations which approximate, to a greater or lesser degree, the model of an independent human rights NGO. The universe of actors is many times greater still if one adds on the ancilliary interest groups and associations that are actively engaged in human rights conflicts but are political, actively engaged in human rights conflicts but are political, rather than human rights organizations. In its two decades of existence, and most consciously in the last decade, a number of strategies and tactics have been used-with varying degrees of success-to try and provide some measure of protection to human rights defenders, and to human rights organizations at risk because of their human rights work, since each tactic of repressive requires some appropriate protective counter measure, the movement has been engaged in a wide range of defensive practices. Thus, the enumeration which follows is intended to be illustrative, rather than definitive, but the methodologies employed can be broadly divided into three categories: The strategy of Public Exposure and Pressure; (2) The Strategy of Quiet Diplomacy; and (3) Technical and Infra-structural support and solidarity.

The Strategy of Public Exposure and Pressure

This strategy proceeds from the premise that, with some notable exceptions-e.g., China in Tiananmen Square, Romania's Ceaucescu in the period prior to her fall, the white apartheid regime prior to the de Klerk regime-governments today are reluctant to be seen to be engaged in repressing human rights defenders or human rights NGOs. It is disturbing to contemplate that the governmental practice of "disappearance" may have emerged in response to the success achieved by the human rights movement in attaching public vilification to governments which locked up large numbers of political prisoners. By using death squads and paramilitary to "disappear" the opposition or to torture opponents in secret prisons, governments could claim "plausible deniability" - they are not involved, they assume no responsibility. It is also disturbing to recognize that governments may be more likely to hire an expensive public relations firm to clean tip their image as did the Argentine Generals during the "dirty war" when, in 1978, they turned to the Madison Avenue firm of Burson Marsteller-than they are to alter their behavior. In recent years, governments have also become sophisticated enough to try to impugn the credibility of the human rights monitors not merely by labelling them as "subversive" (as has been the practice in situations as disparate as the Philippines, India, and South Africa), or by disputing their "facts" (as the El Salvadoran government did With Socoro Juridico in the early 1980's), but by producing their own human rights reports using all the appropriate international human rights language and symbolism. Nonetheless, human rights NGOs must still operate on the assumption that the threat of public exposure is a vital deterrent. It is more effective where the government is sensitive to international public opinion and particularly effective when a government fears that such exposure is likely to lead to a cut off of vital economic or military aid. It may also be effective if the government believes it will lead to black-listing by the UN Commission on Human Rights, an unfavorable report by the Inter-American or European Commission on Human Rights, or condemnation by some other august body. In this sense, timing may be crucial. A report issued just prior to the US certification of El Salvador (as having a good enough human rights record to qualify for military assistance) is likely to be far more effective than the same report issued after the certification process has been concluded.

Fact-Finding Missions and Reports

Accurate and credible information is still the most potent

weapon in the human rights NGO arsenal. Where human rights monitors are under threat, getting the facts and getting them out to the media, to sympathetic governments, to international human rights bodies is almost always the first line of defense. To the extent that one can shine a spotlight on those in danger, that may provide some measure of protection. It is not as good as a bullet-proof vest and it does not always work, but it is an important tactic.

There are a number of variations of importance. The fact-finding mission and report may be simply a staff mission and report. If it is the product of a credible organization-Amnesty International, the International Commission of Jurists, the Watch Committees, the International Federation of Human Rights that may be enough. In other situations, it may be helpful to increase the impact of the report by having the mission headed by, or conducted by, political heavy-weights-parliamentarians, distinguished jurists, Nobel laureates. If the person at risk is a doctor, a mission from a medical association may be most effective; if he is a writer, a delegation including publishers, Pulitzer prize winners, or journalists may cut the most ice. Human rights NGOs have increasingly come to recognize that mobilizing distinguished professional colleagues of the person at risk may be a highly effective means both of capturing media attention and staying the hand of repressive regimes. They have also come to recognize that producing a good report is only the first step in the process; the second, and equally important step, is getting it into the hands of those who are opinion makers, who have political clout, and who will act upon the basis of the information provided.

Urgent Action Networks

The Urgent Action Network, an idea first developed by Amnesty International in 1976, is a tactic intended to permit an immediate and dramatic response to a situation where there is a grave risk that someone will be tortured or killed and where time is of the essence. AI's Urgent Action (UA) Network consists of members who agree to be "on call" to send immediate appeals regarding impending or actual cases of human rights violations. UA appeals are telexed, faxed or mailed from the International Secretariat to Urgent Action coordinators in different countries, who then send the appeal to groups and individuals, Urgent Action participants are asked to send telegrams or letters to the authorities in the countries concerned. When appropriate, appeals by specialist groups, such as health workers, lawyers, or trade unionists are requested. There now exist perhaps two dozen or more urgent action networks, with some variation on the basis model. There are UA networks where members agree in advance to permit telegrams to be automatically sent in their name for certain types of cases. There are networks that are country specific, as with the Christian Urgent Action Network for Emergency Relief in the Philippines. Others are professionally specific as with the Centre for the Independence of Judges and Lawyers, the Lawyers Committee for Human Rights, Physicians for Human Rights, Index on Censorship and the Committee to Protect Journalists. In many instances, an urgent action might result in several hundred or more telegrams or faxes landing on the desk of the Head of State within a 24 hour period. That may be warning enough to call off the executioner or the torturer. One UA network which merits special mention is SOS Torture. Intended to compliment the Amnesty UA Network, SOS Torture is a clearinghouse comprised of member organizations concerned with the rapid dissemination of information relating to torture, summary executions, disappearances and psychiatric internment for political purposes. Unlike AI, which itself verifies all information received from others, SOS Torture-in the interest of speed-sends out information from network members without such verification, relying on the accuracy of its member organizations. SOS argues that the occasional error that may result is more than justified by the increased response time gained for, with torture, it is usually the first hours after the victim is arrested that are the most dangerous. In this context, it is worth noting that modern communications technology-including E-mail and the Fax-has served to make possible an even more rapid turn around time. In 1988, when there were sweeping arrests of social activists in Malaysia, an urgent action network based on E-mail was coordinated from Hong Kong. And in June 1989 at the time of the crackdown in Tiananmen Square, a group of Chinese activists in Massachusetts kept a telephone line to Beijing open for 24 hours, immediately relaying the information they were receiving to the international press while simultaneously keeping activists all across China informed about Tiananmen Square developments by sending news bulletins to fax machines in business offices all over the country. One other USA network that should be noted is that of the Congressional Friends of Human Rights Monitors of the US Congress. Established in the early 1980s as a bi-partisan group with the specific aim of providing support and protection for human rights monitors, the Congressional Friends can send out letters or telegrams over the signatures of-Congressmen and- Senators. Over the past ... years, the Friends has made appeals on behalf of... The model has been duplicated to some extent by urgent action from groups of parliamentarians in other countries.

Human Rights Awards

A third tactic, of rather more recent vintage, is the human rights award, intended to focus media attention on human rights defenders, especially those at risk. There are now 10 or more major awards given out annually in the US-most notably, the Robert F. Kennedy, Carter DeMenil, Reebok, Letelier-Moffitt and the Rothko Chapel awards-and twice or three times that number internationally (including awards by the Council of Europe and UNESCO). Some are given to individuals, some to organizations; they may or may not involve a monetary value. There is increasing evidence to suggest that such awards can play extremely important role in providing defenders and NGOs with legitimacy, credibility, visibility and-because of this-some degree of protection in their work. The Kennedy Award last year to Fang Lizhi undoubtedly played a role in getting the astrophysicist who had taken shelter at the US Embassy out of China.

Accompaniment

Accompaniment-where foreigners escort threatened leaders of human rights organizations, trade unions and peasant organizations, and maintain a watchful presence at demonstrations and in the workplace-is a technique .' first introduced into the human rights movement in Gautemala in 1985 by FBI, Peace Brigades International. PBI was founded in Canada in 1981 by veterans of the Gandhian movement for non-violent change, and is modeled in part on the Shanti Sena-Gandhi's "peace army"-that worked to try and stop Hindu-Muslim violence in post-independent India. PBI, which had been operating in Gautemala since 1983, was convinced that Nineth de Garcia, President of GAM, would be murdered-about a dozen GAM members had been killed since the group was founded-and that human rights work in Guatemala would have to stop unless some means was found to provide at least a modicum of protection for the defenders. Accompaniment began with GAM and was then extended to Amilcar Mendez of CERJ (Ethnic Communities

United in Total Equality), and to other human rights leaders. In 1987 it was introduced into El Salvador, and this past year it was extended to Sri Lanka, Since the program began, more than 275 volunteers have served in Central America, with volunteers serving stints of from two weeks to over 18 months. All PBI volunteers are training in non-violence, all are committed to political "neutrality" for the period of their service. They serve as human shields and, especially, as watchful eyes and cars armed with only a camera. During this period, they are prohibited from engaging in solidarity work themselves. The theory behind accompaniment-which seems to have been validated by praxis-is that the authorities and the paramilitary will hesitate before trying to kill or disappear human rights activists in the presence of foreign witnesses. The technique, is, of course, costly, and PBI volunteers can only provide cover for a small number of leaders. As a consequence, GAM has tried to operate its own program of accompaniment with volunteers who do not get the same intensive training as that offered by PBI-to have additional "peace bodyguards" on call

One interesting variant on the accompaniment technique was recently tested in Guatemala by former PBI volunteers. It involved leafleting tourists in Guatemala, informing them of a strike that was taking place, and asking that they go to the factory to provide a foreign and visible presence, so that the authorities would be reluctant to send in good squads to crush the strike. And apparently, as long as large numbers of foreign tourists did stand a vigil, no action was taken against the strikers. But the vigil could only be sustained for a short period and the strike was busted after the tourists were gone. Discussions are however, underway to explore this strategy further.

12

SOME NOTABLE NGOs

An Association of Human Rights Defenders

This leads to the possibility of considering the establishment of an association of human rights defenders as a mechanism for increasing protection. A number of years ago, there was one attempt (within the UNESCO framework) to establish an association of human rights educators. That effort failed for a variety of reasons, perhaps because the movement was not well enough developed yet. Now, however, I believe that such an effort might be possible, but generalized beyond educators to human rights activists. And, this World Congress might be, able to provide the framework in which such an association-a trade union or at least a union of human rights defenders-might be established.

A High Commissioner or Ombudsman for Human Rights

At a rather more ambitious level, with the changed international environment, it might be possible to consider a proposal made many years ago by the Government of Costa Rica, to establish a new international mechanism: a High Commissioner (or Ombudsman for Human Rights)-an Office that had the authority for rapid intervention on behalf of threatened individuals and groups, Failing that, one should at least attempt to push for a greater role of such officials as the Secretary General of the United Nations, who has never to the best of my knowledge used his Good Offices to intervene on behalf of human rights activists in danger; or the Chairpersons of the UN Commission and Sub-Commission, or relevant officials of the regional human rights bodies. In this regard, one should also note the anomaly that, at present, the only regions of the world which do not have human rights machinery are Asia and the Middle East. The time may be auspicious to devote greater efforts to exploring the possibilities of Asian and Middle Eastern human rights bodies.

Greater Access to International Machinery for Human Rights Defenders

A fourth tactic to consider is how to provide greater access to international human rights bodies to human right NGOs, especially national NGOs. At present, the United Nations and its organs are remote from many national human rights NGOs not merely because of the distance, or the cost of attending UN meetings, or even the lack of information about what is happening in those august bodies-although all of these are critical factors-but also because the UN structure is such that only international NGOs have Consultative Status and therefore the possibility of fully participating .' in the work of such organs. The UN Working Group on Indigenous Populations (a Working Group of the Sub-Commission) which opened itself up to all indigenous peoples' groups, whether or not they had Consultative Status, was a radical and innovative departure in this regard. It means that such groups have direct access, and are not required to have to go through the intermediary of an international NGO, which tends to create a paternalistic dependency between front line national organizations and international human rights NGOs.

And, at the regional level, all efforts should be made to have the African and Inter-American Commission (and any other regional bodies created) recognize the importance of the work of, and accord protection to, 'human rights organization and their leaders.

Human Rights Fund for Defenders

This might be used to enable fact-finding missions to be rapidly deployed when activists are in threat and a mission might save them; or to provide funds for their legal defense, if they are arrested; or to provide funds to enable activists to attend international meetings of significance. How such a fund would be administered, who could draw on it, and when these are technical issues that could, I think, be resolved, and might again (or could again) be linked to the idea suggested above about an association of human rights defenders.

None of these ideas will, of course, provide the ultimate protection and human rights defenders will always be at risk because challenging those who wield power is always dangerous. It, however, behooves us to try and do outmost to make it impossible for governments to threaten the work of human rights organizations and their leaders.

Final Reflections

Even since the Universal Declaration of Human Rights in 1948, the human rights has been recognized in all countries and the 50th Anniversary provides the ideal opportunity to take practical steps to achieve the common standards for all peoples and nations. It is unfortunate that total disregard and contempt for human rights have resulted in barbarous acts which have outraged the conscience of mankind. In an attempt to secure the goals of human rights declaration, NGOs in India are joining together with government agencies to spread awareness on human rights issue to the common man's reach. Violation of human rights is not a new phenomenon in Indian society. In rural areas, its magnitude is very high. A large section of India's population has been living in rural areas. These areas have been neglected in terms of development and awareness on various aspects as compared to urban areas. Although policy makers, social scientist and a group of nongovernmental organization (NGOs) have been playing a tremendous role for its promotion. Yet it remains as nostalgia to the common man. Rural masses are far away from the mainstream of social development. Low literacy levels among them can be adduced as one of the major reasons for its lagging behind.

As a consequence they have to face the onslaught of exploitation of civil rights as well as human rights. By 'human rights' we mean the rights and dignity as has been enshrined in the Constitution of India. The Universal Declaration of Human Rights (UDHR) proclaims that "all human being are born free and equal in dignity and rights". The basic objective of human rights can not be fulfilled if the rural masses are not aware and educated on basic parameters pertaining to health education and other rights. Under this circumstance a large number of non-government organizations (NGOs) have been coming forward to undertake the herculean task of promoting human rights at the grass-roots level particularly in rural areas. This present article is an attempt to highlight the various approach of NGOs that have been initiated in order to promote human rights in the subcontinents.

Non-governmental Organization (NGOs) embrace a bewildering group of organization varying in terms of innumerable parameters. No standard definition can include all organization under the caption - NGO' Essentially, volunterism is a doctrine which held that the will is a dominant factor or it is a principle relying on one's own free will for an action. Voluntary efforts stood for services independent of State. 'Volunteer ' is a person who offered one's services spontaneously without external incentives. His/her work is conscious, automatic and instinctive. A voluntary organization is a conglomeration of volunteers joining hands together with shared values of concern for a specific goal. The raison de'tre of a voluntary organization is based on the principle of interest of a group constituting the organization. They can function based on general interest of a group which formed the organization. Thus a voluntary organization can be private or public based on the interests they serve. The Vigil India Movement, Citizen for Democracy, Association for Protection of Democratic Rights and PRAYAS are some of the prominent organizations working towards India's initiative as far as human rights promotion is concerned.

The Vigil India Movement

This has been rendering good service to the promotion of human rights in the country in a manner which is uniquely its own. It was founded in 1977 at White field near Bangalore. In early stages, the main emphasis of the organisation was to organize training programmes on Socio-economic and political issues in human rights perspective. The impact of the programme gets reflected in remote rural areas. People belonging to a cross-section of society are members of the society. The Vigil India movement's activities are manifold. In 1978 Vigil India movement along with other organizations raised its voice against Preventive Detention Laws (PDL). In 1979, a nationwide signature campaign was organized to press the Government for the ratification of the operational protocol of the International

Conference on Civil and Political Rights. Vigil India has championed the cause of the Adivasis in the Agasthyakoodam forest of Kerala. The organization is also involved in several other issues affecting the Adivasis by its campaign against the ecologically disastrous Agasthyavanam Bio-logical park in Kerala.

Citizen for Democracy

It is a sister voluntary organization of People's Liberty of Civil Rights located at Aligarh district of Uttar Pradesh and promoting human rights activities specially among the minority communities. Their activities include organizing seminars, conferences, street-plays, folk-dances at community level. Institute of Objective Studies, a Delhi-based organization has been working in collaboration with CFD in the field of human rights promotion in India. This organization has been engaged in publishing newsletters, conducting seminars and research work in the field of human rights in India. The IOS has recently launched a crash course for dedicated volunteers in order to promote the human rights in and around the country.

Association for Protection of Democratic Rights

A West Bengal based organization has been working in the field of human rights promotion since 1960. This organization is working to promote the various constitutional rights which has been violated by the police. Moreover this organization has been publishing newsletters in local language and for advocacy activities. Organizing rallies, exhibitions, lecture are some of the prominent initiatives of its sensitisation programme.

Prayas

Prayas, established in 1988, has made a major dent and emerged as a reputed organization in the field of child welfare and human rights. This organization with a model character prescribes a clear direction towards the achievement of juvenile justice in human rights perspective. The philosophy on which Prayas works towards human rights is that children's rights are synonymous to their needs. The recent transfer of juvenile home at Delhi Gate by government of Delhi to Prayas calls for a radical initiative on the part of NGOs in government's policy towards juvenile justice.

In addition, South Asian Coalition on Child Servitude (SACCS), World Vision (India) and the Society for the Promotion of Youth and Masses (SPYM) has been working on human rights in specific areas such as girl child rights, women's rights, etc. No doubt, in the field of promotion of human rights In the rural areas, voluntary organisations contributions are acknowledgeable and of paramount importance. The role of NGOs can be traced in this connection in different manner. Due to failure of political democracy and instability of government machinery, the human rights activities can get affected. The NGOs are more flexible and they have committed, dedicated workers maintaining transparency and accountability in their work. India's commitment to protection of human rights has been a cardinal issue in all the development programmes. The Government, Voluntary organizations and the people at large need to work 'in unison and play a more proactive role as partners and watchdogs in promoting human rights at all levels.

Universal Declaration of Human Rights. At the centre of this education and advocacy campaign is a national human rights Action Agenda that the Institute successfully negotiated with the participation of a diverse group of organizations drawn from a broad cross-section of civil society. The campaign theme - IN YOUR HANDS - echoes Eleanor Roosevelt's belief that "the destiny of human rights is in the hands of all our citizens in all our communities." The coalition has established an interactive website for the Fiftieth Anniversary of the Universal Declaration. The site offers information, news, a calendar of activities, and opportunities for advocacy throughout the anniversary year. An interactive, historical overview of the Universal Declaration of Human Rights is provided for educators, organizers, activists and students. The site also profiles each member of the coalition and provides a web link. A human rights education section, complete with document library, adds to the site's extensive resources. The coalition has also prepared a community action guide called "in Your Hands" for the anniversary. The guide offers 'fifty actions for the fiftieth' - based on the coalition's action agenda. These activities, aimed at ending human rights violations, can be undertaken by local chapters of national organizations, by schools, churches and other community groups. The booklet will be distributed to community organizations throughout the United States. Other resources include a National Human Rights Speakers' Bureau and email lists for news and action alerts (open to subscribers throughout the world).

The following were the initiatives undertaken by various non-governmental organisations in 1998 in connection with the celebration of the 50th anniversary of the Universal Declaration of Human Rights.

Hong Kong Human Rights Monitor

- Launching the worlds first Chinese language database of human rights treaties on the internet.

Human Rights Education Centre of Charles University

- Chairing and developing long term educational project: "Education for the culture of Human Relations in the Multi-ethnic society of Central and Eastern Europe.

- The in-service training of teachers for human rights education.

Human Rights Watch (HRW)

- Organising Human Rights Watch International Film Festival (HR-WIFF)

The Asia - Pacific Human Rights Information Centre (Hrights Osaka)

- Promoting 50th Anniversary of the UDHR in its newsletters
- A Regional work shop to commemorate the 50th anniversary of UDHR in Osaka, Japan.
- Preparation of two publications on the Asian experience in developing human rights education as a component of the school programme.

Informal Sector Service Centre

- A discussion on the impact of Universal Declaration of Human Rights on the lives of the people.

International Institute of Human Rights

- A study session in international and comparative human rights Law.
- A two week Human Rights Pedagogical Training session.

Inter American Institute of Human Rights

- Conducting training courses for various target groups - the police, the armed force, NGOs and indigenous communities
- A special training programme for legal professionals.

International Movement Against All Forms of Discrimination and Racism (IMADR)

- IMADR attaches great importance to human rights education in its over all activities which include promotion of the rights of the persons subjected to racism or discrimination and for the creation of a human rights culture,
- Organising the annual seminar on "Promoting the United Nations decade for Human Rights Education and the 50th anniversary of the Universal Declaration of Human Rights.

Law - The Palestinian Society for the Protection of Human Rights and the Environment

- Organising a cultural competition for Palestinian artists as a means of strengthening the awareness and development of Palestinian cultural rights.

Marangopoulos Foundation for Human Rights

- Publication of the book entitled "Equality and Development: Fifty Years of UN contribution to their evolution".

Memorial - International Historical and Educational Human Rights Charity and Society

- A weekly radio programme: "Democracy, liberty and Human Rights".
- Inclusion of material on the theme: Human Rights: Yesterday, today and tomorrow in the Museum and Library.

Milan Simecka Foundation

- Human Rights education for both basic and secondary school teachers -10 training workshops.

- Human Rights education for secondary school students -6 training workshops.
- Introduction of human rights education component into a University course -6 training workshops.
- A series of articles on human rights.

Norwegian Human Rights House

- All schools are asked to take part in the commemoration by focusing on human rights in their work that year.
- Offering courses on human rights for teachers.
- Providing materials such as books.

Open Education Centre

1. National activities include:

- Preparation of a Human Rights Manual for High Schools;
- Organization of Olympic Games in a Human Rights Regional Competition (October/November) and National Competition (December);
- Organization of a National Debate Competition on Human Rights (November/December);
- National Human Rights Youth Festival (8-10 December), with the participation of young people from Macedonia and Romania;
- Minting a commemorative coin, National Commission for UNESCO;
- Publishing the Universal Declaration of Human Rights; Civic Education - Human Rights in small Bulgarian towns -this is a programme concerning comprehensive civic and human rights education in

the small Bulgarian towns and cities which are now thought to have been neglected in the different educational campaigns.

- National Seminar - The Right to Health - a basic Human Right (Sofia, April 1998).

2. International activities include:

- Debating for Human Rights - International seminar for teachers under the bursary scheme of the Council of Europe (24-28 May);
- Intercultural Education and Human Rights - international seminar for teachers under the bursary scheme of the Council of Europe (28 May/1 June);
- A Balkan Meeting on the 50th Anniversary of the Universal Declaration of Human Rights - Human Rights and the Fight against Violence in Schools (Sofia, 8-12 June 1998);
- Meeting of the Board of the International Center for Teaching Human Rights, Democracy and a Culture of Peace (1822 June);
- Summer University course on Human Rights and a Culture of Peace - 50th Anniversary of the Universal Declaration of Human Rights. Intercultural Education and Building a Culture of Peace (11-19 July),
- International Meeting "Sites for Citizenship" - under the auspices of the Council of Europe (16-20 September),
- Fourth International Conference under the auspices of UNESCO and the Bulgarian Ministry of Education and Science 50th Anniversary of the Universal Declaration of Human Rights and the Development of School Democracy (16-20 September).

Philippine Alliance of Human Rights Advocates (Pahra)

- International campaign to uphold universality especially in the Asian region, where tendencies towards "Asian values" oriented rights are being spread by Asian governments;
- Community based human rights courses are being undertaken in the light of the UN Decade for Human Rights Education. Particular targets are the indigenous peoples of the Philippines, the urban poor vulnerable to sudden evictions, and internally displaced families due to militarization;
- Local policy advocacy work of PAHRA hopes to effect the full institutionalization of human rights education in schools and universities throughout the Philippines.

Public Administration Institute for Turkey and the Middle East

- preparations for a comprehensive conference on issues, problems and the level of development of human rights in Turkey including human rights education (10-11 December 1998);
- conference on NGOs and Human Rights Education (September 1998). Participation and support to governmental agencies and institutions for:
- preparing and conducting human rights education seminars for the education of educators. The existing programme will be implemented on a continuing basis in 1998 for public servants in different ministries;
- effecting the panel discussion on human rights education for high schools and human rights in the family and in schools (15 January 1998);
- radio and television programmes on human rights education;

- education curricula that will include human rights as a course for primary and secondary schools, and the programmes developed for human rights educators by the Ministry of Education.

Raoul Wallenberg Institute of Human Rights and Humanitarian Law

The Raoul Wallenberg Institute of Human Rights and Humanitarian Law plans to implement and pursue the following initiatives:

- continuation of its academic programmes for the dissemination of human rights standards and democratic values in developing countries, funded by the Swedish International Development Cooperation Agency (SIDA). In 1998, several national and sub-regional seminars, courses and workshops are scheduled for different countries;
- in collaboration with SIDA, developing advanced academic training programmes in human rights, normally for 25-30 senior officials and academics. In 1998, a course of this kind will run for 5 weeks in Lund with participants from developing countries worldwide. Similar courses of 3-5 weeks duration will also be organized for participants on an individual country basis. Another annual course is focusing on the equal status and human rights of women;
- jointly with the Institute, Martinus Nijhoff Publishers (in the Kluwer Law International) have started two series of publications: each volume of "The Raoul Wallenberg Institute Guides" is a thematic guide to documents on human rights in a particular field. Volumes on human rights and health, and on minority

rights are scheduled for publication in 1998, In "The Raoul Wallenberg Institute Guides" series, studies are published on subjects related to the Institute's activities, including a compilation of international human rights instruments. Additional volumes are being compiled for 1998;

- the Institute has started to publish "General Comments or Recommendations adopted by United Nations Human Rights Treaty Bodies;"
- continuing support to academic law libraries in Africa and Asia.-16 institutions have received donations of books, periodicals and documents on public international law, with the main emphasis on human rights and humanitarian law. More academic institutions in developing countries will be included in this project in 1998. A similar project has also been initiated for criminal justice institutions in developing countries. In 1998, eight institutions will be provided with human rights material relevant to their activities.

Tavola Bella Pace

Tavola della Pace, in close collaboration with the United Nations Information Centre in Italy and the National Coordinating Committee of Local Authorities for Peace, has decided to commemorate the 50th Anniversary of the Universal Declaration of Human Rights by promoting a "National Human Rights Education Campaign." This initiative will involve hundreds of organizations, local and academic institutions.

- promote an extensive educational campaign throughout the country mainly focused on a more widespread understanding of human rights among the youth and a deeper commitment to uphold those rights;

- extend the network of permanent organizations and institutions at national level concerned with education in and the promotion of peace and human rights,
- promote the inclusion of a peace and human rights education component in the school syllabus at all levels and on a permanent basis;
- strengthen Italy's commitment to promote and defend human rights, within and outside the country and urge the creation of appropriate National Human Rights institutions as encouraged by the UN,

Programme initiatives undertaken during Human Rights Year include:

- setting up a secretariat within the Tavola della Pace intended to:
  - successfully activate educational initiatives in all the Town Councils on the theme of peace and human rights,
  - organize a national archive for coordinating and documenting all the initiatives to be carried out in the course of the year.
  - collaborate in distributing material on themes of peace and human rights and the commemoration.of the 50th Anniversary,
  - organize the effective cooperation and the exchange of information and documents on a regular basis with the United Nations High Commissioner for Human Rights (New York-Geneva), the University of Padua Research and Training Centre on the rights of the individual

and of peoples, the United Nations Information Centre in Rome and all other national, European and world institutions involved in the commemoration of the 50th Anniversary of the Universal Declaration.of Human Rights-,

- September/November 1998: organization of an "International Forum for a Human Rights Culture and Policy" Perugia:
- September/November 1998: organization of a National Human Rights meeting in Assisi - presentation of projects developed by schools;
- November 1998: National exhibition of books and videos on human rights and peace-Perugia;
- December 1998: commemoration of the 50th Anniversary of the Universal Declaration of Human Rights. Presentation of projects on the theme of Human Rights Year for implementation by schools and other organizations;
- organization of a competition for students with the focus on Article 1 of the Universal Declaration of Human Rights
- dissemination of the proposal "An act of peace in each school" in all schools for the protection of human rights,
- dissemination of the following publications: -Universal Declaration of Human Rights;
    - International Covenants on Human Rights;
    - Final declaration and Programme of Action adopted at the World Human Rights Conference in Vienna,
    - Textbook for students at the primary, secondary and high school levels;

- An Atlas of Hope (pinpointing the major problems of our time and the organizations involved in promoting human rights in the world);
- 13 educational charts emphasizing problems linked to the globalization of the economy and to social and economic rights in particular.

13

Red Cross and Red Crescent

Caring for the wounded in war, helping the mentally and physically handicapped, visiting detainees, bringing relief to earthquake victims, restoring contact between relatives separated by conflict, giving courses in child care and hygiene, encouraging blood donation, protecting the population in occupied territory -the activities are diverse, but they all have one purpose: to help those who suffer, without discrimination.

More than 125 years after Henry Dunant's humanitarian action on the battlefield of Solferino, the International Red Cross and Red Crescent Movement is universal: it has over 250 million members and volunteer workers and is active in nearly every country in the world.

A Man, a Book and an Idea

On 24 June 1859, the armies of imperial Austria and the Franco-Sardinian alliance fought a day-long battle near the northern Italian village of Solferino. The casualties were heavy - some 40,000 dead, wounded or missing. Military medical services at the time were virtually non-existent; as a result there ' was great suffering and many of the wounded died for lack of care.

The injured were brought to the surrounding villages

for whatever treatment they could get. In the church at Castiglione, a young Swiss called Henry Dunant, horrified by the agony of the soldiers, began to organize help with the aid of the local people.

Returning home to Geneva, still haunted by what he had seen, he wrote a book about his experience. "A Memory of Solferino", published in 1862, was acclaimed throughout Europe. In it, Dunant put forward an idea for supplementing army medical services in times of war. This would be done through national relief societies which, in peacetime, would train their Voluntary members for this work. Dunant also proposed that the wounded, and all those attending them, should be regarded as neutral, even on the battlefield.

To help promote the alms of the book, four citizens of Geneva -Gustave Moynier, General Guillaume-Henri Dufour, Dr. Louis Appia and Dr. Theodore Maunoir - joined Dunant in setting up the "International Committee for Relief to the Wounded", which later became the International Committee of the Red Cross (ICRC).

In response to an invitation from the International Committee, specialists from 16 countries met in Geneva in October 1863. They adopted ten resolutions that made up the founding charter of the Red Cross, defining the functions and working methods of the Committees for the Relief of the Wounded which Dunant had proposed. Thus the Red Cross was born.

A convention is Signed in Geneva

For the International Committee, the major task still lay ahead: persuading governments that the wounded and those caring for them should not be considered adversaries, since they were not - or no longer - taking part in the fighting, and therefore needed protection. This concept of neutrality would have to be embodied in an international treaty providing for a protective emblem to be used by all armies, to identify medical personnel, hospitals and ambulances.

To this end the Swiss Government undertook to convene, in Geneva, a diplomatic conference, to be held in August 1864. Delegates of 12 governments took part, and adopted a draft treaty prepared by the International Committee. The agreement was called the "Geneva Convention for the Amelioration of the Condition of the Wounded in Armies in the Field".

This treaty, with its ten articles, was a milestone in the history of humanity. War and law had, until then, been considered irreconcilable. The founders of the Red Cross argued, however, that law could apply even during war, and could regulate, in certain respects, the conduct of soldiers.

From then on ambulances, military hospitals and medical staff were to be recognised as neutral and, as such, protected and respected by the belligerents... Wounded or sick combatants, to whatever nation they belong, shall be collected and cared for".

At the same time the red cross on a white ground (the Swiss flag reversed), which had been adopted 'in 1863 as the symbol of the embryo Red Cross movement, was incorporated in the treaty as the protective emblem of the military medical services.

The Emblem

The emblem of a red cross on a white ground was created with a specific purpose: to ensure the protection of those wounded in war and those who care for them. Any abuse of this sign instituted by the Geneva Convention of 1864 - for example, by transporting armed troops in an ambulance, or by flying a red cross flag over a munitions dump - is not only a breach of international law but also threatens the very notion of protection granted by the emblem.

To prevent such breaches, States party to the Geneva Conventions must A issue strict regulations on the use of the emblem. It may only be displayed on vehicles, aircraft, ships, buildings and installations assigned to transport and shelter the wounded, and by the personnel who care for them. It is forbidden to use the emblem for commercial or publicity purposes.

National Red Cross and Red Crescent Societies, on the other hand, are allowed to use the emblem to identify their premises, vehicles and equipment, as well as for their members, who often wear a uniform or badge. In this case the emblem must be small, so as not to be confused with the wartime protective sign.

The 1864 Convention mentioned only the red cross. A second emblem made 'its appearance a few years later, and is still in use - the red crescent. The cross had been adopted as a tribute to Switzerland, and had not been intended to have any religious significance, in 1876, however, during the Russo-Turkish war, the ottoman Society for Relief to the Wounded replaced it by a red crescent.

This emblem has since been adopted by a number of countries in the Islamic world. It is recognized as having equal status with the red cross, and as such is mentioned in the 1949 Geneva Conventions and their Additional Protocols,

A Movement Becomes Universal

The members of the founding committee in Geneva, anxious to make full use of the tide of good will on which the movement had been launched, lost no time in encouraging the formation of relief committees. Such was their zeal, and so great the enthusiasm for the Red Cross idea, that within ten years national committees had been established in 22 European states. It was not long before the universal appeal of a humanitarian organisation free- from racial, cultural, religious and political bias, led to the spreading of the movement beyond the confines of Europe to the Americas, the Far East and Africa.

To ensure cohesion, the new national committees (which became known as National Red Cross Societies) had to be formed according to established and accepted rules. To this end a proper procedure for recognition was introduced. New Societies had to convince the ICRC, as founder of the movement -and custodian of its principles, that certain conditions had been root. In their present form, the conditions state that a Society must:

1. Be constituted on the territory of an independent State where the Geneva Convention for the Amelioration of the Condition of the Wounded and Sick in Armed Forces in the Field is in force.
2. Be the only National Red Cross or Red Crescent Society of the said State and be directed by a central body which shall alone be competent to represent it in its dealings with other components of the Movement.
3. Be duly recognized by the legal government of 'its country on the basis of the Geneva Conventions and of the national legislation as a voluntary aid society, 'auxiliary to the public authorities in the humanitarian
4. Have an autonomous status which allows i to operate

in conformity with the Fundamental Principles of the Movement.

5. Use the name and emblem of the Red Cross or Red Crescent in conformity with the Fundamental Principles of the Movement.
6. Be so organized as to be able to fulfil the tasks defined in its own statutes, including the preparation in peace time for its statutory tasks in case of armed conflict.
7. Extend its activities to the entire territory of the State.
8. Recruit its voluntary members and its staff without consideration of race, sex, class, religion or political opinions.
9. Adhere to the present Statutes share in the fellowship which unites the components of the Movement and co-operate with them.
10. Respect the Fundamental Principles of the Movement and be guided in its work by the principles of international humanitarian law.

A new Society has to be recognized by the ICRC before it can become a member of the League of Red Cross and Red Crescent Societies.

Today there are National Societies in almost every country in the world, with more than 250 million members; they are all united by the same ideals and, a major factor in ensuring unity, by the same statutes and operating rules.

The National Red Cross and Red Crescent Societies:

Originally created for service in time of war, to help the army medical personnel care for the wounded and he sick, the National Red Cross and red Crescent Societies today carry out a wide range of activities in both war and peace.

This development reflects the fact hat military medical services have improved dramatically since the time of Solferino, and also that civilians have increasingly become victims of hostilities, as conflicts are no longer confined to the battlefield.

The National Societies' wartime role as auxiliary to the armed forces' medical units remains essential- but is now just one of many aspects of heir work.

New Activities

After the First World War it was widely believed for a time that war was a thing of the past. Nation Societies wanted to put the training and experience their members have gained during the conflict to use in other ways. Their first objective was to attend to the urgent medical an social needs of populations ravage by the conflict. From then on, Red Cross work has expanded into man spheres of medico-social activity. The National Societies came to play an important role in founding hospitals, training nurses, carrying out education programmes in child care and public health, in pioneering ambulance, mountain and sea rescue services, providing first aid training and caring for the elderly and the handicapped.

Nearly every Society has its Youth section, encouraging even the very young to learn and practise useful skills and to develop early on a sense of humanitarian responsibility. The promotion of blood transfusion services is a vital task for all National Societies.. In some countries National Societies are in full charge of national blood programmes, while in others they frequently have a supporting role, for example in recruiting voluntary donors.

Since the Second World War the National Societies in industrialised countries have further widened their field of activities to help tackle social problems like drug addiction, unemployment and delinquency. In developing countries the National Societies work for improved health and welfare, engaging in projects to combat unnecessarily fatal infantile diseases, give basic health education, mount intensive vaccination campaigns and provide training for medical and social administrators.

A major new challenge faced by many countries in the 1980's, especially in the Third World, has been the enormous increase in numbers of refugees. National Societies are, in many cases, in the front line of providing relief and social services to the new arrivals.

Perhaps one of the oldest peacetime activities of the National Societies is that of helping victims of natural disasters: for this emergency work, as for other aspects of the National Societies' activities, outside support and resources are often needed,- these are typically supplied through the League -of Red Cross and Red Crescent Societies.

The League of Red Cross and Red Crescent Societies

At the end of the First World War large areas of Europe were in chaos -economies had been destroyed, populations were being decimated by epidemics, vast numbers of destitute refugees and stateless people roamed the continent. National Societies turned their attention to helping famine victims and the homeless, especially in eastern Europe.

Few countries had health ministries at the time, and there were no real international bodies capable of organizing large-scale relief operations. Yet it was the creation of one such international organization, the League of Nations, that led to a major development in the Red Cross,

One of the leaders of the American Red Cross, Henry P. Davison, convened an international medical conference in 1919 at which he proposed "to federate the Red Cross Societies of the different countries into an organization comparable to that of the League of Nations, 'in view of a permanent worldwide crusade to improve health, prevent sickness and alleviate suffering"

Davison's proposal gained immediate support- the League of Red Cross Societies was established; with headquarters in Paris. Since 1939 'its permanent home has been in Geneva.

The League's role is to inspire and support the work of its members, and help them to develop their activities. It also supports the ICRC in the development and dissemination of international humanitarian law and the promotion of Red Cross Principles. Through its work the League seeks to maintain and promote peace.

A Catalyst

Among its member Societies, the League acts as both catalyst and coordinator. It is a forum for ideas and for the exchange of experience between the Societies.

The League contributes to the development of new National Societies by providing advisers, equipment and, at times, subsidies. Here, the League acts in co-operation with longer-established Societies able to share their expertise, assistance is also given to Societies in formation, that are still working towards official recognition and League membership.

A crucial part of the League's work is in providing and co-ordinating assistance to victims of natural disasters and epidemics. Since 1923, when an earthquake in Japan killed 200.000 people and made millions homeless, the League has been active all over the world. Statistics show that a significant natural disaster occurs on average once a week and that every three weeks its scale is such as to exceed the damage-control resources of the country in which it occurs. So international assistance on a large scale is frequently required.

In cases like this the League acts at international level as co-ordinator for the emergency operations carried out by the National Society on the spot. Based on information and requests it receives from the afflicted area, it appeals to other member Societies for assistance. It forwards donations, buys food or other supplies not readily available in the stricken area and, if needed, sends experts to help in the relief operations, in particular medical teams.

In countries often at risk from certain kinds of disaster, like floods, the League helps National Societies to minimize the toll on human life by developing disaster-preparedness plans. These include, for example, the construction of shelters and the setting-up of warning systems. The League has also established an international network of warehouses to enable relief supplies to be sent to disaster zones with the minimum of delay

A Wide Range of Duties

Another of the League's responsibilities is to assist refugees outside conflict areas. The League is often asked to undertake operations in partnership with the Office of the United Nations High Commissioner for Refugees (UNHCR).

Health protection has formed part of the League's duties since it was founded and has led to the development of a great variety of National Society activities, in the fields of community health care, health education, blood transfusion services, and, support to large-scale vaccination campaigns. The "Child Alive" programme, launched in 1984, aims to support National Societies and local authorities in their fight against infantile diseases which needlessly kill millions of children every year.

To support the many National Societies that have responsibility for blood services, the League actively encourages the dissemination of the "Code of Ethics for Blood Donation and Transfusion", established in 1980 by the International Blood Transfusion Society.

The supreme body of the League is the General Assembly, where each Society has one vote. The Assembly normally meets every two years, and elects for a four-year term the League's President and Vice-Presidents, as well as the National Society members of 'its Executive Committee. The Secretariat in Geneva employs about 130 staff of 30 different nationalities and a number of technical delegates in the field.

The Secretariat services are directed by a Secretary General nominated by the General Assembly. The League is financed by statutory contributions from member Societies, emergency and development programmes are paid for by special contributions from National Societies and governments

The League is a non-governmental organisation. It has advisory status with the United Nations Economic and Social Council (ECOSOC) and represents the views of its members there and in other international agencies.

The International Committee of the Red Cross

From its modest beginnings in 1863, the International Committee of the Red Cross (ICRC) has developed into an operational organization, working, throughout the world to protect and assist victims of armed' conflict and strife.

It acts on behalf of people who, because of conflict, are left without protection from the acts of their enemies: the wounded, prisoners of war and - civilians displaced from their homes or living under occupation.

The ICRC bases its activities on articles of law which it has itself promoted and developed. Its role is that of neutral intermediary between the victims who have rights and the States which have obligations.

Ensuring the protection of prisoners means that ICRC delegates must visit hospitals, camps, work places, prisons and anywhere else that captives may be held. Whether these visits are carried out under the Geneva Conventions or outside the scope of international humanitarian law (as in the case of "security detainees", the ICRC's work is governed by established criteria:

- delegates must be allowed to see all the prisoners or detainees and be able to talk to them in private, without witnesses,
- they must be given access to all places of detention and be able to make repeated follow-up visits, they must be given a list of the people to be visited (or be allowed to make such a list during the visit).

Their purpose is to examine the physical and psychological conditions of detention, not the reasons for it. Where necessary, relief supplies are given to prisoners and detainees, and to their families if they are in need. Confidential reports are written after each visit and given to the detaining authority, in the case of prisoners of war they are also sent to the government of the POWs' home country.

Relief and Medical Assistance

Given the very nature of modern conflicts, with their inevitable effects upon civilians, the ICRC has had to develop its capacity to provide medical and general assistance to populations in need. Often, the presence of ICRC delegates among the population can in itself be a form of protection against hostile acts.

The Relief Division is concerned with identifying needs and with organizing, managing and supervising programmes of relief: carrying out field surveys, studying local markets and assessing the means of storing and transporting supplies. Relief supplies have to be obtained, through either purchase or donation, and arrangements made for their onward transmission. Donors -governments, National Societies, various organisations such as the EEC and specialised UN agencies must be informed of developments. Stocks have to be managed and relief operations monitored. Delegates must be instructed in organizing logistics and supervising distributions.

The Medical Division has diversified its work to keep pace with changing situations. As well as meeting priority needs for medicines and medical supplies to treat the wounded, the Division has adopted a global approach to health problems affecting conflict victims - epidemics, inadequate hygiene and poor nutrition, for example.

Some victims of armed conflict are permanently disabled as a result of paralysis or amputation. In the past twenty years the ICRC, in addition to providing surgery, physiotherapy and rehabilitation treatment for these cases, has embarked on an extensive orthopedic programme for amputees, making artificial limbs and other devices in a number field centres.

Active in Other Situations

Since the First World War, the ICRC has expanded its activities to include other violent situations such as civil war and internal unrest. On the basis of its universally-recognized Right of Initiative, the ICRC can offer its services even in situations not covered by the Geneva Conventions and their Additional Protocols. Its neutrality and its discretion have enabled it to take humanitarian action on behalf of the victims of most of the internal conflicts this century.

It visits people arrested and detained for political reasons or offences, those known as "Security detainees". These visits are outside the scope of international humanitarian law and are covered by special agreements with the authorities concerned.

ICRC delegates do not concern themselves with the reasons for arrest but, as in their visits to prisoners of war, examine the conditions of detention, distribute relief supplies and make sure that the detainees are able to communicate with their relatives. Since 1945, the ICRC has visited more than 500,000 detainees in about 100 countries.

The ICRC is a private humanitarian institution whose supreme body is an Assembly which co-opts its members from among Swiss citizens (to a maximum of 25). The ICRC President is elected to a four-year term which is renewable. The staff, mainly Swiss, total about 580 at the Geneva headquarters with a similar number in some forty field delegations. Apart from the decision-making bodies (Assembly, Executive Board, Directorate), five departments manage the organization's day-to-day business. They are Operations, Finance and Administration, Principles and Law, Personnel, Information.

The ICRC's activities are financed from three sources-States party to the Geneva Conventions, National Societies and an assortment of donations, funds and legacies.

The regular budget, half of which is financed by the

Swiss government, covers the institution's permanent activities in Geneva and in the field. There are also special budgets to cover emergency operations, these -are financed by specific appeals. The ICRC's accounts are audited each year by two firms, one Swiss, one international. The figures for contributions received and expenditures made are published in the ICRC's annual report,

The Central Tracing Agency:

In the days before the Red Cross and the Geneva Conventions existed, it was almost impossible to find out what had happened to a member of the armed forces who fell into enemy hands. Neither the force to, which he belonged, nor the man's family, had any means of knowing whether he had been found -dead on the battlefield, a nameless corpse, and been, thrown into a common grave, or whether he was lying, wounded but alive, in an enemy camp or hospital.

This situation changed during the Franco-Prussian war of 1870-71. The ICRC persuaded both belligerents to provide it with lists of the wounded and prisoners in their hands. These helped the Committee to answer enquiries from anxious relatives and to forward correspondence between the detainees and their families. This breakthrough was the start of the ICRC's Central Tracing Agency.

The Agency's main tasks are to obtain and record all information which might enable dead, wounded or missing persons to be identified and to pass information to next of kin; to facilitate correspondence between members of families separated by events, when other means of communication have been interrupted; to try to trace people who are missing or of whom their relatives have had no news; and to issue various types of documents, such as certificates of captivity or death, and travel papers. The work is often carried out in co-operation with National Societies, many of which have their own tracing services.

The Agency's files make up a register of human suffering: its 60 million personal index cards, with the names of prisoners, refugees and the missing bear witness to the consequences of a century of strife. At its Geneva headquarters the Agency is adopting new methods for the storage and retrieval of its unique data, but the qualities required for tracing work remain unchanged: patience, perseverance and precision.

International Humanitarian Law & Red Cross

Until the second half of the nineteenth century arrangements made to protect the victims of war were of an informal nature, usually based on reciprocal agreements between army commanders and lasting for the duration of a particular engagement or campaign.

The birth of humanitarian law, under the auspices of the International Committee of the Red Cross, was to change this. The Geneva Conventions would be permanent, international treaties binding on the States which signed them.

The Geneva Convention of 1864 gave protection to the wounded on the battlefield. Its rules were gradually extended to other categories of victim -to lifeboats and to hospital ships and their personnel in 1899, for example, in a Convention signed at The Hague. The provisions of this Convention were improved and expanded in 1906. In 1907 a new Hague Convention defined the groups of combatants entitled, when captured, to prisoner-of-war status and ruled on how they should be treated during their captivity. The 1914-18 war, during which many men were held prisoner for several years, showed a need to regulate life in prisoner-of-war camps as well as the conditions in which POWs should be kept, the work that could be required of them and the means of maintaining discipline. This was accomplished in 1929,

The ICRC's proposals for the protection of civilians, on the other hand, were rejected initially by signatory States. This was to have 24 grave consequences in the Second World War .when millions of people died in Nazi concentration camps and the Red Cross, with no legal rights in the matter, tried in vain for four years to come to their aid. It was only in the last months of the war that ICRC delegates were able to get inside some of the death camps and to use what meagre resources they possessed to help those who had survived.

The Four Geneva Conventions of 1949

Shaken by the horrors of the Second World War, governments met for a new diplomatic conference in 1949 and adopted the text of a convention, drafted by the ICRC, relating to the protection of civilians in wartime". It contained precise rules for the protection of civilian internees and on the rights and duties of an Occupying Power,- it prohibited reprisals and deportation.

At the same time, the diplomatic conference revised the texts of earlier conventions and aligned their provisions- they then became the four Geneva Conventions of 12 August 1949. The 429 articles they contain guarantee the protection of the wounded and sick in armed forces in the field (first Convention), of wounded, sick and shipwrecked members of armed forces at sea (second Convention), of prisoners of war (third Convention) and of civilian persons in time of war (fourth Convention).

The Role of the ICRC

The four Conventions mention the ICRC they give it numerous and extensive rights on which to base its action. Article 126 of the third Convention, for example, stipulates that the delegates of the Committee "shall have permission to go to all places where prisoners of war may be, particularly to places of 'internment, imprisonment and labour, and shall have access to all premises occupied by prisoners of war- they shall also be all' owed to go to the places of departure, passage and arrival of prisoners who are being transferred. They shall be able to 'interview the prisoners and in particular the prisoners' representatives, without witnesses, either personally or through an interpreter"

Article 3, common to all four Conventions, sets out a certain number of regulations applicable to civil wars in the territory of a signatory State. Here the posit on of the ICRC is weaker: its ability to act depends on the goodwill of the authorities, for the article simply indicates that an impartial humanitarian body, such as the International Committee of the Red Cross, may offer its services to the Parties to the conflict"

Yet, although the 1949 Conventions have been 'instrumental in saving innumerable lives, they have provided inadequate protection for victims in the new forms of conflict that have arisen since 1945. For this reason the ICRC proposed, in 1965, to examine ways of extending the rules of humanitarian law, and to submit proposals to the signatory States.

This process culminated in the Diplomatic Conference on the Reaffirmation and Development of International Humanitarian Law Applicable in Armed Conflicts, held in Geneva from 1974 to 1977 and attended by the representatives of about one hundred governments.

Two Additional Protocols

Two Protocols additional to the Geneva Conventions were adopted on 8 June 1977. Protocol I covers international armed conflicts, and Protocol 11 armed conflicts not of an international character.

Protocol I introduces a number of improvements: while giving greater protection to civilians, it also takes into account problems currently besetting all States and accordingly makes international humanitarian law more universal in its conception and its formulation.

The improved protection for civilians extends to the direct effects of hostilities (under the Conventions it applies only to abuse of power by the enemy). Civilian medical units, as well as medical transport, establishments and personnel, are now entitled to the same protection as that granted to military medical personnel, installations and transport. Various rules have been introduced on the conduct of hostilities, in particular the prohibition of certain methods of combat and of attacks on civilians.

One of the provisions increases the categories of people entitled to prisoner-of-war status when captured, while others allow stricter checks on the application of humanitarian law. Protocol I also prohibits the use of starvation as a weapon, bans reprisals and facilitates the channeling of relief supplies to civilians in time of war.

The scope of the four Conventions and of Protocol I has been extended to cover struggles "against colonial domination, alien occupation and racist regimes as understood by the United Nations Charter".

Protocol II, which is shorter, supplements and develops Article 3 common to the four 1949 Geneva Conventions, which had previously been the only provision applicable in non-international armed conflicts. Among the main improvements of this second Protocol are fundamental guarantees for safeguarding all those not taking part in the hostilities. Rules for the protection of the wounded, sick and shipwrecked and of medical personnel and installations, on the entitlement of the latter to display the distinctive sign of the red cross or red crescent, and on the general protection of the civilian population have been incorporated from Protocol I, though 'in less detail.

A "Humanitarian Strategy"

In the period following the adoption of the two Additional Protocols there have been signs of a decline in the value put upon the application of international humanitarian law. This has been shown by serious and repeated violations of the 1949 Geneva Conventions. There has been a reluctance too on the part of certain authorities to allow the ICRC to fulfil its humanitarian mandate in situation not covered by the Geneva Conventions., such as internal disturbances,- humanitarian concerns have often come a poor second to political, and security considerations.

The ICRC's response to these obstacles has been to draw up a "humanitarian strategy II containing specific solutions to these and to similar problems which may be faced in the future.

The strategy requires the support of the entire Movement. It is primarily aimed at governments of States which have signed the Conventions and the Protocols and therefore share a moral responsibility both for respecting the existing law and for seeing them respected. It also provides for making the ICRC's work better known and understood and for spreading knowledge of humanitarian rules and principles, among members of armed forces and throughout all sections of the population - universities, schools, the general public. The spread of knowledge on a large scale essential. If the rules are to be observed, they must first be known and understood.

Statutes and Structures

Through its humanitarian ideals, the International Red Cross and Red Crescent Movement unites millions of members of every race, creed and social background.

Known to many by its former title -the "International Red Cross" - the Movement's component bodies are the International Committee of the Red Cross (ICRC), The National Red Gross and Red Crescent Societies, and The League of Red Cross and Red Crescent Societies.

Like those of any institution, its coordinating bodies and legal frame' works are reviewed periodically to keep them in line with changing needs. For the first 60 years of the Movement's existence, the ICRC acted as co-ordinator, on the basis of resolutions adopted at International Conferences. Formal statutes were introduced for the first time in 1928, following the founding of the League in 1919.

A new body was established - the Standing Commission of the International Red Cross - to prepare the International Conferences and act as co-ordinator. The Statutes were reviewed in 1952 with attention focussed on filling certain gaps and correcting inaccuracies in existing texts.

A review in 1986 made sure that the Movement had a solid, internationally valid legal structure. The Statutes were made easier to follow through a re-arrangement of the provisions, and some new texts, adopted since 1952, were introduced.

At the same times the title "Internatioal Red Cross and Red Crescent movement was adopted reflecting more accurately today's realities."

The Standing Commission

The Red Cross has three statutory bodies to enable it to determine the main outlines of its thought and work and to provide the links that are vital to unity among its components. They are the Standing Commission, the Council of Delegates and the International Conference of the Red Cross and Red Crescent.

Comprises nine members: two from the ICRC, two from the League and the other five elected in a personal capacity by the International Conference. Their term extends until the following International Conference. The Standing Commission elects its own Chairman and meets every six months. Its main task is to prepare the International Conference and ensure co-ordination. The Standing Commission awards the Henry Dunant medal to people who have shown exceptional courage while serving with the Red Cross, or devotion to its cause.

The Council of Delegates

Constitutes the assembly of the "Red Cross family", its members being representatives of the ICRC and of the League, as well as delegates of all the recognized National Societies. It meets every two years and is often called on to give an opinion on doctrinal points or on any other subject of common interest to the Movement. In the preparations for the International Conference, it is responsible for adopting the provisional agenda and for proposing the names of Chairmen of Commissions.

The International Conference of the Red Cross and Red Crescent

Generally meets every four years, bringing together delegates of the ICRC, the League and the National Societies, as well as the representatives of States party to the Geneva Conventions. The Standing Commission invites observers from government, non-government, regional or specialized organizations particularly interested in humanitarian problems. The International Conference is the supreme deliberative body of the Movement and as such determines major policy options on questions of principle and in the field of international humanitarian law.

Bibliography

Alston, Philip. *The United Nations and Human Rights: A Critical Appraisal*. Oxford, UK: Clarendon Press, 1992.

Alston, Philip and Mary Robinson, eds. *Human Rights and Development: Towards Mutual Reinforcement*. New York: Oxford University Press, 2005.

Anaya, S. James. *Indigenous Peoples in International Law*. New York: Oxford University Press, 1996.

An-Na'im, Abdullahi A., ed. *Human Rights in Cross-Cultural Perspectives: A Quest for Consensus*. Philadelphia, PA: University of Pennsylvania Press, 1992.

An-Na'im, Abdullahi A., ed. *Cultural Transformation and Human Rights in Africa*. London: Zed Books, 2002.

Askin, Kelly D. and Dorean M. Koenig, eds. *Women and International Human Rights Law*, 3 Vols., Ardsley, NY: Transnational Publ., 2000.

Bailey, Sydney D. *The UN Security Council and Human Rights*. New York: St. Martin's Press, 1994.

Banda, Fareda. *Women, Law and Human Rights: An African Perspective*. Oxford, UK: Hart, 2005. *Pollution*. San Francisco, CA: Sierra Club Books, 2005.

Chesterman, Simon. *Just War or Just Peace? Humanitarian Intervention and International Law*. New York: Oxford University Press, 2001.

Clapham, Andrew. *Human Rights in the Private Sphere*. New York: Oxford University Press, 1994.

Cottier, Thomas, Joost Pauwelyn, and Elisabeth Bürgi, eds. *Human Rights and International Trade*. New York: Oxford University Press, 2005.

Dunne, Tim and Nicholas J. Wheeler, eds. *Human Rights in Global Politics*. Cambridge, UK: Cambridge University Press, 1999.

Eldridge, Phil. *Politics of Human Rights in Southeast Asia*. London: Routledge, 2002.

Emberland, Marius. *The Human Rights of Companies: Exploring the Structure of ECHR Protection*. New York: Oxford University Press, 2006.

Flekkøy, Målfrid Grude and Natalie Hevener Kaufman. *The Participation Rights of the Child: Rights and Responsibilities in Family and Society*. London: Jessica Kingsley Publ., 1997.

Frost, Mervyn. *Constituting Human Rights: Global Civil Society and the Society of Democratic States*. London: Routledge, 2002.

Gearty, Conor. *Principles of Human Rights Adjudication*. New York: Oxford University Press, 2004.

Gewirth, Alan. *Human Rights*. Chicago, IL: University of Chicago Press, 1982.

Henkin, Louis. *The Age of Rights*. New York: Columbia University Press, 1990.

Keal, Paul. *European Conquest and the Rights of Indigenous Peoples: The Moral Backwardness of International Society*. Cambridge, UK: Cambridge University Press, 2003.

Kent, Ann E. *China, the United Nations, and Human Rights: The Limits of Compliance*. Philadelphia, PA: University of Pennsylvania Press, 1999.

Kent, George. *Freedom From Want: The Human Right to Adequate*

Food. Washington, DC: Georgetown University Press, 2005.

Keown, Damien V., Charles S. Prebish, and Wayne R. Husted, eds. *Buddhism and Human Rights.* Richmond, England, 1998.

Kolodziej, Edward A., ed. *A Force Profonde: The Power, Promise, and Politics of Human Rights.* Philadelphia, PA: University of Pennsylvania Press, 2003.

Korey, William. *NGOs and the Universal Declaration of Human Rights: 'A Curious Grapevine.'* New York: St. Martin's Press, 1998.

Kymlicka, Will, ed. *The Rights of Minority Cultures.* New York: Oxford University Press, 1995.

Mullally, Siobhan. *Gender, Culture and Human Rights: Reclaiming Universalism.* Oxford, UK: Hart, 2006.

Nino, Carlos Santiago. *The Ethics of Human Rights.* New York: Oxford University Press, 1991.

Ratner, Steven R. and Jason S. Abrams. *Accountability for Human Rights Atrocities in International Law: Beyond the Nuremberg Legacy.* New York: Oxford University Press, 2nd ed., 2001.

Reichert, Elisabeth. *Social Work and Human Rights: A Foundation for Policy and Practice.* New York: Columbia University Press, 2003.

Schoenberger, Karl. *Levi's Children: Coming to Terms with Human Rights in the Global Marketplace.* New York: Atlantic Monthly Press, 2000.

Scott, Craig, ed. *Torture as Tort: Comparative Perspectives on the Development of Transnational Tort Litigation.* Oxford, UK: Hart, 2001.

Sigler, Jay A. *Minority Rights: A Comparative Analysis.* Westport, CT: Greenwood Press, 1983.

Sohn, Louis. *Guide to Interpretation of the International Covenant on Economic, Social and Cultural Rights*. Ardley, NY: Transnational Publ., 1993.

Steiner, Henry J. and Philip Alston. *International Human Rights in Context: Law, Politics, Morals*. New York: Oxford University Press, 2000.

Steiner, Niklaus, Mark Gibney, and Gil Loescher, eds. *Problems of Protection: The UNHCR, Refugees and Human Rights*. New York: Routledge, 2003.

Sullivan, Rory, ed. *Business and Human Rights: Dilemmas and Solutions*. Sheffield, UK: Greenleaf Publ., 2003.

Talbott, William J. *Which Rights Should Be Universal?* New York: Oxford University Press, 2005.

Taylor, Paul M. *Freedom of Religion: UN and European Human Rights Law and Practice*. Cambridge, UK: Cambridge University Press, 2005.

Teson, Fernando R. *Humanitarian Intervention: An Inquiry into Law and Morality*. Ardsley, NY: Transnational Publ., 3rd ed., 2005.

Tolley, Howard B., Jr. *The International Commission of Jurists: Global Advocates for Human Rights*. Philadelphia, PA: University of Pennsylvania Press, 1994.

Tomasevski, Katarina. *Economic, Social and Cultural Rights: A Textbook*. Dordrecht: Martinus Nijhoff, 1995.

Tomuschat, Christian. *Human Rights: Between Idealism and Realism*. New York: Oxford University Press, 2003.

Wellman, Carl. *The Proliferation of Rights: Moral Progress or Empty Rhetoric?* Boulder, CO: Westview Press, 1998.

Wheeler, Nicholas J. *Saving Strangers: Humanitarian Intervention in International Society*. New York: Oxford University Press, 2000.

White, Richard Alan. *Breaking Silence: The Case That Changed the Face of Human Rights.* Washington, DC: Georgetown University Press, 2004.

Wilson, Richard A., ed. *Human Rights, Culture and Context: Anthropological Perspectives.* London: Pluto Press, 1999.

Wilson, Richard A. and Jon P. Mitchell, eds. *Human Rights in Global Perspective: Anthropological Studies of Rights, Claims and Entitlements.* New York: Routledge, 2003.

Woods, Jeanne M., Hope Lewis, and Ibrahim Gassama, eds. *Economic, Social and Cultural Rights: International and Comparative Perspectives.* Ardsley, NY: Transnational Publ., 2004.

Zeleza, Paul Tiyambe and Philip J. McConnaughay, eds. *Human Rights, the Rule of Law, and Development in Africa.* Philadelphia, PA: University of Pennsylvania Press, 2004.

Index